The Burning Child

Essays on Mental Health and Illness

by

Thomas Simmons

authorHOUSE™

1663 LIBERTY DRIVE, SUITE 200
BLOOMINGTON, INDIANA 47403
(800) 839-8640
WWW.AUTHORHOUSE.COM

First published by AuthorHouse 12/19/05

ISBN: 1-4208-6359-2 (sc)

Printed in the United States of America
Bloomington, Indiana

This book is printed on acid-free paper.

Cover photograph of the author at age 14 taken by Mary Powell Simmons in Los Altos, California, circa June 1972.

"Siddhartha" first appeared in the former Sunday magazine of the San Francisco Chronicle and Examiner, then known as California Living, in January 1985. It was reprinted in California Childhood, ed. Gary Soto (Berkeley: Creative Arts Book Company, 1988).

For Bruce Springsteen

In the garden of Gethsemane
He prayed for the life he never lived
He beseeched his heavenly Father
To remove the cup of death from his lips

-Devils and Dust

Table of Contents

Acknowledgments

Given the dominant subject of this collection of essays, one might well imagine a curmudgeonly or otherwise purely performative hostility in these "acknowledgments," which as a genre are routinely devoted to the author's grateful feelings for those who have helped him. Much of this book concerns ways in which the author explicitly was not helped, or was harmed. Yet in the end the book is about living, not dying, and dear people along the way have contributed to that outcome.

Though the debt is many years old now, I remain grateful to Dr. Eric Chivian of MIT and Harvard, Nobel Peace Prize winner and physician in the finest Hippocratic tradition, for attending me during the year-long crisis that preceded the events in this book, from the fall of 1991 to the spring of 1992. Dr. Peggy Baker, formerly of Iowa City and now of Minneapolis, was, like Eric, a kind soul, and her kindness made an important difference in 1995 and 1996. For most of the past three years, Lisa Bard, LMHC, of the heavily-overworked Poweshiek County Mental Health Center, has provided a locus of stability during some of the darkest moments of my experience of depression, and has managed to do so in spite of erratic scheduling due both to exigent circumstances and financial difficulties. Her wisdom and kindness reflects the same psychic gifts I received from Eric and Peggy, and I cannot but be grateful for them.

James Larew, attorney-at-law in Iowa City, offered kind counsel at important moments, friendship in dark moments, and monetary support when the worst financial crises occurred; if I am pleased to have been able to make good on his financial loans, I also hope this moment of thanks will reflect the pleasure I have taken from his wise and gentle company. Lesley Wright and Laura Rigal have both helped me to begin to relinquish adversarial positions, and the ensuing intersubjectivity filled dark corners of my psyche at times with unexpected light. I am grateful to them for that peace. Orion Jones, my research assistant for a different project on what has come to be known as the "post-traumatic culture," which I finally chose not to turn into a book, nevertheless provided helpful research into the literature of depression and post-traumatic stress disorder, as well as finding David Lee Miller's book, which I had somehow overlooked. A small portion of Orion's research makes an important appearance here, and he deserves the credit for that.

Finally, I acknowledge my most profound debt to my three children— Nathaniel Wright-Simmons, Georgia Wright-Simmons, and Thomas Rigal—who, with their intelligence, wit, tenacity, idiosyncracy, and personal strength, regardless of age, have reminded me over and over of how the power of love can be second to none, and how—though love may not of itself heal all wounds—it nevertheless becomes the invitation to a familial gathering where one knows one's absence would be, not only an affront, but a cause for much soul-searching. Though I feel certain they already know this at some level, my love for them is such that it will always be present, wherever I may be, in whatever way it may most comfort them; but I myself, for their sakes, will never be too far away.

Thomas Simmons
Grinnell, Iowa
April 2005

Preface

It would be disingenuous to begin this book without warning the reader that it has its harrowing moments. Yet those who come to these pages should know from the outset that the narrator wishes to find a path to life rather than to death. Though this may seem like a remarkably blunt and unliterary distinction, it is essential to understanding the overall trajectory of the book. To the kind of people William James described in *The Varieties of Religious Experience* as "healthy-minded," or even to those suffering from mild depression, the idea that life itself is an unmanageable and grotesque illusion, a travesty of unbearable valuelessness into which one has been abjectly hurled, is fundamentally inconceivable; to the suicide-to-be, it is second nature, an indisputable reality.

Confronting the never-desired seduction of that dark vision, this book remains dedicated to the living and to life, not to death or the dead. Against considerable odds, its narrator looks again and again for ways to refuse what may seem the ineluctable blessing of oblivion, and if that refusal seems at times hollow or provisional, it rests on a strange confluence of hopes and perplexities—very much the hopes and perplexities one finds in the one work that shows up most often in these pages, a work in certain ways uncharacteristic of its author's career—Harold Bloom's *Omens of Millennium*. For if it is indeed true, as Bloom argues, that what one might identify as an endemic American religiosity is at its heart gnostic, then behind my own punitive religious upbringing, somewhere, was a reality of absolute comfort: my soul, or whatever term one wishes to use for that essence, remained and remains with God—as does yours, if you follow this intuitive path—co-eternal, uncreated, and safe in defiance of all evidence to the contrary in this world where we are hurled toward destinations scarcely imaginable. At the same time, if one follows Bloom's lead toward the work of Henry Corbin on Islamic Sufism, or toward Bentley Layton's edition of the nominally Christian gnostic scriptures, one comes to understand that, however this world may appear, and however profound its agonies may be, its fundamental challenge is the challenge of the resurrection before death, not after: the knowledge that one is eternally alive at this moment and by that *gnosis* or knowing lifted, to a greater or lesser degree, from the diurnal darkness.

Perhaps very little of this book, at any given moment, would reflect such a profound hope, and yet, despite the variant agonies and mysteries of each essay, the possibility that life and not death is a given, and worth fighting for—or surrendering to—must, at some level, be my chalk circle. To say this is not, however, to denigrate the alternative which so many lovely people, both celebrated and largely unknown, have taken. Indeed, one might argue that our fascination with certain prominent figures in the world of literature and culture—Sylvia Plath and Anne Sexton particularly—is a way of deflecting or transferring our own anxieties about decisions they made, as they crafted rich and vivid literary lives, confronted and overcame familial upheavals, betrayals, and imponderable obligations, and yet, in the end, as Sexton wrote in "Wanting to Die," understood that the fundamental question was not "why build," but rather "which tools." "Suicides have a special language," as Sexton explains, but that point needs no explanation to anyone who has walked the immaculately thin line between life and death.

If I have chosen, for as long as I can foresee, to remain on this side of that line, my decision has much to do with the private implications of all that I have said above. And if, in this book, one finds it ironic that no chapter is devoted to Plath or Sexton, I could say that, on the one hand, I find their work and their lives in some ways too familiar, having taught them for the past five years at the University of Iowa; but I could also, perhaps with greater clarity, say that some dimensions of their lives and work inhabit private zones of my own meditation, which even the most ardent autobiographer would be reluctant to reveal. Then, too—while the advent of the second wave of feminism brought in its wake a multitude of writings about women, women's modes of despair, suicide, and redemption—no equivalent body of work exists for men, men like me, for whom suicide is one of the leading causes of death: it is the black hole of literary and cultural studies at present. And so the two men who occupy the latter third of this book—though neither, arguably, was a suicide—hold their place of respect because I saw something in their lives for which this culture still has no answer, and in crafting a provisional answer I found myself thrown back to certain ancient texts and immanent ideas. There are still some spiritual allies, as unlikely as they might appear, who work in the background to say that we grieve for a reason, and their subtlety in this world marks both our own struggle against trauma and our own hope for a restoration that could be, at any moment, this moment.

Foreward

This book is the work of someone who is at once chronically and acutely ill, and as it is autobiographical, one might assume it to be a confrontation with death, a reconciliation with life and the leaving of life, a meditation on terminal illness, or a combination of personal meditations and research on the provenance, growth, and treatment of a specific disease. In a way, it is all of these, but in another way, it is none of them. Perhaps the most important justification for this paradox is that the author himself does not, in any particular way, appear profoundly ill; indeed, most days, he appears to function like any other relatively normal, happy, healthy person. Thus, in a strange way, the circumstances of his life seem to go both with and against the grain of the book: he is both himself and an other, the ordinary man and the one in danger of dying.

The peculiarity of this comes from the nature of the disease: it is not cancer, or heart disease, or diabetes, or AIDS, but rather depression. As a popular subject in this culture, depression is, ironically, one of the best: to be depressed tends to signal a certain sensitivity, the hint of unusual hardship or trauma in one's background, the possibility of an entirely appropriate alienation from the modern world, and a mental condition increasingly susceptible to helpful treatment. But this is not the kind of depression I'm talking about, nor is it the subject of the book. According to a number of medical studies, most depressed patients come out of their labyrinths of darkness within six months to eighteen months of its onset, relying on a combination of drug therapy—particularly the relatively new selective serotonin re-uptake inhibitors, the SSRI's—and psychotherapy.

For these people, depression is a serious condition, a significant and potentially fatal health hazard, but it is treatable. Among writers who have written directly about their experiences of depression, perhaps the two most famous are William Styron and Elizabeth Wurtzel. For Styron, though the journey through depression could scarcely have been more harrowing, time eventually did heal; for Wurtzel, struggling with suicidal impulses on the other side of the Atlantic and in desperate need of treatment, the then-new drug Prozac turned out to be the miracle that it tends to be for anywhere from 40% to 60% of its users. These were stories with endings that, if not happy, were at least hopeful. And advances in "atypical" antidepressants, including such drugs as Welbutrin, Serzone, some medicines originally designed as anti-psychotics, or Remeron, have raised that percentage even higher.

For a small group of people, however—studies suggest it to be anywhere from 13% to as low as 6% of the depressed population at any time—nothing works. Time does not heal; medicines do not ease the darkness or despair; psychotherapy seems to run in circles. And as medical bills mount, the body attempts to adjust to one drug regimen after another, and the patient copes with the reality that, once again, another attempt has failed, the actual practice of healing becomes part of the punishment. This is known in the profession as "dysthymia," defined as a serious depressive episode lasting more than two years. In my case, the "serious depressive episode"—to the extent that the current one can be dated accurately—began in June 1995, and has continued unabated since then. It is, as I write this, April 2005, almost ten years since I began to feel a kind of globe of darkness separating me from the rest of the world, and a corresponding labyrinth of darkness within. No treatment—and there have been many, more now than I can count—has helped; I live, as one therapist noticed recently, largely by pure stubbornness, which itself is a trait of arguable virtue under the circumstances: from some psychoanalytic points of view, it is this very stubbornness, this refusal to cave into the Ardennes of absolute despair always just across the no-man's-land from my soul, that prevents my healing: only by effectively permitting myself to be annihilated, this view goes, would I find the base ground of healing. Meanwhile, the cost of the hospitalization and treatment necessary for that, combined with the possibility that it, too, would not work, would lead to a combination of exorbitant hospital bills and such an unpredictable job situation that I might wind up, if not homeless, then so close to the edge of physical survival that life itself, ironically, would not seem worth living. And so that envisioned treatment, the one held out as the last best hope, is ironically also the one most likely to lead to suicide.

If these seem to you like remarkably dark thoughts, they should. They are. Yet my intention here is not to lay down a roadmap of hopelessness and despair from some self-indulgent belief that, simply because the story is mine, and because it is too great a burden to carry, I should pass it along to others. Rather, this is a story of what it is like to continue living when something innate says that one does not belong here, or cannot truly survive here, or is irrevocably in the wrong place at the wrong time, always. Clearly, if I were truly without hope, the end would be swift. But that purpose has not yet manifested itself.

I spoke earlier of a certain stubbornness that keeps me going, but that both says too little and too much. From birth, as this book will explain—and as three of my other books have considered in one way or another—I was raised as a Christian Scientist. While this religious background is too broad, with too complex a history to summarize in a preface, it's fair to say that the two main functions of Christian Science in my life were to make me, from consciousness on, doubt the reality of the world around me, and to know myself as inexplicably flawed because, unlike other Christian Science children and adolescents, I rarely if ever responded to the healing power of Christian Science prayer. I was always the one unhealed, the one in days of pain, the one bleeding heavily from a head wound at the age of three, the one on the verge of death from pneumonia at the age of eight, the one chronically underweight, beaten, bullied, abused. If there were a black sheep in the fold of Christian Science, I was that one. The last fifteen years have begun to reveal that, in fact, I was not just "one": many children had similar experiences, and as they grew into adults— Barbara Wilson, Caroline Frazer, Nathaniel Lachenmeyer (writing about his schizophrenic father, the sociologist Charles Lachenmeyer, raised as a Christian Scientist) and several others—revealed pathologies similar to my own. But the consequence of years of feeling not-at-home in my body or in the world was a set of quite specific psychological symptoms: dysthymia; post-traumatic stress disorder; a profound anxiety disorder;

intrusive thoughts, obsessions, compulsions; and sudden, startling losses of concentration, the terror of any teacher, so that, at any given moment, I may forget, not only the sentence I am speaking, but what the entire discussion was about, and what the class itself is about. If I continue to struggle consciously for clarity and connection against these opponents, it is because some part of me simply cannot believe that, having survived so much pain in childhood and adolescence, I should survive it by losing most of what I struggled to achieve as an adult.

The underlying question, however, so clearly worth asking, is simply this: why bother? If, from the moment of awakening, one is plagued with dark thoughts and memories of pain from the terrible failure of Christian Science, if one's legacy of failed romantic relationships and divorce has yielded financial bankruptcy and a minimal mode of survival, despite a professor's salary, if one routinely has trouble concentrating and, occasionally, must take one or two-week medical leaves simply because one cannot, for that period of time, think abstractly, if two of one's three children are largely grown and away, if the third child lives 70 miles away with his mother and visitation or custodial opportunities—though blessedly unmanipulative—are nevertheless somewhat complicated, if one lives in a part of the country one never really chose—but moved to for the job, for the sake of a family that was about to break apart in any case— and if one cannot afford to move back to the one place one loves, if one has few if any friends…why bother? Why not honor oneself for all years one has survived terrible odds, give oneself credit for accomplishments in the face of obstacles others might have found insurmountable, bless one's children, acknowledge the impossibility of the present, and accept the blessed relief of suicide?

This book is, in its own accomplishments and its flaws, an attempt to answer that question. Depression, as most people now aver, is both inherited and circumstantial: one may have a genetic predisposition toward depression, but a certain array of circumstances as one grows through childhood to maturity will tend to draw that predisposition into the foreground while placing a "normal" array of human feelings—happiness, joy, contentment, appropriate pride in appropriate accomplishments—well into the background. With a Christian Science upbringing, it is of course virtually impossible to know anything like a medical history; virtually no one that I know of back through my grandparents ever went to physician for any ailment. If the "illusion" or "claim" of a backache or a fever or difficulty breathing arose, one either prayed on one's own or called a Christian Science practitioner, who prayed to know that the patient's life was purely good and spiritual and purely in God's hands, and no mortal illusion of illness could touch it. Ideally, these prayers washed over the patient—either in person or from miles away over the telephone—with such renewal that all symptoms of the illness vanished. Alas, it was not often the case in my life, but what has been striking over the years are small discoveries suggesting that prayer did not meet the needs of other members of my family. There is some evidence that a relative of my father's was hospitalized for a period of time, when I was very young, for treatment for alcoholism; my brother struggled with alcohol for years; my father was an alcoholic when he died of pneumonia in 1998. I went from not drinking, as a devout Christian Scientist, through the age of 25, to the present, when I now think of myself as a rather quiet and retiring alcoholic, addicted to the very California wines that were in vogue in the 1980's, when I was largely not drinking. There is evidence, too, from the behavior of my father's father and my father, of depression and post-traumatic stress disorder from World Wars I and II: the rages, the occasional, apparent disconnections from immediate reality to some internal, half-remembered trauma, the withdrawals, the surface congeniality combined with an inability to make friends.

On my mother's side of the family, both depression and bi-polar tendencies clearly were more than circumstantial possibilities: my own mother's darkness for days at a time could not be construed, finally, as a sequence of bad moods, while her mother's dark days—ironic, since she herself was a Christian Science practitioner—alternated with days of manic energy, vast highs when anything was possible, when God might appear on earth. Naner, as we called her, was alternately dark and dismal, neutral, lively, unrestrained, hopeful beyond all reason, insanely busy, and messianic. It also seems that, on my father's side, there was a history of heart disease, while on my mother's side, there was a history of cancer, heart disease, and bizarre malfunctions in various internal organs (my uncle Sandy, a funny, witty young man pressed early into the service of the Christian Science church, became the First Reader of his branch church—a very high honor—before he had reached 40, then died within a week's time of dual kidney failure: he was not rushed to a hospital, of course, until his virtually lifeless body signaled that a week's worth of prayer had not yielded the divine result, and by that time he was beyond the help of medicine as well). If one likes to gamble with high odds, or a deck stacked against one's very being, my deck is very much tainted. I like that, in a way: having always felt that, at some level, I was playing against high odds, this adult knowledge of the nature of some of those odds is actually somewhat soothing. But, hereditarily, the evidence here is not hopeful.

And then, of course, there were the circumstances, the journey I was on—presumably a journey toward greater and greater revelations of the truth of Christian Science and Mary Baker Eddy's vision. Somewhere I stepped off that path, perhaps very early on, without really knowing it, trying harder and harder as an adolescent to be a "good" Christian Scientist, until the weight of that burden became too great to bear. One of my current students, in a two-dimensional mapping project of the known universe—not so much temporal-spatial as illusory-metaphorical-real—presented "hell" as the domain of humans who are not necessarily evil, but who carry burdens too heavy to bear. It seemed to me one of the best definitions of hell that I had ever read. Hell, of course, is here and now, if one is living that way. But there may be heavens here and now as well.

In a remarkably eccentric and brilliant 1989 novel, *Sexing the Cherry,* Jeanette Winterson writes,

> Every journey conceals another journey within its lines: the path not taken and the forgotten angle. These are the journeys I wish to record. Not the ones I made, but the ones I might have made, or perhaps did make in some other place or time... .I discovered that my own life was written invisibly, was squashed between the facts, was flying without me like the Twelve Dancing Princesses who shot from their window every night and returned home every morning with torn dresses and worn-out slippers and remembered nothing (Winterson, 2).

In other books, I have written narratives of what has been, more or less, a single journey: the journey through the pain, lies, manipulations, and broken promises of Christian Science toward a life more capacious, more rich with possibility, more human, and more humane. If that story has failed, one might argue that the narrative itself—to the extent that it was my narrative, the life that I embraced—was at once too naive and too limited. Even when, as an assistant professor at MIT, I was completing my first book, *The Unseen Shore: Memories of a Christian Science Childhood* for Beacon Press in Boston in 1990, I was still largely unaware of the powerful ways in which depression had been working through my life as a specific and diagnosable illness, leading me both to states of mind and to decisions that undepressed people would not have experienced or made; I had only barely heard of "post-traumatic stress disorder," and associated it specifically with Vietnam veterans, not realizing that, as an identified and treatable illness, it also manifested itself among victims of non-military trauma—rape victims, victims of domestic abuse, abused children, survivors of catastrophic accidents—and, though less common in America than depression, was still markedly prevalent in the general population. I did not, when I was writing that book, really know that I was sick; I only knew that I was unhappy, and that my journey seemed to be going radically in the wrong direction. Yet it was still one journey, discrete, a journey through darkness into a light I had not yet seen yet felt I could predict.

What has come to pass in the 15 years since the publication of that book is not more light, but much darkness, with random shafts of light from directions I had not expected. And so there is this book: a book about darkness and random shafts of light. In *Sexing the Cherry*, the elusive twelfth dancing princess, Fortunata, moves with remarkable ease in and out of our known universe, sometimes appearing as a body, sometimes appearing as her essence—space and light—and her only liability, depending on how one reads the text, is that she does not truly understand love. It is the male protagonist's Jordan's great fortune or misfortune—depending again on one's interpretation—to encounter Fortunata and to know her above all as integral to himself yet separate, true to her own existence, and fundamentally real in a way his being craves by its very nature. Yet they can spend no more than a month together, and while one might argue that he loves so profoundly that, reincarnated in life after life, he always returns to her, she is never quite sure what to do with him. But perhaps that is in itself a sign that the question here is not a question of love, but rather a question of possession or attachment: Jordan becomes karmically attached to Fortunata; Fortunata exists beyond attachments. It may be in the nature of many Western readers to see the experience of being "beyond attachment" as having its own drawbacks. We don't discuss this much, and to raise it, as I have, as a subject among Buddhists or Hindus is to invite gentle remonstrances of condescension and encouragements to see the beauty behind non-attachment. So it may be. Yet one of the most beautiful things that Fortunata does is to teach at "a dancing school in a remote place," where she teaches her students "to become points of light."

It would be too simple to say that the narrator of this collection of essays is another incarnation of Jordan; among other things, that would make this book in some way a work in service to *Sexing the Cherry*, and since that is not true, an element of deception would inevitably creep in. Nevertheless, it is possible to be profoundly wounded in this world and yet still to suspect that great secrets are at hand, within; that the world itself, its linearity and chronology, its noise, its preoccupations, its judgments, its need for step-by-step instruction toward some greater career path, its fascination with self-improvement, its insatiable desire to consume, its intellectual desire to measure and quantify and label productivity, its general appearance as an enormous steam engine run on microchips—all of this finally is distraction and—well, if not illusion, then something akin to it. Perhaps one would not see or sense the world in which there is no time, but only light and the dance of those points of light, themselves both conscious and beyond consciousness, if it were not for the ordinary world. And if one despairs over the ordinary world, and condemns oneself for that despair, as depressives often do, the reality is that there is much to lament: not for nothing do the great spiritual teachers of the world warn against acquisitiveness, grasping, pride, lust for wealth and power, the dominance of the ego: these lead to the contemporary world as a parody of God, which might well be defined as the world in which God is Las Vegas, whose circumference is everywhere and whose center is nowhere.

Good luck to all of you out there in the well-watered Nevada desert that is everywhere. You're going to need it.

But a trace of an alternative vision can keep one alive: is that a good thing? It seems to me still that, to the extent that consciousness, both through itself and through relinquishing itself through certain acts of meditation, can make contact with worlds like Fortunata's, then there is something to be said for consciousness. To be fair, there is also something to be said for oblivion: release from all remembering and thinking, from all that human consciousness would seem to imply, has attracted many brilliant and lovely people, and some of them make major or cameo appearances in this book. Still, certain kinds of adventurers believe until the last moment that there is a thread to be followed; the thread of a fictional dancing princess, for example, who teaches her students to be points of light, has non-fictional analogues in the sacred texts of the Hopi, in the Kalachakra initiation of Tibetan Buddhism, in the myth of Shambala and the multiple ways in which people have internalized that myth, in the fragmentary insights into Siberian shamanism in the Altai mountains in Siberia; what these few examples have in common is a certain isolation from the contemporary world; an experience of having been, politically or militarily, conquered (as the United States Army nearly erased the American Indian, as China continues to try to erase Tibet); and an experience of the reality of the tradition continuing, despite all material, human destruction, despair, and death. For a child who began life with an odd combination of great, unhealed pain and a serious interest in all kinds of adventuring, as I did, the thread of what remains is a thread of life, not death.

The essays that follow are thus threads. They do not treat the subtitle of this book—"Essays on Mental Health and Illness"—in a formal, analytic way, but that subtitle informs each essay: in each case, an essay confronts some dimension of health or illness. Underlying each of these essays are two extremes and one relatively practical question: when does pain become too much pain? When does rapture—such as Dylan Thomas' rapture in his poem "And Death Shall Have No Dominion"—have the potentially accidental yet deadly side effect of making this world irrelevant? And what, finally, is an "adequate" world, a world in which one can claim to live with some sense of protectedness while nevertheless pursuing the goal of a point of light? That last question may be the most suspect of the book, for the point may be, finally, for a depressed person to learn that no amount of earthly protection is "protection"; earthly life is fundamentally nothing but danger. And if that is the case, one can only embrace the loveliness one finds in unexpected places, the thread that never quite breaks, and follow it, despite all pain, toward a light one cannot identify or name. That is certainly one kind of objection to the third question here; perhaps it will turn out to be correct, or perhaps, by the end, a different vision will emerge. As this preface is being written, with the book about three-quarters finished, I cannot yet say how it will end. It may not end— the first book I have written without a true conclusion. From a writerly point of view, such a possibility is maddening. From the point of view of one looking out beyond the horizon, however, the first days of a crescent moon make the horizon irrelevant.

First-person narratives, as a genre, have their waxing and waning, and it seems to me that we are in a waning time at present, after two decades of fascination with personal narrative; or perhaps it would be more accurate to say that our personal narratives have now gone primarily visual, into TV and cable shows like *Fear Factor, The Bachelor,* or *The Apprentice,* and written, meditated versions have become tedious. If so, this book, like other books both more or less worthy, will languish on shelves or in computer files in warehouses around the world. One could defend oneself slightly, perhaps, with Henry David Thoreau's dry wit at the beginning of *Walden,* when he notes that he would not write about himself if there were anyone else he knew as well. Equally interesting, however, is Michel de Montaigne's 1580 note "To the Reader" of his *Essais,* in which he says, "This book was written in good faith, reader. It warns you from the outset that in it I have set myself no goal but a domestic and private one" (Frame, 2). In hundreds of pages of meditative essays that we sometimes still teach as precursors to the modern essay, Montaigne examines his own psyche, his life, time, soul.

Yet he wins the sneering opprobrium of Jean-Jacques Rousseau two centuries later: in his *Confessions,* Rousseau dismisses Montaigne's meditations as highly artful—which is to say, contrivances or lies, infinitely inferior to Rousseau's own confessions of grandeur and abasement, worthy and despicable motives. The oscillation that began once Rousseau set both a high-water mark for revelation and a charge against the grace of Montaigne has never really been resolved, and perhaps never will be. About the best that can be said of the essays that follow is that they, too, were written in good faith, and if they seem at times to be more about dying than about living, it is because they wish to find, against now-heavy odds, what is left to build—what kind of life is worth living, not only for the narrator, but for anyone in exigent or complex circumstances. Such exigencies inhabited 16th and 17th century France in their own way, and all of 19th century Europe, and Japan, Russia, and China in the early part of the twentieth century, and much of the world between 1940 and 1945, and Tibet in 1959, and much of the world now: there is, in short, much in this book that could be transposed across time and space to other conditions, other characters, other exigencies. Thus, perhaps, it is, as a book, a kind of placeholder, a marker of a certain kind of reality with others layered above it and below it. Or perhaps it is a digression, a long ramble away from a kernel of truth that came quite early in my own life, a kernel as old as the Word itself, but presented to me with such virulent ferocity that, in the end, the only alternative was to walk away; and yet, stubborn, persistent, that Word followed, like a point of light, not before me but behind me, not guiding me but reminding me that not every blessing is in the future, and time does not always run only in one direction, and the best dance may be long past, yet one unseen partner away.

Part I:
The Burning Child

The Unbroken

In a recurring dream, I pick up the telephone receiver at a ringing pay phone somewhere in the mountains—Aspen, Colorado comes most often to mind in waking hours. When I answer, it is Jim Croce singing "Operator," his second big hit in 1970. I'm riveted to the song, in which the singer eventually tells the operator not to make a call to the woman he's loved and lost. He wants to tell her he's fine, he thinks, but over the course of the song he realizes that it's not true: "I've overcome the blow," he sings, "I've learned to take it well,/ I only wish the words could just convince myself/ That it just wasn't real;/ But that's not the way it feels." He can't reassure her, or himself, that he's overcome the loss, because he hasn't; implicitly, in the song, she has. She's on to a new life. He's turning away from a telephone. I listen to this entire song in the dream, enraptured, and then in the background there's the high-pitched hum of a small aircraft engine being run up to full power for take-off. The sound gets louder as the song comes to an end, until at last we're in the last measures of the song and then, suddenly, there's a kind of fast cracking sound and something like a mechanical gasp and then there's only static. I wake up from the dream remembering September 20, 1973, when Jim Croce died in an evening plane crash in Natchitoches, Louisiana. He was always flying in and out of small airports in small planes, doing small shows at local venues and colleges even after he'd made it big. On September 20, his plane hit a tree on takeoff.

For a long time I had a different memory of this. I remembered that Croce had just done a big show in Aspen, and was flying out of the stylish but tricky Aspen airport in a private jet when the jet crashed into a mountain. Between 1978, when Croce first began to come back to me as a memorable voice, and recently, in March 2004, I was convinced that Croce had died leaving Aspen. My dream seemed to figure a mountain range, and when, every now and then, I drove past the Aspen airport, I wondered which mountain he'd hit. My dream never made it clear; only by looking up Croce's life did I find, to my shock, that he hadn't hit a mountain. My dream was, say, three-quarters accurate, historically. But what does that say about dreams?

* * *

My father was a flight instructor during World War II in the Naval Reserve. As a teenager growing up in Ardmore, Pennsylvania, he had loved machines of all kinds, but airplanes particularly; he talked some older men into teaching him to fly at the North Philadelphia airport in exchange for odd jobs around the FBO ("Fixed-Base Operator," the technical term for a small airport). That was in the late 1930's, when he was 17 and 18. By the time World War II broke out in 1941, he was a 20-year-old pilot with more time on his logbooks than most of the pilots already in the military. He had taught himself barrel rolls and Immelmanns and a host of dogfight maneuvers, how no one now knows or can remember: in experimenting, given the private planes available at the time, he must have cheated death a hundred times, perhaps every time he flew. He was like that. He lived best on the thin edge between life and death. That thin edge was where everything came together for him. It was like a fluid in physics, like plasma: it went everywhere through him, shot through his body the way plasma shot through the bodies of the Columbia astronauts in January 2004, burning them in a flash. But the earthly plasma of my father's life, though just as quick, was life-giving, life-sustaining. Before and during the war—before he fell to ordinary life—he walked back into the world each day having touched the authenticity of the edge between life and death.

* * *

"The authentic is a line from one thing/along to the next; it interests us," writes William Stafford in the opening poem to his 1973 collection *Someday, Maybe.* The authentic—that vexed concept, utterly anathema to contemporary cultural studies. We learn now that nothing is authentic; everything is provisional, culturally-dictated, meaningful in its own context even if that context is unanalyzed, yet much more meaningful in its arbitrary value if the context comes under the scrutiny of a post-structuralist analysis. But authenticity as a concept has been in trouble for a very long time. Its appearance in the title of Lionel Trilling's 1972 *Sincerity and Authenticity,* though it might seem a sign of importance, actually signaled a crisis: Trilling could define "sincerity" across its existence in English from the last third of the fifteenth century, but he could not, in the end, define "authenticity." The protests and upheavals of the 1960's and early 1970's had left him profoundly shaken as a liberal academic and social critic; nothing in his pantheon of cultural heroes, of whom Matthew Arnold was always first, seemed up to the challenge of the Students for a Democratic Society, the Student Nonviolent Coordinating Committee, the assassinations of Martin Luther King, Jr. and Robert F. Kennedy, the National Guard shootings of four students at Kent State in Ohio, the outbreak of student strikes and insurrections in protest both against those deaths and against the American government itself. In a society seemingly out of control, Trilling found himself called upon to give the Charles Eliot Norton lectures at Harvard in the spring of 1970. He could not, in the end, accomplish the restorative task that he appeared to have set for himself, and part of the problem was that, everywhere he looked, nothing was authentic.

* * *

We walk through a world of dreams in which people appear out of the darkness to speak to us. Many of them have no corollary we know of in the phenomenal world. I, for example, know no wealthy widows, but one came to me in a dream last night, or rather invited me in for drinks at her penthouse condominium in a city somehow a hybrid of Boston and New York. We were to have dinner and attend a show later. But as we talked over martinis, she looked at me sadly and said, "You and I are about the same age, but you are broken. No woman my age will be able to fix you, and it would take an exceptional younger woman to know how to deal with your sadness. I'm afraid you'll have to reconcile yourself to being alone." With that she rang for her personal attaché—no one seems to have butlers anymore, even in dreams—and she invited me to spend the evening out on the town alone, enjoying myself as I might.

In the aftermath, the city shifted to Seattle, the waterfront at night, and I was walking alone among stacked containers and idled cranes, the huge cargo ships not quite at rest. Everything creaked and groaned, and yet there was an immense silence. No other humans came, although I saw shadows scurrying in the darkness under freeways and felt afraid, as if, if I turned in the wrong direction or even the right one, I might be beaten or raped, or simply—simply! A lapse into my childhood—tormented. Finding my way eastward, up a steep hill, I came to a line of men snaking around a corner. At one end was darkness; at the other, the lighted entry to a shelter. The men's clothes were old and various and dirty, and many of them carried sleeping bags, bed rolls, or duffle bags. I waited, wondering if I should stand in line.

The first part of this dream was a dream, although I have been running the woman's words through my head all day. I can hear the voiceover of wise friends' words telling me to scrutinize the dream, to be suspicious of its strictures—why the refusal of the older woman, why the near-sanctification of the younger woman? Is that not a cultural cliché? Is the dream itself the saga of a mind working out its own limits, its own prejudices, against the nearly-infinite variation of possibility? Might the dream be a warning *against* the very observations the widow made? Perhaps; at the very least, the dream might be understood as an odd encomium for aloneness, a warning not to seek salvation through another. And yet, clearly, love was the underlying problem—both erotic love and *agape*, the love that we give and receive freely as we can, the unselfish love that restores and preserves. It is easy to overlook the possibility that the speaker of this dream, the widow, though seemingly well-shielded, was herself broken.

The second part of this dream was also a dream, but it really happened as well, on a fog-enshrouded night in Seattle in the spring of 1996. I dreamed a dream, and I dreamed a real thing that became a dream. Where was the authentic, from one line to the next? Was it the line connecting, as a continuum, consciousness and unconsciousness? Was it the line of brokenness, stretching from the wise, sad woman in the dream to the re-envisioned reality of standing in a line of homeless men? And what was the real story of each of those men, that night I was actually there, and what were their dreams?

The story of brokenness...an inheritance I received from my father. "The word 'authenticity' comes so readily to the tongue these days and in so many connections that it may very well resist such efforts of definition as I shall later make," Lionel Trilling writes, "but I think that for the present I can rely on its suggesting a more strenuous moral experience than 'sincerity' does, a more exigent concept of the self and of what being true to it consists in, a wider reference to the universe and man's place in it, and a less acceptant and genial view of the social circumstances of life" (Trilling, 11). Though not a definition, it's an interesting list in relation both to brokenness and to the idea of an inheritance:

*) a more strenuous moral experience than sincerity

*) a more exigent concept of the self

*)a wider reference to one's place in the universe

*) a less acceptant and genial view of the social circumstances of life

I will begin last to first, roughly.

* * *

It is possible, after many crises, to own a story of brokenness so seemingly continuous and so vast in relation to one's own life that no other story, and certainly no story of love, even comes close. But this distinction—between a story of brokenness and a compensatory story of love—places love itself on the "genial" side of the "social circumstances of life." At some point, one must admit whether that is where one can really place love. My father's love, for example, had nothing of the genial about it. It was raw and angry and interior and embittered—indeed, few people would call it love, and many more would look for some synonym for "abusive" to describe it. Yet it was from my father that I learned the possibility of a "less acceptant and genial view of the social circumstances of life," in part because, after his service in World War II, he performed so skillfully the roles of an accepting and genial man. He was the quintessential salesman, an Arthur Miller character quick to make his own stage.

Each morning, as I came up from the basement where I ate my breakfast—to avoid the inevitable fights between my older brother and sister and my father—I would see him put his long, heavy overcoat over his business suit and stand on the curb, waiting for the carpool of colleagues to collect him. The grim determination in his face was identical to what I had seen on television of military men standing at attention. Yet at office parties or Christmas parties, I was always astonished to see him smiling and vivid, telling stories and laughing as if that were his natural default. He was a product manager, which was, as far as I could tell, a little like being in the no-man's-land between two warring armies: his job was to take customer requests for carpet designs down to manufacturing plants in the Carolinas, where the engineers would explain why the request was or was not impossible. Apparently he was good at it, defusing arguments and resolving complaints with great skill; he kept that job for years until we moved to California, where he acquired another job almost identical to it at Ampex Corporation, which made magnetic recording tape for the music industry. But I remember my father coming home most days sullen, exhausted, and seething. He would often fall asleep in his own father's old chair—part of our weird assortment of furniture—before dinner was ready.

Weekends, which were his time, were of three kinds. The first was home improvement or repair; since our house was very old and we didn't have much money, my father did everything from plumbing to re-tiling the bathroom to re-wiring parts of the house to repointing the brick on a high, wobbly ladder. These projects usually involved an enormous amount of rage. Often you could hear my father swearing wildly throughout the house as a tile cracked in the wrong place or a circuit shorted out or a pipe fitting failed. A great improviser, my father could not be reconciled to failure; obstacles to his useful plans infuriated him. I remember hiding behind his chair in the living room, listening to his torrent of invective. He would sometimes smash the very things he was trying to fix, and I was never clear whether that rage at some point would be directed at me.

The second kind of weekend was hobby weekend, when my father used to build Heathkit electronic devices—oscilloscopes, AM/FM receivers, amplifiers—and during these weekends his mood was rarely different from his home improvement battles. It was as if, whether he was supposedly enjoying himself or working, the underlying substratum—the line connecting one thing to the next—the key piece he refused to show outside the family, was breaking, broken, fracturing anger. Except for his voice, the house would be silent. My brother and sister would have gone out to visit friends; my mother would go shopping for as long as she could; I hid.

Only on the third kind of weekend—the weekend on the water—did anything change. Somehow my father had scraped together enough money for an old 14-foot fishing boat with a 40-horsepower Evinrude on it; this he used in the summers for waterskiing. The family was drafted to drive the boat, watch for other traffic, and—sometimes—to ski with him. If our fall, winter, and spring weekends were reminders that our domestic world, so dependent on my father's business world, was nevertheless falling apart and dangerous at every turn, our summer weekends were reminders that my father could feel joy, and that his happiness translated to us as safety. He and my mother had both spent their childhoods in Avalon, New Jersey—they had met on the beach there—and as we piloted our old boat through the back waters of that island town, I had the feeling that my father, too, was going back in time, riding the wake as if he were still a pilot, bearing down and flying into the air over choppy water, teaching himself tricks—360-degree turns, sometimes in sequence—as we watched from the cockpit. He was a wing-walker, a barnstormer, his medium shifted from air to water...but since, in practical terms, air behaves as much like a fluid as a gas, there is hardly any difference between them. And joy is joy, and love is love, and in the midst of each one knows no distinctions, only happiness.

Still, the most compelling memories of this time bring with them—as the experiences themselves brought with them—a savage division between one's performance for the judging world and one's internal or domestic being...too much rage within signals such an inauthenticity without that, witnessing it as a child, I could never really believe that "the social circumstances of life" were true or safe. This is ironic, because home was the source of unsafety—but I did not really know that then. Seeing the divisions in my father, I saw something damaging about the person he needed to be in the world, or thought he needed to be, in order to survive, and thus found myself emulating him…quiet and well-behaved, I was in fact anxious, suspicious, and always looking for signs of brokenness in the world. And I always found them.

* * *

What, then, was real? I did not learn the meaning of the word "exigent" until high school, but I knew the experience of exigency early on, and had someone explained briefly Trilling's "more exigent concept of the self" to me, I would have understood it as early as I could have understood language. It never particularly worried me whether there was one true self; in fact, it may seem strange to suggest that a child would even think about these things. But, as a particular kind of child—a Christian Scientist—I was from the beginning preoccupied, in a way not unlike the early Puritans in America, with the state of my self, with its real being, with the unreality of the mortal world, and with the presence of God in my life. These thoughts were so overwhelming, when I was six or seven or eight, that they would, eventually, sicken me—drive me to symptoms of influenza and exhaustion—and then, after a fitful rest, I would awaken to something hazier, something less distinct in myself… something contingent, growing, not yet finished. In that self there was hope. The growth itself implied someone I had not yet met, someone who was not a given but was always becoming more himself, even if that goal might never be reached. Easing back into a day of that self, I would make things—I would make worlds.

I started with towns and farms, Matchbox-sized. Before they became like every other toy, Matchbox cars and trucks were crafted in Lesney, England, for children with an eye for detail: the perfect, tiny world of the "Hoveringham" dump truck or the Singer Sewing Machine service truck or the 1962 VW with its tiny engine under a rear hatch that opened—all these, slowly gathered at forty-nine to fifty-seven cents apiece, became the floor of my room. I built houses, shops, and barns out of cardboard and scotch tape; I used construction paper to make fields, forests, construction sites. The cars and trucks and tractors and travel trailers and boats and motorcycles multiplied; I made freeways, highways, side roads. To walk in my room, for many years, meant to learn how to turn your feet sideways to fit on small roads, to step between houses and garages. There were no people in my cities; they were an absence. Their habits, their drives, their labors, their recreations, had as their signs the vehicles they used or the buildings they inhabited. A humanless world peopled with human signs...for someone for whom humans were so untrustworthy, so liable to rage and unhappiness, so unable to sustain love, the sign was an enormous relief.

Then I built cities...Venice, all of it, map-perfect, from cardboard and scotch tape, with gondolas and canal-side cafes with little tables, stretching all across the room; then Moshe Safdie's "Habitat '67," each cardboard block hand-made to nest precisely against its mates, higher and longer and vaster than anything Safdie actually built, an entire city of rectangular apartments, doing things no solo rectangle could manage...a geometric trick of humanity, people signaled by rectangles...and then different versions of the same concept, a series of pyramids interlocking, each one about three inches tall, stretching eight feet by twelve feet around my room...Days and days of quiet work after the annoyance of school, after a longing for people who never quite seemed to be there. In building, my self went out into all that I had made, and my lonely self found company in the exigent souls of all the people who lived in the Matchbox cities, or in Venice, or in Habitat or its successors, people who had lost sympathy with the genial world I was supposed to inhabit, and who had willingly come to a different world.

* * *

Over Christmas 2003, my new partner traveling in England, I sent her an average of a poem a day for twenty-one days. She had a laptop computer, and we e-mailed daily; she loved her new collection of poems, she said. Though she was vague about where she was at any given moment or what she was doing, she would usually fill me in on the Brontes' house, or her great-grandmother's grave, or a certain pub in Leeds...usually, she said, she simply felt too abstracted in her life abroad to know what to say. It was a trip she had planned before we'd met, a present she was giving herself for having graduated as a "returning student" from college, and while she'd been looking forward to it for months, she sounded at times as if she were between two worlds—which, in my state, I took to be a kind of compliment. Our time together before her trip had been filled with pleasure, and she had spoken euphorically before leaving of her return, when we would live together in my house; I was counting the days. At one point she arranged to return early from England to live with me. Abruptly, on the day she was to return, she sent a cell phone text message announcing her plan to return on her original date instead; she would also be on the go, she said, with only occasional access to e-mail and text messages. Perplexed and momentarily sad, I wrote a short poem I could quickly send:

> You can carry this little poem
> anywhere, in the Underground, in the
> Up Above, in the Here and Now, in the
> Great Beyond, it is always what it is,
> the words of ordinariness and wonder
> saying, we are ordinary, we are wonderful,
> we are love, everywhere, everywhere.

What a relief it had been, after our autumn e-mailing and the ensuing time we'd actually known each other, to feel the "dear ordinary," as Marilynne Robinson calls it, begin to creep back into my life past years of drought. It was almost too much to hope for, yet it was there, it felt there…it felt, how should one say it, authentic. With this woman I could be ordinary and wonderful, as could she; the days we lay in bed for hours, talking, in December, before she left—those were days in which exigent selves began to feel weighted again in the best possible way, to return to earth to be like the ghosts in Wallace Stevens' "Large Red Man Reading"— or rather, to be like them if they had gotten what they wanted, to return to the poem of life. Two selves crafting one another make a world somewhat insulated from Trilling's "social circumstances of life"; one's expected behavior or unexpected behavior no longer is really the subject. Nor is the anxiety chronically anxious children feel when they face the reality of "one's place in the universe" when that seems shriveled, harshly-judged, and grudging. This woman and I began to feel, finally, less exigent, and though a wise person might have questioned that transition, I embraced it. The plans we made—a life together in my house in the spring, and then perhaps a move to Chicago so that she could begin the MFA program in poetry at the School of the Art Institute of Chicago, while I arranged a somewhat complicated but manageable commuting schedule to Iowa City—they were good plans; they were the plans of a new couple, neither young nor old but seasoned and capable of making a serious and lovely life together. Certainly there were complications; the Chicago-Iowa City arrangement was not ideal, and I was tired from the financial need to teach year-round for many years; I needed comfort as much as she did. But comfort seemed to be the bedrock of our time together in December. I could not have been more thrilled.

I had no idea that, all the while I was writing her and sending her my poems, both long and short, simple and complex, and writing her daily e-mails and awaiting hers, she was traveling with another man, with whom she'd left from Los Angeles. They were visiting his mother and traveling around the country. This came out months later, though only a few weeks ago, but after she had left me in Iowa to go to him again in L.A., and then apparently had come and gone and returned to some part of his life, through waves of other boyfriends and girlfriends in West Hollywood in a story whose thread I cannot follow because I can no longer bear it.

* * *

What is left to build?

Love has, sometimes, as one of its traits, a tendency to make the self less exigent rather than more. If one has felt oneself to be, unhealthily, lighter than air for some years, lost in the multifold layers of the self signing its connections and displeasures to the less-accepted world, what a relief to feel things settle, the signs becoming readable rather than inscrutable or hostile, the world one's own world. But if love is connected to the realm of the authentic, then, Trilling would seem to imply, love is connected to selves that continually shed themselves, remake themselves, become other than what they are. Love makes the self an other.

Post-modern diction...it has an odd habit of turning up when one least expects it. In her anthology *Levinas and Lacan: The Missed Encounter,* Sarah Harasym invites a number of scholars to consider what Emmanuel Levinas, the ethicist, and Jacques Lacan, the post-Freudian psychoanalytic theorist, might have said to each other about the Other who is always among us, whose presence is our gift and our mark of Cain and whose unknownness is our greatest pain. It's tempting to turn to such a book as an intellectual deviation from the devastating grief, still profoundly recent, of discovering that one can try to build a city of love, but—unlike the cities from one's childhood—one is likely to fail. Consider the "Other"—a term at once so vivid and so empty that there seem to be almost as many interpretations of it as there are visions of the self. But in "Levinas and Lacan: Facing the Real," Donna Brody brings forth an oddly gnostic view of how both of these seemingly remote thinkers envision an other that itself is both present in our kernel of being and almost infinitely remote.

For Lacan, the "Big Other" (upper-case other) is the domain of the unconscious subject, beyond all conscious imagining or meditation, beyond any person's ability to conceptualize an other self: it is the domain that both underlies and disturbs all consciousness. For Levinas, otherness or "alterity" is, at its heart, unthinkable. "the Other or the face is situated altogether beyond time, as anarchical, immemorial, hyperoriginal or exorbitantly prior; a protolocution preceding but leaving a trace of itself in all modes of the Same" (61). How fascinating to see tame academic language forced to confront ultimate mysteries—thus neologisms or neologistic concepts such as "hyperoriginal" or "exorbitantly prior"— yet, nevertheless, the curiosity here is that intellectual life can so easily resemble a journey of the soul (which intellectuals may or may not accept as an entity). We live in a domain in which something we cannot imagine, a disturbance of the waters of the unconscious, nevertheless colors our views of sameness, of ourselves and our impressions of others like ourselves, and demands of us at the last an allegiance to a form of knowing beyond the mind's capacity to render and an object of knowing beyond the body's ability to resemble.

The Other that is always with us is our face before a god infinitely distant, who did not create this world, who has no place in this world, who did not place us in this world, yet whose very being troubles and infiltrates ours until the moment when, at one with departure, we find ourselves leaving this creation in mind or in deepest feeling for the presence of home, the location beyond ordinary space and time of the mansion that is uniquely ours. Late in the day, darkness falling, loneliness growing like a mist from the ground, we turn wearily from the toys of the day and find ourselves rocketing forward, like someone fainting just before she hits the ground, and there, finally, is the Face that is not our face, the consciousness not our consciousness, and a place prepared at the table, nevertheless recognizable as a table and a place, for us, for our consciousness as it shifts over into the reality it had forgotten it possessed.

The most exigent possible view of the self.

* * *

Croce is calling. Again I am answering, but this time it is my father's voice speaking. I overhear. They are talking about loss, about all the lost souls. They are talking about Croce's lost lover, about my father's students, gunned down in dogfights, about my father's kidnapped innocence, his dreams, Croce's last flight which he has not taken yet but has already foreseen—he has written a song about it, and he sings it to my father, who already knows that Croce will die.

I want to tell them things. I want to warn them both—stop now. Wait. I want to tell them of dreams, of brokenness and of waking to a self both oneself and something distant, redeeming. I want to tell them about the authentic, about the exigent self and about Stafford's line from one thing to the next. "Look," I want to say, "This is all the authentic is—a line from me to you, or from you to each other, or from my lost love to your lost love to the next love who will not be lost. Believe." But they do not hear me, because they do not need to believe. They are both already elsewhere, where belief is irrelevant. They are wholly Other now.

I want, still, to tell them about flying, about how I too acquired a pilot's license and flew for several years, how I avoided disaster and, in tight spots with recalcitrant airplanes, remembered things my father told me to get the plane back on the ground in one piece. I want to say, "Look, a line runs directly from you to me," because I doubt that he ever believed it...I remember his incredulity when, shortly before he died, he learned I was taking flying lessons. "You?" he said." "How can you fly? You're the one in the family who always got carsick. How can you even stand being in a plane?" Such support...but in a way he was right: I was the least likely member of the family to earn a pilot's license, yet perhaps the most stubborn, the most hopeful that, in learning to fly, I could make my way back to him, building the city of our lives anew and becoming, not the son he regretted or tolerated, but the son he wanted.

I want to tell him, and Croce, of my flying dreams, the ones that began shortly after I took up flying and then stopped abruptly a year later: the ones in which, a beautiful body, I lean out of a high tree and keep leaning, falling into air as I feel myself clinching for the inevitable disaster and then, effortlessly, extending my arms and sailing upward on rising currents of air, flying naked among the crowns of trees and then above them, far above them, rising and falling by my own will and the power of the air sustaining me. The inrush of power in those dreams was enormous: I would wake in a sweat, not of fear, but of strong hope, as if a force unknown to me yet intimately related had made contact with my consciousness, infusing it with hyperoriginal strength, exorbitantly prior being above and beyond all normal expectations, and love, love radiating out through the body itself to soar in, through, and above the creation. In these dreams, everything was beloved, and I was both loved and lover. There was no harm to be found anywhere.

Then the dreams stopped.

I want to tell them both about these dreams, about the line of connection I felt between them and my own fragile, ordinary life at the time as an assistant professor of humanities at MIT, about how confused I became when I could draw the line from the dream through me and out into the world but only so far...could not reach, in the end, a guardian spirit or even a fellow dreamer, could not say to Croce or even my living father at that time, "Where does this line lead? What is the authentic that comes from it?" For the authentic, as the line from one thing to the next, interested me all the way down to the darkness of dark water, like a mooring line slowly descending into the darkness under the surface...to follow it would have been interesting indeed, but not something I could imagine in this life. So I turned back—seeking ordinary things, seeking love, raising my children, keeping a job. But in the end, as always, love became the weak link, the exigent part of the self looking for something to balance or further alter its exigency, an other linked to the Other who disturbs all our waters yet whose presence marks some of us for kinship. I looked for kinship. I did not find it.

* * *

Croce is saying good-bye; my father is walking out of the dream. I hear the aircraft engine warming up. I say, "Good-bye," not to either of them, but to the woman, the one who even now, months later, thinks everything is fine, the one who thinks she herself is fine and I'm stupid for not getting over what was clearly not meant to be, the archetypal lover whom Croce realizes can never be called because she will never believe the extent of the damage as she moves on and on, in gyres rising through other men and aspirations to a high point that may yield grace or downfall, those gyres where we men are stations of ascent as we spiral downward. The gyre and the vortex. The woman cannot hear me; she is two thousand miles away, surrounded by admirers in a West Hollywood bar. Croce is climbing into the small plane on the tarmac at Natchitoches, Louisiana, and my father, at the edge of the dream, is turning to wave good-bye. I can see the trees at the other end of the runway. "Wait, Jim," I yell, trying to run toward the plane, but my legs are weighted with iron and make me move like a prisoner. Jim turns and smiles, waves; he knows what's coming. I stop. "I only wish my words could just convince myself/ That it just wasn't real,/ But that's not the way it feels," he sings quietly. "Is it?" he asks. "No," I say. "That's not the way it feels." "We think by feeling," he says. "What is there to know?" "Wait," I say. "That's someone else." "That's everyone, man," he says. The plane begins to taxi. The dream ends.

"Love your ties to their last splendor and you will be free," French writer Edward Jabes once wrote. The authentic is a tie, an exigency with strong bonds; the world is a set of landmines; the authentic might be a line strung back from soldiers at the head of the minefield, so that others can follow without triggering the switches. But there are no soldiers at the far edge of the field, only enormous body counts, black bags, choking smoke ahead. Behind, a garden; here, a line of some kind, asking for the moral strenuousness capable of saying, I will follow this line into darkness, and there I will find a home. The builder of cities, the pilot, the dreamer, all hold the same thread the way daycare children hold a line that connects them as they walk down a street, so that none will get lost. But by the time we are seven, that line is gone, and a different one replaces it: you can see it from the heavens if you fly in your dreams, a line like a contrail heading into the darkness of space, or a buoy line heading down into the depths of the ocean. And all of these, one knows instinctively, are nevertheless metaphors, versions of sameness that point to the Other we all must ultimately find, because He troubles our waters always, overturning, overturning, overturning until he comes whose right it is, and until she comes who sees the same exigency and embraces it. Let lovers fall from the sky toward cities of cardboard and crystal, so fragile they break into light when hit, and let the light, with all its sharp edges, be the advent of the real. That would be enough for me, now, as I turn from the edge of consciousness back to the edge of language, to write, not this, although this says perhaps everything I ever wanted to say, but a poem, which will say something different.

On Being Left Behind

It happens so gradually, sometimes, that only at a certain moment on a certain day—looking up from a book one is reading, a set of papers one is grading, a class syllabus one is preparing—does one see the rows of colleagues' new books, enough of them to remain daunting and thus unread, but there—present, accomplished, finished. One's own books, those with one's own name on the spine, stand as they have stood for the past three, four, five years...four of them, largely unnoticed, with no newcomer to affirm or redeem them. After this moment, perhaps not by coincidence, the scree of silence becomes an avalanche: colleagues inquire: where is the new book? What are you working on now? Do you have a publication date? To which one answers, there is no new book, I'm working on silence now, there is no publication date. One has been left behind.

I should have said: I have been left behind. It's a very stark thing to say, virtually an admission of a failed career. Seeing it in print is all the worse for all the purported promise of the beginning—the first two, first three books, really, from prestigious publishers—two trade, one academic; perhaps, at the time, one might have understood it to be a bad omen that the books sold so badly, attracted on their own so little attention, like the truly socially inept, who really do haunt the walls and corners of parties, waiting for rescue. But at the time, those books of mine appeared to promise a golden career, a "shelf of books," as James Baldwin once said.

What happened?

Should I say, simply: I grew tired of the noise, including my own?

* * *

Once, years ago, when I was twenty and in the midst of what is commonly called a nervous breakdown, though as a Christian Scientist I could never have admitted that, I desperately and rather recklessly accepted an offer of travel from the Stanford Overseas Studies Center, and after three surreal days in Paris, found myself in Hyde Park in London. I was completely exhausted. It was a beautiful June day, and Hyde Park was full of the British—British sunning, British walking, British sitting and discussing one thing or another, British walking dogs, British children playing. All the noises were British, and the trees in the park seemed to swell with the sound they absorbed, transforming it into a kind of second shadow that dogged the actual shadow on the ground, the way a second cloud, slightly more pale than the first, will rise behind it...It occurred to me that never again would I be able to get away from people; there would always be people. Here in England, where I had almost no money and could not travel except to the Stanford campus, then at Cliveden House, I was surrounded by people, as I had been surrounded in Paris...there was no way to escape them. And all of their noises came to me, as I lay down in desperate weariness on the grass, as a cacophony of meaning, of many, many meanings I could not quite catch or assemble, or more thought than I would ever know or wish to know, or more disorder than I could ever imagine. I lay in a great field of entropy in which the illusion of order maintained itself by good British grace. Closing my eyes, I repeated to myself, "silence, silence, silence, silence, silence." Eventually the sound of my silence began to drown out the ambient British noise around me, until, after perhaps an hour or so, all I could hear was a kind of dull hum inside my head. I knew then that I could get up, ride the tube to Paddington Station, and take the train to Maidenhead, where a shuttle to Cliveden would pick me up. It was a last-ditch effort to stay sane in an insane time, having done a crazy thing—having traveled halfway around the world—to get away from my own terror of only seeming to be mortal, of being actually spiritual but not being able to realize it, of having failed at every test Christian Science set before me by which I ought to demonstrate my worthiness as a spiritual idea. All I had was that dull hum that got me back to a place as foreign to me as the moon.

Cliveden was a mansion, most recently owned by Americans—William Waldorf Astor having purchased it in 1893 and then having deeded it to his son, the second Viscount Astor, and his wife, Nancy Witcher, Lady Astor, ironically herself a Christian Scientist—and its cornerstone had been set shortly after the British Revolution, in 1666. But it was also an estate, with a large formal garden behind the house, a secret rose garden hidden among towering boxwood walls to the front of the house, and over 800 acres of forests, grasslands, and secret groves scattered about. The River Thames flowed lazily by all day and all night, as it might have in an A.A. Milne story, never seeming to change pace in its age; the students I was with, all from Stanford, attended classes and made elaborate plans for three-day weekends on Mallorca, in Barcelona, back in Paris, in Dublin, in Prague. Alone and poor, knowing virtually none of the people with whom I'd happened to ship out, I was left to myself. And being left to myself, I turned to the woods around the mansion as my home. I became, I suppose, a kind of wood elf.

A day might go like this: I'd wake up around 8, dress and go down to try to manage something with the classic British breakfasts we had—kippers, fried tomatoes, congealed oatmeal, dry cereal, occasional streaky bacon—and then I might or might not attend one of my classes on 19th-century British history or Anglo-American law. Let's say, for the sake of curiosity, that I did attend both classes, being uncommonly dutiful that day, finishing at about lunchtime. The one good fortune of the Cliveden kitchen was the cook's desire to serve as few people as possible; thus he would willingly prepare bag lunches ahead of time for anyone who preferred to take lunch out of the dining hall. That usually was me. Grabbing my bag lunch, I would head out the side door, near the garage, and walk across the crushed-stone driveway to the far edge of the giftshop (for Cliveden was also a National Trust property, and thus open to the Great British Public on weekends) where the forest began. Then I would simply walk. I would walk until I was tired; I would walk until I saw something of interest—a fieldmouse whose whiskers I could just see beneath a leaf, or a tiny nest of fieldmice nearby, or the eyes of deer among the low branches, or the sharp light of a foxtail disappearing beneath the bracken. I saw a great deal for a non-naturalist. But what I saw I saw in a great silence.

Often I would cross my path several times, finding broken twigs or flattened leaves I was sure I had made—or the actual imprint of my Brooks running shoes in a patch of mud somewhere a mile or so away from the house. In theory it would have been possible to lose oneself in those woods, to follow them farther and farther into property that technically became someone else's, to follow still farther north, toward Reading but skirting it, toward Oxford, into the Cotswolds, into the Midlands, into the Lake District...if the point had been distance, there was distance to be had, and if the point had been stealth, I had learned it by that time. But in a sense, the point was mapping—not externally, not even informally in a journal or notebook, but internally, in memory. I was mapping the Cliveden forest so that, for the rest of my summer, no matter what else happened inside my own mind or in the din of the student world I inhabited or the greater din of London, where I was occasionally obliged to go for Trips of Historical Interest, there would be a terrestrial paradise of a sort where I would be able to place myself at any moment and announce to myself that I was home.

In this way, of course, I was left behind. I went on none of the three-day extravaganzas across Europe or Ireland; even if I had had the money, I would not have gone—could not have gone, could not have endured the tension, the continual presence of others, the need to converse, the fraudulence of social intercourse. I also frequently missed classes, preferring the forest to whatever lesson plan happened to be on the docket for that day, and my absences were noted and commented on, though—because under pressure I was always able to write some kind of paper or another—I never ran the risk of failing. This is curious in retrospect, because had I failed I would have been sent home—that is, back to California—where, one might argue, I would have actually been at home, and would have been happier. But one's remembered landscape is not always safe at every moment, and my remembered landscape of California included places of great danger—a church I was expected to attend regularly; Christian Science practitioners who wanted me to tell them that I was well, that their prayers had healed me; anxious parents who did not know what was wrong with me; a legacy of decline and despair at a university many considered to be great. No—a return to California at that moment might well have been fatal. And yet, while I was willing to call some attention to myself simply by failing to attend classes at Cliveden, I had some sufficient sense of propriety that, having turned in my assignments, I was left to myself. It was a simple fact that no one there really knew what to do with me. Unfailingly polite, asking for nothing, dating no one, traveling almost nowhere, and rarely seen, I was the ghost man of Cliveden. But all that time I was learning the forest and making it my home.

There was time later, in the October after that summer, when people from Cliveden had a reunion at Stanford. Having returned at that point, and having learned something quite remarkable from Cliveden—that my internal mapping skills could be translated and transposed, could work as well in the Pacific coastal range as they worked in England—I was safer mentally and emotionally than I had been in years. So I went to the reunion, which, in the character of a college party, quickly became a rather drunken comparison of exploits—how many trips to the Continent, which professors slept with, how many partners, who hooked up with whom. The stories genuinely amazed me: so much life had been going on, so much sex more or less right outside my door (and sometimes on my side of the door, apparently, as I slept through my roommates' couplings), so much travel, so many things seen, a huge world rendered, for all of these people, more accessible, part of a great adventure. They thought I was funny at the reunion: I was the charming reticent, the one people apparently wanted to date but could never find, the one who never seemed to travel but was always gone. "What were you doing all that time?" Someone asked. I thought about the map in my head, how even then, at that party in a trailer court at Stanford, I could close my eyes and see specific quadrants of the woods, see how the trees touched or didn't touch, see how the most recent storm had brought which branches low, see the robins and the squirrels and the handful of foxes, always just out of reach... "I wasn't doing anything," I said. "I was just walking." "All that time." "Yes." And then the conversation turned to someone else, the woman who'd walked in on one of our tutors having sex with another student. It was a good story, if one liked those kinds of stories, and I did, in a way. Clearly I had pretty much missed everything. I had been left behind. But I had a map in my head that would not otherwise have been there of ground that, when examined minutely, turned out to be ever more minutely beautiful. And so that was my journey, my far travels, my adventure. It hardly bears mentioning. It is best honored, perhaps, in silence.

* * *

If you are prone to anxiety, as I am, being left behind never really loses its characteristic implication of fear...One's childhood fear of being left at a gas station or roadside restaurant metapmorphoses into a fear of being abandoned in marriage, a fear of one's parents dying, a fear of unemployment, of being spun suddenly out of what one knows has never really been a safe universe into the radical unsafety of every blessed day. On the other hand, growing used to such things, it sometimes comes as a shock to see, in the distance, as clouds form before a major thunderstorm, the darkness of a new possibility: the specific reality of being left behind in a specific way, of actually losing one's job after years spent trying to keep it, trying to make it work; or the specific reality of an oddly-shaped mole on, say, one's mother's arm, something that grows strangely and with unusual darkness and leads to increasingly less-revealing clothing, and then to hunching and pain, and then to such pain that she cannot get out of bed...The clouds of melanoma swelled over my mother despite every overt denial from her and from my father, despite every private prayer I prayed that whatever it was that was happening wasn't as bad as I feared it would be. Her death took nine months, in a life symmetry that would have been lovely had it not been horrifying; she died in excruciating pain, with no morphine to ease it, in a Christian Science care home in San Francisco. It was 1980; she had just turned 60; she had joked with us the year before that longevity ran in her family, that she would outlast us all, that she would live to 120.

I have a map in my mind of my mother's death, of the days of her dying in those nine months, that isn't so dissimilar from the map of the Cliveden forest or the Pacific coastal range from Portola Valley to Pescadero. The internal map is always, at heart, a map of terrain: sometimes the terrain is physical, while at other times it is psychic, as fear or sadness or joy or gut-wrenching anxiety become analogues of themselves, grassy fields or orchards or rivulets running into underground streams, emerging again in torrents at the end of a dark valley...yet this is not entirely accurate, for the psychic map is not merely an allegory, in which mountains take the place of joy and underground streams take the place of sorrow. The psychic map is exactly that—a map; feelings acquire spatial reality, they lie next to each other easily or uneasily depending on where they came from or how they have been brought to bear on one another. It is difficult to explain because it cannot be illustrated: there is no picture for it. Yet it exists as image, nonetheless.

And so, in a sense, one can always find one's way. "The valley of the shadow of death" is, by contrast, an allegory of feelings rendered in landscape, the fear and darkness of death scripted into a narrow passageway between mountains whose peaks are invisible among the clouds. One reads such a psalm for comfort, as my brother and sister and I read psalms and poems at my mother's odd, hand-me-down funeral, but even Psalm 23 only hints at what one can construct as a map of one's own being. One can always find one's way, even when the allegory falls apart and there are no mountains for fear and trembling, but only the topography of fear and trembling itself.

Yet behind all this mapping, and its distinctions, is the reality from which we cannot turn: we are all ultimately left behind. The last time I saw her, a couple of days before she died alone in her room at around 1 in the morning, my mother pointed to the full moon outside her window. I have never looked at the moon since then without thinking of her, nor have I ever wondered if she was there, having somehow mapped herself into the life of that hard demi-planet. At the same time, what one sees and what one hopes for are not always a match, and sometimes one has to look into the darkness of the night and see what is actually there—great quantities of empty space between vastly distant stars, places where, if we ever do travel, though we have already mapped many of them, we will leave our planet behind, perhaps in some sense leave ourselves behind. But who can say, really, if a leave-taking is the end of one's being or the beginning of something new? The question, really, perhaps, is stranger and less of a cliché—it has to do with the one who does not leave, the one who stays behind. What is left for him? For her?

* * *

Topographical studies have changed greatly with the advent of satellites and global positioning systems. Now it is possible to map terrain with an accuracy cartographers never before imagined—down to square inches, if one so chose. A map of a city block, should one choose to print it out, might take two hundred wall-sized pages...the map would be on the scale of 1:1, or even more remarkable, on the scale of 10:1—the actual world in which one lived and moved and had one's being magnified ten times, so that even blades of grass became mappable, became in a sense immortal. For it is in the map that things continue to have their existence apart from however they live in the world; the world of the cartographer never dies.

Perhaps, then, I am wrong to think sentimentally about the prospect of being left behind: the perception is wrong. Perhaps I myself am a cartographer's dream, as you are, and we are mapped in our movements and directions in a scale of 10:1, so that, should anyone care to look carefully or adjust our proceedings,they will find us larger, clearer, more distinct in our perfections and our imperfections, more present even than the lifesize world would have us appear. To a cartographer of the human, "life-size" is a matter of opinion, not a given, and the phenomenal world is really merely a matter of scale: change the scale, and one sees different things about the people in it; change the scale radically, and one may see into the human heart.

It is there, beating and not beating, itself and its allegory... unlike the mapping of the world that goes on in my mind, this mapping conflates the literal and the metaphorical, so that what one sees under the microscope of the greatest cartographer is really a body in motion, modeling through its motions the realities of fear or hope or love or anxiety or loneliness or desperation...all present as the heart pumps blood through the arteries, as the lungs rise and fall, as the chemical reactions in the liver purify the blood. It is all there; nothing is left behind.

I imagine this cartographer, who does not exist, whose tools do not exist, but I find myself mapping him, the great gnostic, the medium, perhaps, between all that we are when we feel ourselves most alone and all that we are in actuality, in the different scale that would, if we could see it, show us truly to ourselves as complete, having survived our wounds, upright, not burdened with the fierce weight of so many good-byes, of so many moments of having felt left behind. I imagine this cartographer taking such quiet pride in his work, seeing how little it actually took to lift human beings up to the destiny that was always theirs…it was, in the end, simply a matter of scale.

In the meantime, staring out the window of my old house in Grinnell, Iowa, at a day of thunderheads and racing storms, I contemplate the possibility that, having been insufficiently "productive," I may be asked to leave my job; I consider the prospect of not being able to pay my family's bills; I contemplate being progressively less-known, no longer a writer of books, no longer keeping up, falling behind, left behind, silent. The world in which I work has established itself along these lines, and because of those arbitrary but binding latitudes and longitudes, some of us will drop off the grid; some of us will be lost.

How will it be, then, I ask myself, as I return back across the years to the grid of Cliveden in my mind, to the fieldmice and the foxes and the young robins and the other denizens of the forest, each crossing and re-crossing paths I myself have crossed, none of them still alive, yet all perfectly preserved in the map I have held for them all these years: to what will I return, when I finally am left behind? How great will the welcome be? How great, at last, the silence? And will there be, in fact, someone else already there, who also saw the trail beginning from a very different vantage point and followed it back to a place that will never not exist?

The Burning Child

Somewhere a child is skating alone on a pond. It is late afternoon, late December, and if there were any other skaters, the cold has driven them away. The child skates on. It is nearly dinnertime; soon people will be looking for him. Though a half-moon has risen in the sky, the night is dark, so dark that the child, looking down, believes himself to be skating on an invisible dark field, or on air, or in the firmament close to the earth but above it or below it...the firmament leading to the moon. He looks up, and the dark sky is there; he looks down, and behold, the dark sky is there, too, with one exception: there are no stars below. In the clear night above, he sees the stars.

Curious, he begins to skate farther out on the long pond, out toward the part that has not yet had time to freeze. He skates past the orange plastic cones and warning signs; he can feel the ice shudder a little under him, hear little cracking noises. Skating more slowly, he looks out to the water he can already see, so cold it will take his life, if he should simply slide into it, in less than three minutes; the shock of falling itself might bring unconsciousness. But there, at the edge of the ice, as water flows over the thin surface on which he stops, as it begins to crust around the still blades of his skates, he sees himself, the moon, and the stars in the darkness below, and sees himself standing on a plane that does not exist, a magic carpet, an arbitrary division between the upper and lower heavens. Satisfied, he begins to turn. The ice beneath him does not so much crack now as simply fall away, and suddenly, fully aware of peril, he tries to step back to the stronger ice a few feet from him. With each step he seems to sink...now the water is flowing over the tops of his skates onto his socks, his feet. Now he feels fear.

There are two endings to this story. In the first one, the child returns home, knowing something he did not know before, but weighted also with a new and deeper fear of the world. In the second one, the child is never found.

Neither of these stories is a dream. But let us say that, after returning home, the child makes feeble explanations to his harassed and not terribly interested mother, runs a bath upstairs and warms his feet in the tub as he thinks about the world falling away from him, and then awakens each night for the next two weeks with the same nightmare, a version of himself coming to him from the further darkness of the ice, reaching out just as he sinks below the surface of the water, never saying a word. Each night the child awakens to the vision of his own eyes, bright with terror, growing slowly dim in the darkness of the broken ice; he awakens in animal shock to the vision of his death, which did not occur. Though dreams subside, the vision never leaves him; it comes back to him at odd moments of his adulthood, when he is out on a date, starting a new job, teaching a class, taking his own children to an ordinary playground in the middle of summer. Suddenly he will see it all again. But in all his visions, and in all of his earliest nightmares, the boy sinking below the water never calls out to him, never gives him a sign other than his outreached hand. After many years, the man the boy became comes to believe, not the dream, but only the story of the dream, and his own story of once having skated too far out and having only just barely made it back, having kept the whole ordeal secret from his parents for fear of retribution. In the end, it is just a story.

There is a terrible mourning, on the other hand, for the child who is never found. Other skaters tell police of a boy skating out beyond the orange cones; they tell the story of him at the edge of darkness. Divers launch from the shore and drop down from an aluminum police boat heavy enough to break the ice at least halfway around the lake, but the murky water and thick weeds at the bottom defeat them…or perhaps, as the police chief suggests later, drowning was not the child's end, there was a kidnapping, or the child walked off into the woods. When the snow melts and the ground begins to thaw, police drag the lake again and search in ever wider circles out from the lake to the forest beyond; the child's name is familiar to every police station and every sheriff's department around the country as a missing child, a probable kidnap victim. But he is never found.

Curiously, no one in his family ever dreams about him; it is as if he had never existed. As his brother and sister reach the age of full consciousness, four or five, they have some memory of a third person, and ask about him, but their parents tell them they are mistaken; they are the only children, there never were any more. Every photograph of the child is excised from every family album, removed from every wall; distant relatives are forbidden to speak of him. Growing up largely on their own, the son and daughter diverge: the son becomes reclusive; the daughter, exceptionally extraverted, a cheerleader, has many boyfriends, a small handful of lovers by the time she is sixteen. She feels alive, almost for the first time. The son plays elaborate on-line computer games of battle and conquest with unknown compatriots around the world. He has a compulsion for secrecy and a yearning for almost any kind of knowledge; when his parents are not at home, which is most of the time, he explores every square inch of the house, cataloguing in his mind the location of every book, every article of clothing, every toiletry, every photo album, every piece of debris in the basement and attic. One day, combing through his parents' dresser, he finds, at the bottom of one of the drawers, what he knows he has been looking for for years. It is a picture of a boy, about eight years old, who looks like him but is not—a difference in the eyes, the gaze, as if the child were searching for something, or about to ask for directions. Ironically, in the picture, the child carries a pair of figure skates under his left arm.

After this, the son begins to spend time at the lake; he understands there is something there for him to find. One late October, in his sixteenth year, he walks as far as he can along the long side of the lake and finds an old rowboat that someone has not yet bothered to drag up to shelter for the winter. Neglect hovers over this end of the lake. He has known this for some time, though it has not particularly registered; now, however, he launches the boat onto the lake, judging how far its cracked seams will tolerate his journey, rowing himself to mid-lake in the cold night of stars with water flowing over his running shoes. Peering over the side, he sees himself, but not; that is, he is younger, or feels younger, or sees himself as other than he is. But it cannot be; it can only be a reflection. And yet it is not; it is also more.

From that time on the son moves through his world without loneliness, all his reclusiveness, his reading, and his lakeside ponderings loyal to him now the way friends might be loyal, as he looks for the face of the person in the lake. One thing leads to another, as is the way in stories, but also the way in life, when one is truly living, when one ironically cares little what the next thing may be. Where the son winds up, his younger brother has gone before; though the son never dreams of his brother, the brother has managed to lead the way.

* * *

It is not possible to say whether the drowned child ever existed, or whether, in looking into the lake, the son found himself awakening to a life that was all his, yet only partly his—his to live, yet belonging partly to another. I do not mean to tease on this subject, nor am I, autobiographically speaking, the son: I have no memory, hidden or otherwise, of a brother who disappeared while trying to find the surface of the stars. But I have memories of awakening, and awakening: the harsh memories of too many mornings awakening alone, too aware too quickly of all that has happened in the past twenty years of communal and solitary awakenings; and other kinds, more generous or gentle, in which I seem to be in the company of others, or some other, companion. This evanescence is both the evidence of loss and the hope of redemption: redemption from loneliness so great as to be an illness, redemption from the isolations occasioned by failure—repeated failed relationships, a tremulous relationship to my work, a loss of voice, of self—and redemption from the lust for dreams, for meaning coming from afar or within. Too many dreams, each night, yield a cacophony: it becomes impossible to sort the images; no narrative emerges. If one dream awakens a dreamer, against his will, to confront the reality of his own death; if, in one dream, a figure emerges from the darkness with a message; then one awakens to the reality of mortal life and knows at once its limit and its extension. One has a story to interpret, and in interpreting, as Harold Bloom has said, one prophesies one's continued life beyond the ordinary limits of the body. The body is the medium, but in the end it is only that.

But cacophony, without story, yields a kind of continuous pain in the head, a throbbing of the sort one imagines, say, the disciples of a great leader feel when the leader goes away—dies, vanishes, abdicates...the nature of the departure itself is almost immaterial; it is the absence of the leader and his story that leaves a hole as deep as grief. One knows one has, almost, the material of meaning, but it does not come together; one cannot awaken to a series of imponderable interpolations, images raised upon images as Rome was raised upon the ruined foundations of empire. What is the new story above the layers of silt? What is the old story, desperate to be told yet quiescent, untold?

But in a way, one might argue, this entire story is an allegory of awakening by a voice that, for whatever reason, has chosen not to speak thus far in the first person: something in the act of awakening frightens this voice, as the boy on the ice was frightened just as the ice was giving away under his feet. Why should this be surprising? It is at this moment, if one follows the second version of the story, that the boy confronts his death, his child's sensibilities suddenly grown ancient as an old man's.

And all is right there, almost but not quite instantly, with just enough time for the boy to flicker in and out of consciousness, to know the absolute and appalling authority of the unknown.

* * *

When I was about eight, I contracted a bad cold that turned into bronchitis, then into pneumonia. I learned of these diagnoses only years later, of course, since in Christian Science neither "bronchitis" nor "pneumonia" existed. What happened at the time was infinitely more subtle: one day I felt too sick and feverish to go to school; my mother prayed for me and called a practitioner. About five days later, it hurt terribly to swallow—first solid foods, then even liquids. More prayers. By the end of two weeks, it had become difficult to keep any food down at all, it was difficult to drink without the sensation of drowning, and it was difficult to breathe. Already a rail-thin child, I was losing weight rapidly. My mother continued to call practitioners as if nothing really were wrong, and contined writing daily notes to school apparently simply saying that I was to be excused from my third-grade classes on the basis of a religious exemption. Most of the day, and then day and night, I lay on a couch in the small third-story room where we had our one black-and-white television; for the first week or so, I could concentrate on it, then its noise became an irritant, then I simply stopped noticing.

Sometime in the third week I stopped noticing quite a lot, or rather, began noticing small things but in a different way: the specks of dust on the carpet, for example, became very interesting, the way friends many years later who'd taken LSD described their fascination with ordinary objects—red digital clocks, mitred wood trim corners, the floral design on plates. Sometimes it seemed that the dust was able to fly, and I would picture it flying, not disintegrating in the air as dust does but cohering, like a small space ship or other extra-terrestrial vehicle. At other times, as the dust did seem to disintegrate in the sunlit room, I would seem to see an ocean, the ocean in New Jersey where I played in the summers, or the backwaters of Seven Mile Beach, where my parents would sometimes take me in their boat…Apparently, at times, my mother would come up to check on me, to see if the latest round of prayers had restored me to health, and I would croak something to her about the water and how it just kept going on and on. She would always leave quickly, I remember.

I did not realize until years later that, starving and dehydrated, I was beginning to hallucinate, slipping out of normal consciousness into an awareness of another, absolutely present reality that simply happened to be encased entirely in memory: memory made present through the progressive destruction of the brain. As it lost its essential nourishment, my brain released its defenses in every way it knew how, releasing me— but how odd it is now even to write a sentence such as that, a sentence implicitly equating the contents of consciousness with the neurochemical behavior of a dying brain; one could as easily argue that the brain was releasing itself to the reality of all that existed both beyond it and within it, to every vestige of experience that implied a greater experience, a long continuation. I would be surfing. The wave would swell up behind me as I sat on my board, then leaned forward into the irresistible swell, paddling hard to keep the tip of the board up and in the air, to keep from slipping backward across the backside of the wave…and every time, suddenly, every ride was perfect, the board slanting down just a little as I got to my feet, rocking back slightly as the board began to drop down the front of the wave, as I set my rail and began to ride, the wave curling over and over above me but never collapsing…In some of these reveries, I remember, I rode the same wave for what must have been hours; I have some recollection of starting a ride around noontime and ending it just as the winter sun was setting, around five. In all of those journeys across and through the water, I had a sense of being released into something absolutely true, something reliable and secure in the world, requiring my body yet a somewhat different body from the one I had—or had had; I had no further sense, much of the time, of my ordinary body. Nor was there any such thing as an "astral body," even if I had known the word "astral" at that point. I had my own body, but released from all expectation, merely itself, in a world merely itself. This was always enough until something came to break the spell—my mother, my father after a day's work to see how I was, my brother or sister…and then, suddenly, the appalling pain returned, the almost unbearable difficulty in breathing, the throat that seemed to be on fire all the time, the terrible sensation of something in my stomach, consuming itself, my arms and legs flailing in exhaustion and fright. Though people always triggered this, the terror was never knowing when it was going to end, never knowing when what I thought of as the dream would return; sometimes I would gasp and flail all night, or until, in the deep darkness, I passed out, and then came to again as a child sitting with a surfboard on a beach, waiting for the next wave.

Then, late in the third week, my mother did something utterly out of character. Although, among the Christian Scientists with whom I grew up, no one ever admitted not being healed of something, there were, it turned out, two doctors in our town with some sympathy for the Christian Science way of life; they were willing to step in if something, for some unknown reason, went awry. My mother appeared one morning in the upstairs room, wrapped me in blankets, and carried me to a man named Dr. Rohrmeyer, whose offices were a few blocks from our house. I remember bits of this... the pale green of the office walls; the nurse's attempt to weigh me, as I could barely stand; low whisperings between my mother and the doctor; odd fragments of conversation—"He weighs less than any child I've ever treated," "Another couple of days and he'd be past my help"—oddly, these didn't mean much to me. In some sense I already was no longer there. But Dr. Rohrmeyer gave my mother some capsules—powerful antibiotics, as I learned later—and my mother, knowing I couldn't swallow easily, ground the capsules up into a paste, mixed it with a small amount of water, and had me drink it. The revolting bitterness of the mixture, like a poison, slowly returned me to life. The surfer boy and his ocean began to fade; I began to return to pain, and an awareness of time, of long hours to fill, and hunger, desperate hunger that for several days nothing could allay, and the terrible pain in my throat that only gradually subsided, the mucus I could barely cough up or swallow. Time returned; my body returned. The weight of the return was fierce, the way I thought gravity must affect our Mercury astronauts when they came back to earth.

But over the course of a week, I got better. Presumably one of the things my mother and Dr. Rohrmeyer discussed was my hospitalization, which for my mother would have been an intolerable solution because it would have acknowledged in a very public way the failure of Christian Science to heal me. She would have been mortified at church. So the treatment I received was, in reality, itself a very iffy thing, and again, only years later did I learn how remarkable it was in some ways that I got "better" rather than "worse." All I really knew, however, was that where, before, I had been in a visionary world of great happiness and beauty, I was now back in a Pennsylvania winter with a pained body that could barely carry itself to the bathroom and back. The disappointment was tremendous.

Yet, because I began to improve, my mother gave thanks to the Christian Science practitioners, said nothing about the medicine, and urged me to eat so that I could return to school as quickly as possible. Accordingly, sometime in the middle of the fifth week of the illness, I put on my school clothes and let my mother drop me off at the public school I attended in the middle of the city. She did not come in with me; I carried no further note regarding my absence; in my own mind, I was very sad to be back, for the school was old, decrepit, and violent, with more than its share of angry, violent children; also, although I did not know it at the time, my eyesight was failing—by the spring I would finally get the glasses I had actually needed for two years—and going to school was an ordeal of never being able to see what the teacher was doing, and thus being reprimanded frequently for being "dumb" or "stupid." If heaven had been a vision of the surf in the depths of my illness, hell was school.

I walked into my classroom, began to hang up my coat in my cubby— and heard a scream. A little girl, one of my quasi-friends, was staring at me, screaming. A group of students gathered around her; then she pushed through them and ran to hide behind the teacher, who rushed toward me. She stopped about three feet from me, just looking.

"What in the world are you doing here?" she said.

"My mom said I'm supposed to be here," I said. I looked into her eyes, which were at once frightened and angry—a look I had not seen before. I had to appease her somehow. "Look," I said. "See? I'm all better." She turned instantly, went to the front of the room as if nothing had happened, and called the class to order.

She had to do this several times over the next hour, as small groups of students drifted away from her attention to stare at me. Never in my life had I had so much attention, but the stares were not kind; they were not welcoming; they were frightened.

During a quiet moment that morning I leaned over to the boy who sat next to me and asked him what was the matter.

"The teacher told us you were dead," he said. "She said you died last week."

I considered this. I looked over the whole room of people and suddenly, deeply—as only a child can feel something profoundly—realized how I looked to them, and how I was no longer supposed to be here.

It was years before I realized that, to them, I was the burning child.

* * *

Considering the compelling place it holds in Freud's psychoanalysis, the story of the burning child is riddled with anomalies. As David Lee Miller writes in *Dreams of the Burning Child*, "It is a father's dream, but not Freud's. In fact it was reported to him by a woman patient—yet it was not hers either. She heard it in a lecture, and carried the dream from doctor to doctor. 'Its actual source,' writes Freud, 'is still unknown to me'" (Miller, 177). How curious that the dream that came to play such a dramatic role, not only in Freudian dream analysis, but in the analyses of others—of Jacques Lacan, of Cathy Caruth, of Harold Bloom, of David Miller himself—should have no identifiable origin. It is itself, in an iconographic sense, the burning child of analysis: appearing out of nowhere, a story with no source, like a child emerging from the darkness of death back to life, it invites a fear and trembling in our own identities. Miller makes this point later in his chapter on the dream proper, when speaking of one of the dream's salient features, the open door between the father's vigil and the dead son; "For Freud," Miller writes, "the open door is a threatening signal. He seems to know on some level what lies suspended across its threshold, waiting to be born: an ancient ritual in which the son's death at once destroys and guarantees the father's identity" (185). But Miller observes how ominous this idea remains whether or not the dream-door is opened or closed: "closing the door," he says, "will not quench the flames...our very mental health would be threatened if 'this moving dream' ever crossed the threshold into 'the power of movement'— as indeed it might if the censorship, that critical watchman, ever went to sleep without closing the door" (Miller, 185).

What is the "official" version of this dream? It comes from Freud's *Interpretation of Dreams:*

> The preliminaries to this model dream were as follows. A father had been watching beside his child's sick-bed for days and nights on end. After the child had died, he went into the next room to lie down, but left the door open so that he could see from his bedroom into the room in which his child's body was laid out, with tall candles standing round it. An old man had been engaged to keep watch over it, and sat beside the body murmuring prayers. After a few hours' sleep, the father had a dream that *his child was standing beside his bed, caught him by the arm and whispered to him reproachfully, "Father, don't you see I'm burning?"* He woke up, noticed a bright glare of light from the next room, hurried into it and found that the old watchman had dropped off to sleep and that the wrappings and one of the arms of his beloved child's dead body had been burned by a lighted candle that had fallen on them (*Interpretation, 547-48*).

Cathy Caruth, one of the best commentators on this moment in Freud, raises both implicitly and explicitly the ways in which this dream is connected to Freud's sense of thanatos, the death instinct which, perhaps paradoxically, is not so much interested in death per se but in a release from consciousness, the end and rest from all human endeavor. "If the father dreams rather than wakes up," Caruth writes, "it is because he cannot face the knowledge of the child's death while he is awake" (95). "The dream thus tells the story," she continues, "of a father's grief as the very relation of the psyche to reality: the dream, as a delay, reveals the ineradicable gap between the reality of a death and the desire that cannot overcome it except in the fiction of a dream" (95).

Perhaps. And, yes, perhaps the psyche, with its own denotatively-troubled relationship to "reality," would look upon the reality of the child's death as unbearable, and as resolvable, in a sense, only in sleep, the domain-in-waiting of thanatos. But this act of interpretation on Freud's part—via Caruth—is, as Harold Bloom would say, itself prophetic, and not in a way that Bloom admires: Freud's interpretation prophesies a world in which reality is fundamentally unbearable, in which the spiritual life has no place except as a complex of psychic phenomena, in which death is an end we both crave and fear, in which dreams give us consoling fictions that, rightly understood, only ameliorate our grief, ease our neuroses, or liberate us briefly from psychoses or sociopathies under which we otherwise labor as lunatics. If one takes Bloom's point—and the point is heavily debated—that to interpret is to prophesy, then in relation to this dream it remains particularly important that at its center is an absence—an absent dreamer, an absent subject; there was a patient, but not the patient who dreamed the dream; the burning boy is as enigmatic to a sensitive reader as the burning bush for Moses, at once evanescent, utterly present, entrancing, and terrifying.

Imagine if that were one's own identity—evanescent, utterly present, entrancing, and terrifying. Imagine if one knew that about oneself years before one ever learned the story of the burning child. Imagine if one pictured oneself, over and over, coming back from the dead on a specific morning, the morning of an eight-year-old's seemingly ordinary return to school, after his own seemingly ordinary near-death. Imagine if one woke in the night, from time to time, year after year, with the sensation of burning.

* * *

Bloom asks us to believe that the burning child is the astral body, "and not to read him as a prophetic image is to miss him" (Bloom, 124). But prophetic of what? To Bloom, the answer is almost too obvious: the burning child is burning with the flame of the spirit, the unquenchable gnostic identity of resurrection, proving even in this seemingly ordinary case his triumph over death every bit as remarkable as that of Lazarus, or of Jesus, proving through the device and medium of a dream a spiritual truth so basic to reality that we almost cannot stand the light it emanates; so basic to every moment in which we live, and move, and have our being that we in our mortal dress can do little more most of the time than forget, or look away, because the reality of our own spiritual being is almost too much to bear, the gift we never asked for that can never be returned, the promise never broken, the much-sought-for-and-never-found cohesion ironically right there, all the time, within us and around us.

But doubt is death, or rather, doubt is slowly dying, the act of dying slowly...it is the child skating to the edge of the lake, beyond the cones of safety, looking into the beyond because he can, not thinking—as a child will not think—that some danger may ensue, that some transformation may occur for which he is unprepared, for which his little animal body and emerging consciousness has not yet fathomed the possibility. As water pours over the tops of his skates, he is not thinking of transcendence; he knows the animal fear of thanatos.

And that same child, if rescued or self-rescuing from the lake, a few days or few months later, catches cold, and becomes ill, and then more ill, fading in an out of consciousness as the prayers of believers ineffectually surround him...who is he? If he dreams of himself among the highest, strongest waves, riding the crests in a barrel of sunlight, is he already manifesting Himself to himself? Would there not be some consolation, some cohesion from the sequence of dreams in his near-death state, a pure line of vision to hang onto like the invisible rail onto which one drops, as a skilled surfer, in the dead center of the crested wave? Or would the child be too young to absorb all this? Would he, as luck might have it, return to this world glad for the pots and pans in the kitchen, the Matchbox toy cars and trucks in his bedroom, his sandals in the summer, his dog, his cats, his parents' motorboat, his models of motorcycles, his G.I. Joes? What would he do if he had somehow known that those images of pure, terrible water in his fading dreams were his own awakening, as Lacan would have it—that his dream, himself as the astral body, depended not upon sleep but upon awakening, and in his repeated awakenings to the altered states of a dying consciousness, might he have understood himself to be manifesting to himself the reality of his true being, a conscious force prophesying the life of consciousness beyond all human sequence, space, and limit? "...no one," Lacan writes, "can say what the death of a child is, except the father qua father, that is to say, no conscious being. For the true formula of atheism is not God is dead—even by basing the origin of the function of the father upon his murder, Freud protects the father—the true formula of atheism is *God is unconscious*" (Miller, 185). This child who, on the verge of death, saw a world he would willingly enter and then returned to the present world, this child has spent most of his life wondering if God is unconscious. For what was real in that dying child's dreams, and what was illusion? Where was God, if the child were to die into his vision of a beautiful wave running off the canvas of life? Where was God, if the child were, as he was, brought back from his beautiful vision to the essential ugliness of a working-class Pennsylvania county seat in the middle of winter? Amid the cacophony of spiritual noise, my mother's prayers and thanks to practitioners and my renewed Sunday School lessons, the renewed teaching of Lazarus and of Jesus after three days in the tomb, where was the astral child?

It is spring in Iowa, thirty-nine years after my near-death from pneumonia. This winter, at the edge of darkness, I walked out onto a pond—not a skater's pond, not even a particularly well-known pond by any local standards, just a pond outside of Grinnell—and I walked out to where the ice changed from cloudy white to pale white to translucent, where I could hear the crack and see the water begin to curl around my boots. I stood there for awhile, waiting for something to happen, but nothing did. The evening grew darker. The blessing, such as it was, was of a quiet world, a world of what Robert Frost once called "roughly zones," roughly zones of health or sickness, roughly zones of help or hurt, roughly zones of death or survival. I was crossing a zone, again. I was hoping, after all these years, and all the ensuing stories, some of them good, many of them hard or sad, to remember that, in a prophetic sense, thirty-nine years is as a half-hour, or less, and even in consciousness, should one choose, one can make them flash by as fast as a car swerves to avoid one in the street—that fast, thirty-nine years goes by. And so the astral child should still be here, at this extremity of this minor pond in a place relatively little-known; one meets oneself, in prophetic theory, at the divide and the reunion, the recovery of the moment of terror and wonder. One is oneself and, if one remembers the story, one's brother; one becomes one's own brother, the lost one looking and looking and finally seeing beyond a shadow of a doubt the shadow that is also light, that says, "Come here."

But I had forgotten one crucial thing: I was not that astral child, but rather the absence of the child; no prophecy descended upon me; I did not foretell my immortality, or the death of my mother from melanoma at age 60, or the death of my father 14 years later from pneumonia, or the partner who might lead me out of loneliness years later, or the divine spirit who would never leave me comfortless, not through all the years of hardship I had yet to face. I was only myself, and at my extremity I was in the loveliest of all places, on a board at the top of the most beautiful wave in the world, where living or dying was no issue at all—only motion, the moving wave as the moving dream dropping me down into the roar of life. Others saw me as the astral child; others interpreted, saw me as one come back from the dead. Wherever I myself had been, it was in many respects no different from the place I found myself thirty-nine years later—on ice actually sinking under my feet, water once again coming over my boots. Again, I didn't tell anyone. I stepped quickly and fortunately back to ice that decided to hold, and came back, ran a bath, warmed my frozen feet, made a dinner, looked at pictures of my own children, each at that time happily at home with their respective mothers, and then looked again at the last page of Bloom's chapter on Freud. Whom would I rather meet—the burning child, the astral body, or the child I hallucinated, on the verge of the best wave ever ridden? Would I rather meet the child who knew he was the prophecy, or the child who had no idea? Surprisingly, I realized, the decision was simple. We are, in the end, who we are because that is what we are. Some burn; some perish; some resurrect; some ride a killer wave in perfect balance until, caught in the light at the end of the pipeline, they emerge into something they cannot see. Blinding light is not a prophecy, nor is it a given of the "New Age" vision of near-death experiences. Sometimes it is simply what a child sees when he is, for whatever reason, denied everything else, and it is what his adult self sees in memory, thirty-nine years later, on a dark winter night in Iowa, when there is no light anywhere.

Hiding

My five-year-old son Thomas, unlike his older brothers and sister, has been slow to take to the game of hide-and-seek. The problem is straightforward and interesting to my mind, though to Thomas' it comes in the form of a paradox that confounds and frustrates him. Thomas is a remarkably sweet and somewhat fragile boy; he craves attention and reunion, even if the separation is brief. Thus, for him, the sweetest moment of hide-and-seek is being found. He wants me to find him when we play; he wants others to find him—his siblings, his mother, his friends—when he plays with them. But if they find him, he loses the game. Being found comes with a cost: winners are the ones who hide so skillfully that, after many minutes of searching, the other players give up, call for the hidden one to emerge, and decide among themselves who's going to hide next. Winners are hidden till the very end; technically, they are never "found," but merely give themselves up to discovery so that the game may end.

To make connections is to lose; to disappear is to win. The person who disappears most effectively is, according to the game, the most successful player; the one who half-hides, who leaves a bit of his yellow shirt exposed behind the green ivy or fern, who whistles just as everyone else is turning away to look elsewhere—that player, who gets the attention of being found, also gets the language of loss, the teasing or mild reproof that comes with breaking the rules ("You're not supposed to want to be found!"). Watching Thomas, I can't help think how confusing this cultural message—among so many messages—must be to him. Shouldn't we all want to be found? Isn't there something fundamentally artificial about the desire to disappear? Why should vanishing so successfully from human company be the same as winning? Isn't contact a miracle? Shouldn't we all want to lose?

And yet there are those who remain hidden forever. What do they win?

* * *

It is a strange thing to come to Freud specifically, and psychoanalysis in general, relatively late in one's life, as I did because of my religion. It's hard to imagine anything that could strike a naive young adult so truly as those moments in *Civilization and Its Discontents* or *New Introductory Lectures on Psychoanalysis* when Freud proposes the ways we hide from ourselves. How powerful is the id, driving us instinctively toward both eros and thanatos, and how devastatingly furtive: how many lives historically have passed through domains of eros where no fulfillment could be possible, how much crippling of the ego came from these almost inarticulate convulsions? How many specific Paolos and Francescas lie behind the allegorical pair in *The Inferno*? And what of thanatos—not really the "death instinct," as it is commonly misunderstood to be, but rather a wish to return to the primal state, the pre-conscious state, or the state preceding being—the being of the self: one can almost hear the jumping-off point both for Jung and for mystics who might wish to see in certain aspects of thanatos a vindication of their own weariness of human confusion. No, dissimulation is the way: humans continually hide from themselves. And yet, curiously, it was Freud's mission to try to diminish this process of concealment: like Thomas, he found the most successful hiding to be, not the greatest success, but the greatest neurosis or, in some cases, psychosis. To hide is to invert the self, to subject it to forces inimical to it, to lay it before an altar not of its own choosing. Freud, too, ironically—the reputedly distant man, the cautious analyst, always scientific—craved contact; one sees just how much, for example, in Hilda Doolittle's (H.D.'s) memoir *Tribute to Freud*. There, though Freud is clearly "the doctor," a kinship emerges between doctor and patient whose eros is unmistakable. He cherishes her visits just as she cherishes his wisdom, or rather the way his wisdom augments her own. Each is hiding to some extent; each is yearning to emerge, to be seen, to come out from what Ezra Pound once called—ironically in his poem "Francesca"— "the confusion of voices." Hiding is the human condition; being found is the miracle. Most children, however, seem to learn this the other way around.

* * *

In his 1908 short story "The Jolly Corner"—the first Henry James I ever read, as a sophomore in high school, though I no longer remember why—the protagonist is an American who's spent more than a third of his years "in Europe": a true expatriate, having apparently made himself along lines so continental that he bears almost no trace of his American heritage, nevertheless returns to New York to inspect his "property," the childhood home deeded to him upon his relatives' death. Suddenly the home, his first home, is his. At first it's more or less an annoyance; nevertheless something about the house holds Spenser Brydon's imagination, and over time he finds himself exploring the house in the evenings, at night, searching for something he senses is quite clearly there. In "The Jolly Corner," one of James' last stories, James returns to a style of fiction at once muted and sensational, like that of his dark story "The Turn of the Screw": at some point, in both stories, one begins to sense ominously that the protagonist may not live. A sinister force is at work, something malevolent working through the doors, the windows, the voices and presences of the past. In "The Jolly Corner," however, the tension rises in part because it becomes clear that what Spenser Brydon is tracking, during his late-night explorations of the house, is himself. The man who might have stayed in New York instead of departing for the continent, the man who might have made an entire life here, who might have been successful at some unknown business, who might have fallen in love with a remarkable woman, who might—in the end—have come to know himself as quite different from the man he became—this man is still present; he is not a minor obsession or matter of amusement. He haunts the house, seeming at times almost to taunt Brydon to find him. He is the disappeared alter ego of Brydon, the man so well hidden that Brydon, for all his years abroad, scarcely even guessed his reality. Yet he is real, and at one extraordinarily moment, as Brydon stands on one side of a door at night with darkness all around, he realizes that, should he open the door and pass into the next room, he will confront the other man who has hidden so well. And if he does so, he—Brydon, the expatriate—will die. Only one can live; the emergence of the hidden one will spell death to the one whose life seemed so real and vivid only a short time ago. And yet the temptation to sacrifice oneself so that one's other self becomes fully fleshed is so sensual at this moment that one feels it, senses the size and fragrance and sounds of the room, almost tastes the taste of the stale house air in New York.

What holds Brydon back in this extraordinary moment? It is "Discretion"—James' only word for it, his only attempt at explanation. Discretion, the willing choice of good behavior in which some secrets are never revealed, becomes the saving grace; sufficiently discreet to avoid the monstrous confrontation, Brydon nevertheless faints from the strain, only to be brought back to himself by the housekeeper, Mrs. Muldoon. She is the one, intriguingly, who serves as the amateur psychiatrist in the story, observing that what Brydon has done through his near-confrontation is actually to re-imagine himself, and to integrate that other, hidden self into his true being. Is she right? And is it really discretion, and that alone, that keeps Brydon from opening the door? Or is it fear—fear of the power of the one hidden, the one whose life feels so complete, almost as near as touch, and yet as separate as a robber? And how willingly should a reader take Mrs. Muldoon's consolations, which—especially now, in the early 21st century—have all too much the ring of psychological consolation, the studied language of revelation that actually stands in for—rather than confirming—true revelation? How ironic that Mrs. Muldoon should come to sound like the cheap psychologizing for which many of us have paid so much actual money over the years, respectful of our interlocutors' advanced degrees on the walls and their shelves of therapeutic books. No…Brydon came up against a much more formidable complement at the climax of "The Jolly Corner," and his swoon—a beautifully British tradition, going back to *Pearl* in Middle English or *Piers Plowman*, both around 1360—marks the advent of the unbearable. The difference between Brydon's world and the world of *Pearl* or *Piers Plowman* is the absence of a deity or angel for Brydon: all is secular. In *Pearl*, the dreamer's daughter, dead at age three, comes to the border of the river of the Heavenly City to assure him that she is well and that he, too, is cherished of God and will be well both in his human life and beyond. In *Piers Plowman*, a series of guardians come down to the plowman who has lost himself, who has found some part of himself to be hidden or inaccessible in the corruption of the medieval church; these guardians bring him back to a more comprehensive being, revealing what was hidden. Reaching out for what one cannot see, in these archetypally British works, one receives a benediction. In James, the stunningly modern Victorian, one sees the extraordinary power of the hidden; one confronts an absolute limit; and one has the consolation of armchair psychology that one has, after all, integrated the other self into oneself. But whether that is true or not depends wholly—at least in "The Jolly Corner"—on a depth of inner sensibility for which Brydon shows no aptitude. No: the secret of "The Jolly Corner" is the secret it never gives up; someone essential is always there, but—knowing the finished form of the protagonist, knowing intimately his limits, his predilections, his discretion—never comes out of hiding.

* * *

In an odd and perhaps ominous way, this brings us back to the key question of hide-and-seek: at what point, ingeniously or even perfectly hidden, does one whistle so that someone, already walking away in dejection, will stop, listen closely, and begin the search again? Can one whistle for oneself?

Sometimes, when I've hidden skillfully behind an unlikely bush in the backyard and Thomas has searched with increasing dejection for a few minutes, he will begin to walk slowly toward the house, no longer calling "Dad?" At that point, the game might as well be over, for if one of its peculiarities is his distaste for never being found, an equal peculiarity is the possibility that someone else will hide too well for him to find... Really, in the end, it is a game whose psychological perils are hardly ever discussed because they touch so directly on what we most fear about being human: abandonment. At this point in the game with Thomas, however, I whistle. At first it's just a low, quiet whistle, almost like a bird rustling in the tree; if he doesn't quite hear it, I up the volume a little. Eventually, usually just as he reaches the house, he catches the sound—and this is true even if we've played the game before, even if he's been right at this point before—there's a moment, for him, at which the sound of a clue comes through. He turns and runs, yelling "Whistle again, whistle again!" And just at the right moment, I do.

We laugh about this afterwards, as we play the much more satisfying and less threatening game of chase: I chase him around the yard until I almost grab him and then, dodging me ingeniously at the right moment, he announces, "Now I'm it," and suddenly I have to flee. Sometimes he tackles me by the legs and we go down in a wrestling pile, a small boy and his father in a tickle match to see who will give up first. I always do. He's happy. No tricks are being played here: there's no one out there, somewhere, whom he might miss.

I wonder, over time, if hide-and-seek will become more bearable, or if we'll soon give it up because, for a sensitive child, its implications are just too ugly. What intrigues me is how I used to play it with my brother and sister, and how I would react at not being able to find them. Thomas and I have a different relationship from the one I had with my brother and sister, however: for one thing, I essentially hated them, and they hated me, and not finding them was almost always as fulfilling as finding them. For another thing, they often played tricks, so that, for example, when I found my brother, he would dart out of his hiding place with pocketsful of hard, young acorns, their pointy tips as sharp as thorns, and throw them at me as hard as he could. Finding could be the most dangerous thing on earth right at that moment. So I never had the context of wondering, as Thomas does, what it might be like not to find or not to be found. That came much later, and it came primarily through two sources: religion and love. In my religion, which preached the power of love to heal anything, I was the anomaly, the unhealed child; this meant that, whenever I was sick, all the adults left the room to pray for me without having to witness the "lie" of my sick body, and so I found myself abandoned whenever I was in great pain. There was no self-pity about this, only terror, because it was How People Acted: if you needed them, I learned, they left. Perhaps it was that very matrix of abandonment that primed me, as an adult, to distrust love so much: if someone loved you, eventually he or she would leave. Sometimes I was left; sometimes, sensing an end coming, I left first. "Working things out," as certain kinds of romantic partners try to do, was a hard concept for me to grasp, because it meant trusting very deeply in the imperfections of the other person, trusting that—even if the result were a dissolution—the process had been, in some way, healing. The resonance of Christian Science was too great; I could never quite believe it. But I learned that people hid in love, and they hid as well in thanatos, though in a different way.

* * *

Toward the end of *The Scarlet Letter*, Nathaniel Hawthorne wonders aloud whether love and hatred are, at bottom, essentially the same. Driven by the same power of passion, they differentiate only in the nature of their human circumstances. I remember reading this first as a sophomore in high school and being appalled: any sane person would know the difference between love and hatred. But eros and thanatos, as concepts slightly adjusted psychologically, raise Hawthorne's question again: one can hide in each. In love, one can hide in the power of the passion, the love of being in love, projecting—if that is what one has done, since so many criticisms of contemporary love center on our tendency to project what we wish to see on the beloved—one's deepest hopes on someone who, for whatever reason, is more than willing to receive them: whether we fall in love with ourselves, like Narcissus, or whether we make a partial connection with some other person, we fall in love with the protective shadow that comes down upon lovers and separates them out from the ordinary run of people. This is the dark and distrustful version of the phenomenon; there is also, though much more rarely in my experience, the love of two people meeting, the love Jessica Benjamin describes in *The Bonds of Love* as being the apotheosis of human erotic experience: two selves perceiving each other with joy, asking each other not for versions of oneself but for more difference, more of the beauty of the other; this connection over the thrilled of shared experiences and highly-differentiated pasts becomes a benediction of what Benjamin calls "intersubjectivity," two subjects in communion. The intimacy of this communion is not unlike the intimacy of a confessional, or indeed—though it is public—communion itself, in which, for a brief moment, the congregant receives the body and blood of Christ under the blessing of the priest. How odd that, in a line of people in the dark nave of a church, each person should be so profoundly hidden in the putative love of Jesus! Yet that is the premise...one is wrapped in holiness as one is wrapped in a successful human love, hidden away yet present, a living paradox, delighted and at rest.

At rest…For some humans, after years of disappointment, that element of rest in love is one of the most compelling. That element as well may be what most connects love with thanatos, for in rest love brings the soul back to some primal state almost, though not quite, synonymous with non-being; the point, really, is that it scarcely matters whether one "is" or not. The love that one finds so spiritually healing and consoling seems not to distinguish being from non-being, and has no room for the fear of death; death is swallowed up in life, or life is swallowed up in death; either way, a peaceful state reigns. Eros and thanatos secretly meet; the lovers never betray that hiding. And they, too, may inadvertently disguise what moves each of them the most, which is an impulse at once toward life and toward death. For once, those forces rest in harmony.

* * *

But then there is that vexing question of whistling for oneself, calling oneself out of hiding. It comes back to me now as I think of playing with Thomas, a delight I take for limited amounts of time each week in a custodial arrangement that followed an unsuccessful relationship begun, as always, with much hope. The fact is that, loving one's children, one must be careful not to love them too much, to make them stand in for whatever essential relationship has failed, leaving one fiercely exposed. They see, or sense, the exposure, even at a young age: children know this pain of not being hidden, this pain they do not feel but their parents do. At a certain age, far along, it becomes discussable; otherwise one must learn to deal with it oneself, learn to whistle oneself out of hiding, to witness oneself, as far as one can, in the state in which one actually finds oneself.

I would be lying if I said I had any facility at this. Part of the reason I so love hide-and-seek is that it reminds me of the general nature of my life, in which the most wounded part of me has finally, after 48 years, learned some extraordinary facility for hiding. I whistle, quietly at first, then more loudly, giving my position away; but I never show up. Or almost never. I would like to call this discretion, as Brydon does in "The Jolly Corner," but in fact it feels more like compassion of a profound and avowed sort, like the compassion one takes as a vocation in a monastery: leave the most injured so that their injuries remain unseen; pray for their wellbeing without them knowing. Yet how is that different from what people did to me as a child? Is there not some profound irony in the fact that I now treat myself the way adults treated me when I was two or three?

* * *

In the end, the truest version of this is the least discussed: the winners do vanish. They are never found. James Taylor runs a version of this through the lead track of his old CD *Never Die Young.* In this song, the two lovers move so far away, up and out into space, that "we who couldn't bear to believe they might make it,/ We had to close our eyes." Our faithlessness forces us, in shame, not to see the departure. The ones who vanish are the faithful. They are the true lovers.

One should, in the contemporary culture, "interrogate" this so avowedly romantic point of view. For it establishes as primary only one kind of relationship—two people only for each other—and we know, in our cynical way, that in this culture that works only 50% of the time, or less. Meanwhile there are other relationships—the children who seek their parents but cannot find them, or parents who seek their children: non-custodial fathers, or mothers whose primary relationship has shifted permanently from the absent father to the children. For any one of those, one person vanishing breaks the circle: the fragile loop of hope loops all the way around each of these people, hurt one way or another by abandonment, and thus the greatest fear is vanishing, the greatest need to be found.

And yet I wonder about being found, as I wonder about Jesus' return from the dead. Those 40 days before he ascended must have been a trial— so many people in awe, so many versions of doubting Thomas. All along he had said he would leave another Comforter, "who will abide with you forever, even the spirit of truth." Yet no one, with the possible exception of Mary, had believed him. So much unbelief! So much need to find and be found! One can imagine his relief when, in the end, he was simply lifted up into the illumined version of what we would call heaven. For him there was no difference between being lost and found; ultimately we are all found somehow, each lost sheep returned; yet among humans the division is stark. One cannot help but notice Jesus'weariness at different times during the three years of his ministry, when it seems to him that the spirit he knows so well is, like a second-party check, difficult to cash: he keeps trying to transfer it, and yet the all-powerful spirit seems to have trouble settling in to the lives of those who, normal as they are, only want to believe. They want to be found.

There is the pure loneliness of hiding and the exigent loneliness of needing to be found. In relationship, as humans, we live in exigent loneliness. If, for one moment, we could be what the Sufis call "alone with the alone," we would live in the here and now all fully hidden without fear of loss. Yet for now, compassion, both human and divine, would tell us that it is infinitely better to whistle, to bring people back, to let them find you, to ask them to be found.

The Disappearing Mother

"A lot of people I talked to about Denny seemed to be continuing the analysis of the people in the 'Big Chill' session who tried to figure out why he had taken his own life. Some of them asked me if he had AIDS, and I sometimes answered, 'He didn't need AIDS.' I don't know what he had, but I know what he didn't have: his health, his work, somebody to share his life with. For those of us who define our lives in terms of our families, he was unimaginably alone. And he didn't have that sense of worth that translates into capital to draw on in hard times—those moments when you have to make some adaptation to life. I don't know where that sense comes from, but I suspect part of it is reflected in a phrase Robert Keohane used in talking about what Denny lacked: 'this kind of underlying self-confidence that whatever he's doing must be right because his parents taught him when he was two that it was.'"

—Calvin Trillin, *Remembering Denny* (209-210)

"We have already postulated that self-esteem depends upon 'building-in' or incorporating a sense of being unequivocally loved for oneself. Since a mother is, in childhood, the most important source of unequivocal love, it is natural enough that her disappearance should interfere with, or prevent, the incorporation of love, and hence make self-esteem more difficult to attain or preserve...I am inclined to link [Thomas Traherne's 'dependence upon external objects' to achieve some blissful illusion of unity] with a lack of 'good objects' within the psyche: a failure, in early childhood, to incorporate the mother's love and thus ensure a continuing source of self-esteem from within.

—Anthony Storr, *Solitude: A Return to the Self* (125, 141)

I have been avoiding writing this essay my entire life. At the same time, it may be true that I have written the shadow of this essay into everything that has come before—every published poem, essay, or book, and every rejected poem, essay, or book. The published work, consensual public evidence of high achievement, sits in one pile; the unpublished work, private evidence of what one person has called "an increasingly failed career," sits in another, much larger stack. One might argue that a reasonable man or woman would never weigh these respective stacks, but take pleasure and reasonable pride in the published work, while recognizing both the unseen achievements and the noted shortcomings of the unpublished work. The idea that all of it together represents one thing—in a sense, one giant avoidance—seems to me interesting. As with all giant avoidances, there is an enormous reason for it.

* * *

All but one of the adults I've polled on the subject find that their earliest memories start at about the age of three or three-and-a-half. Most have the odd experience of remembering that, at age three, they remembered something earlier, but they can no longer remember what that was. My son Thomas, now five, was born with underdeveloped lungs and kept for several hours after his birth in a warm incubator with a brilliant light above to stimulate his body. Throughout his first year-and-a-half, he was fascinated with ceiling lights; he would stare at them for minutes at a time, and the most magical thing in the world for him was to learn to flip the light switch in a room. He would do this continuously, on and off, on and off, while I asked him if he had any memory of a very bright light at some time in his short life. He nodded vigorously and, as he learned to talk, learned "off" and "on" as quickly as he learned "Mom" and "Dad." Now, however, he says he has no memory of this at all; lights don't interest him much, whether on or off; he thinks it's funny when I describe to him his one-and-a-half year old self, standing on the back of a couch in the living room, flipping the light switch.

I have very clear memories going back a little further than most, back to the age of two-and-a-half. It's an open question whether I remember these because of some synaptic quirk or whether I remember these because they were particularly traumatic. What I know is that, at a certain moment about a year after I had learned to walk, my legs stopped working. I simply lost all sensation in them. I can remember waking up one morning not being able to feel the lower half of my body, rolling onto the floor, and calling for help. I can remember my mother chiding me for teasing her, insisting that I get up and come down to breakfast. Only when she saw me dragging myself across the floor with my arms, my legs trailing behind with no reflex or motion of their own, did she realize I was serious. She did then what she did always, or almost always, for the rest of my life, as long as she was in it: she went into another room and called a Christian Science practitioner.

No one knows what this was about. My sister and brother, the only remaining sources of information, were at that point about 12 and 11, already enmeshed in the incipient rebellions that would become full-fledged battles in a couple of years; they paid attention to me only when they needed a target for teasing or harrassment. Neither of them can remember much about it. "At one point you were walking, and then you weren't," my sister said. "I remember having to carry you upstairs to the sick room and back down. You lost a lot of weight." But no one can remember why. My mother, I remember, was convinced that I had been stricken with polio, and when—two weeks later—I was suddenly able to walk again, she rejoiced at what was clearly a perfect Christian Science healing. My brother has never voiced an opinion on the matter; my sister thinks my temporary paralysis was a response to some trauma—

something I had witnessed, or something that had happened to me, that harmed me sufficiently to cause a profound psychosomatic response. I have the vaguest memory of my brother's friends being very interested in my body, and a place they all used to hang out in the park across the street from our house, and bushes we used to go into, but when I return to that memory there are huge gaps in it—blank spaces where I simply cannot see what, if anything, happened. So there may have been a physical trauma. I very much doubt the polio "diagnosis," which would have had other symptoms, and because there are no medical records, I have no way of knowing what a physician might have said. But I remember suddenly not being able to walk. And I remember my mother leaving all the time.

* * *

Different psychologists argue fiercely over the power of the mother during the first years of a child's life. What most people consider mainstream psychology—the work of Daniel Winnicott, Anthony Storr, or Robert Firestone—argues emphatically for the importance of the mother-child bond in the first years; a disruption of this bond will cause, as Storr says, an absence of "good objects" in the psyche, a failure to incorporate the mother's love and thus a failure to have that essential self-esteem that most children acquire. Feminist psychoanalysts dispute this in a number of ways: Luce Irigaray deconstructs the gender dynamic of the mother-child dyad, interrogating it as a kind of adult male fantasy, and Jacques Lacan explores the complexities of self-fashioning in a way that includes but refuses to limit itself to parent-child bonding. At the same time, first-person accounts of children raised in motherless homes—raised by fathers or relatives—indicate that what is at stake is not necessarily the "mother-child" dyad, but rather a clear and reliable connection between the stable, nurturing adult self and the emerging self of the child.

Nevertheless, if one was born into what was, at one time, a "traditional" American family, as I was, with a father who went off to work most mornings and a mother who stayed home with the kids, one's primary bond was with the mother. Mine was. Or should have been. And I feel certain she wanted, more than almost anything, for that bond to work. But she herself was in bondage to two mothers, neither of them stable, who had never let go—one her actual mother, an obese Georgian named Mary

Goode Powell who, as a Christian Science practitioner with a devoted following, had many responsibilities and an absolute faith in Christian Science as "the way, the truth, and the life"; and Mary Baker Eddy, Discoverer and Founder of the Christian Science Church, dead in 1913, technically, but in another sense never dead, at least not in our household, always alive and present and judging, always full of admonitions about Malicious Animal Magnetism or false beliefs, always chiding my mother for her shortcomings, her imperfect faith, the errors that impeded her healings, her multiple faults that, while "unreal," nevertheless kept her in some degree separate from God.

Enslaved by these two women, one occasionally present, the other a continually present ghost, my mother scarcely had a chance to learn what it meant to live one's own life for one's self. At her center she was empty, brutalized, and terrified. Despite her best intentions, that is what she had to offer her children. And when things got out of hand, as they often did, she would disappear—to some other room, with the door closed—to call a Christian Science practitioner. No matter how young we were, regardless of the possible danger of leaving an infant alone in another room, she took to heart the Christian Science insistence that childhood illness actually has nothing to do with children but is in fact a manifestation of some error of thinking within the parent's mind. Thus, at the first sign of illness—when other children are cuddled and tended, hugged, wrapped in blankets, taken with care to the doctor or the hospital, attentively tended—we were left alone.

My brother and sister had each other; what I remember most about my early childhood, other than partial paralysis at age two-and-a-half, is aloneness. Blank, meaningless aloneness. Sitting on a wooden floor in a room watching a shaft of sunlight move slowly toward me. Being told not to move. Feeling terrible in some unnamable way. Feeling absolutely without protection, without hope, without comfort, without love. Knowing all that, being two-and-a-half, and being able to do not a thing about it. All I can remember knowing is that there could be no world worse than this, no place worse, nothing as painful as the nothingness all around me. And, of course, those feelings never really went away, and as psychoanalysis is rarely full of surprises, the return of those feelings in my late middle age is something any analyst could have predicted. What is dishearteningly predictable as well is that no one has been able to offer a cure. Perhaps there is none, if one learns the world from the very beginning in a certain way. Perhaps one's only hope is to re-learn the world at an old age—or to consent to a long dark night of the soul, rather than a therapeutically quick one: I remember reading William Styron's *Darkness Visible* with astonishment in the spring of 1992, amazed at how my symptoms echoed his: my aloneness seemed a little less painful, less pressing. But for all the treatment he sought and received, for all the treatment that failed, eventually time came to his rescue...over a period of about six to eight months. Six months, as I recall...an eternity of profound depression. And then his body slowly began to heal itself. But for me, that all began in 1991...deepened precipitously in 1995...and it is now 2004...13 years...and no healing, nothing resembling healing, for all the 20 or so antidepressants tried without success, for all the various treatments...some bodies, apparently, cannot heal themselves, and thus far mine is one. Some of that may be genetic; some of it may come from those earliest encounters with the person most charged with my care, and my complete conviction, by the age of three, that this was a world of emptiness, terrors, terrible physical pains, and nightmares, and I wanted none of it. Had death been offered to me clearly when I was eight, I would have accepted it.

* * *

If this seems like an attack on my mother, I should step away and suggest that what I intended was actually something rather different, for if she disappeared regularly when I was in crisis—and she did—her own life was characterized from the start by sudden entrances and exits, brief periods of bliss, and then exigencies, disappearances, a re-writing of her past. She was who she was when I showed up in her life in part because her parents had forced her to erase the part of her life that she most loved, the part before Christian Science entered the picture. But that's the part I think about most when I think about her. Because I feel fairly sure that, between the time of her birth and the time she was six, even though her own mother was quite troubled and possibly manic-depressive, my mother had periods of true happiness.

She was, rather prophetically in a way, the product of an unintentional one-night stand. Unlike contemporary one-night stands, however, the one between her father and mother had been scripted quite differently, at least as far as my grandmother's father—my great-grandfather—was concerned. The Goodes lived a generally quiet life in turn-of-the-century Hawkinsville, Georgia, but they had northern relatives: in the summer of 1919, one of these relatives invited the Goode family for an extended stay in Washington, D.C. While they were there, my grandmother met an apparently delightful young man named Hunter Dunlap Scott, and after spending some time together the two of them promised to correspond when my grandmother returned to Georgia.

My great-grandfather, however, was in every way a southern patriarch, the son of slaveholders, a staunch Confederate, and absolute master of his household. Among other things, he read all the incoming mail, whether or not it was addressed to him: he liked to keep abreast of the family news. Thus when, one day, Hunter wrote a letter inquiring how "the baby was coming along"—referring to a conversation he had had with my grandmother about a friend who was recently married and pregnant—my great-grandfather made the assumption, which he characteristically did not bother to confirm with anyone, that my grandmother was pregnant and that Hunter was the father. On a pretext, he invited Hunter to come visit the family in Georgia. As his correspondence with my grandmother had become increasingly compelling, Hunter was only too delighted to accept, and arrived in Hawkinsville about a week later, sometime late in the month of October 1919.

What he encountered was psychotic. My great-grandfather met him at the station with a hired hand and a loaded shotgun, and proceeded to drive him to the house, where he encountered my hysterical grandmother, pleading with her father not to go through with his plan, my furious great-grandmother, two friends of the family whose mental states can only be imagined, and a justice of the peace. Before this justice, Hunter Dunlap Scott was married to my grandmother, Mary Goode, whose distress must have made the minimal service purely surreal.

That night, Hunter fulfilled what he considered either his duty or his right from the appalling events of the day. The next day he got on a train back to Washington, and filed for divorce—an uncommon proceeding at that time, but not difficult, given the number of ways in which the marriage itself was both a civil and also, though it was never prosecuted, a criminal violation. However, on the night he slept with my grandmother, they conceived my mother, Mary Scott Goode. She was born nine months later, to a mother of about 20, a grandmother of about 40, and a grandfather somewhat older, on July 20, 1920.

For whatever reasons, perhaps related to the family's genetic predisposition toward depression and alcoholism, only the latter of which might have been diagnosed at the time, my great-grandfather did not live beyond my mother's first year. His death, after his legacy of terror to these women and this child, was, by all family stories, a great blessing. Suddenly Mary Goode, his wife, later called "Mama Goode," was freed from a tyrant; her daughter, Mary, was similarly freed; and the child, Little Mary, also called Polly, grew up in a matriarchy almost free of the drama attached to her birth, despite whispers around town. My great-grandfather had left a small legacy; the house was free and clear; for six years, from 1920 till 1926, my mother grew up in a pretty part of rural Georgia, seasonably cold in the winter and humidly hot in the summer, alive with forests and creeks and paths into and out of the woods. Though Southern Baptists by predilection, neither Mama Goode nor Mary Goode was particularly religious; my mother, on the very rare occasions she talked about her first six years, talked in ironic tones about being "a little heathen," but it was clear she loved it: adored by two women who, themselves released from bondage, were settling into a quiet life of reading, gardening, visiting neighbors, and tending their remarkable child and grandchild, my mother must have started life feeling relatively safe and in love with the world. I nevertheless suspect problems, never discussed, from that time: whatever Mary Goode had been through at the hands of her father had clearly scarred her, and as a young woman her manic depression or bi-polar disorder would have been already evident: surely there were moments when my mother came home from one of her early explorations of the woods to find my grandmother weeping uncontrollably, or frantically cleaning house, or simply lying in bed all day, as she had the day before or would the next day. But Mama Goode, who seems to have been within the generation that missed the family genetic curse, was by all accounts steady and loving, and would have muted my mother's encounters with Mary Goode. Though flawed at its heart, the world then could not have been much better for six-year-old Mary Scott Goode.

But it is difficult to find a life without errors, and many if not most of those errors begin as hopes. A young, unmarried woman, my grandmother knew herself to be an anomaly, and though the family did not discuss the circumstances of her marriage, it was clear that, from north to south, a feeling arose that Mary Goode needed relief from her anomalous situation. The family had other northern relatives, in Philadelphia, and Mary Goode had even studied piano for a time at Curtis before my mother's birth. Thus, in 1926, the Goode women and child traveled north to Philadelphia, where my grandmother was introduced to another nice young man—not quite as young this time, but certainly both dignified and vivacious, with a sparkling sense of humor and excellent prospects—Thomas R. Powell of the Philadelphia Powells. T.R., as he was known, was beginning to make an excellent income as an insurance salesman; though on the road a great deal, his accounts were settling down into profitable consistency, and it seemed likely he would move fairly soon to a managerial position in the Philadelphia office.

Most important, he was a member of a relatively new American religion, founded by a woman in Boston and called Christian Science, that taught how we might all be released from our illusions of need, lack, and physical or mental illness simply by knowing the spiritual truth of our being as Jesus taught it. At that time, Christian Science was the fastest growing religion in the United States, outstripping all mainstream Christian denominations as well as the Church of Jesus Christ of the Latter-Day Saints, and newspapers routinely ran news articles on the public lectures of Christian Science practitioners. T.R. captivated my grandmother both with his salesmanship and with his astonishing doctrine of how he, she, my mother, and everyone else were actually already spiritually perfect, perfectly cared for, in perfect health; all we needed to do was to realize it. The impression, as far as I can tell from the family stories, was akin to a tidal wave: Mary Goode had no strength to resist it. By the end of the year, she and my six-year-old mother had moved from rural Hawkinsville to Philadelphia.

It's difficult, with no diaries or written records from that time and with all relatives who might have known the truth now dead, to piece together what those first years in Philadelphia were like for my mother. Certainly, at the most basic level, the shock would have been great: my mother lost her key stabilizing influence, her grandmother, who stayed behind in Georgia; she acquired a father, or rather stepfather, who was the first man with whom she'd ever had to have sustained contact; she went from a rural environment, full of secret playgrounds and hiding places, to a city; and she went from shoeless childhood to fully-dressed school life, as her parents enrolled her in the premier Quaker school of the day, Germantown Friends. Moreover, and perhaps most important, she began faithfully, with an enforced faithfulness, attending Christian Science Sunday School, and having the Bible and Mary Baker Eddy's text, *Science and Health with Key to the Scriptures*, read to her daily until she herself could read; then she was obligated to read a portion of each book every morning before going to school. At that point she would have begun to learn that everything she had known or intuited in Georgia was false; the material world was false, a lie; only the spiritual world was true; and only through ardent prayer could we come to see the spiritual world in place of the material one. In truth, said Christian Science, there was only one world—that of the spirit—but our mistakes made us believe in two. My mother's new job, as a six-year-old, would have been to erase the reality of her past from her mind, and supplant it with a vision of spiritual perfection from her brand-new religion. It would have been a little like handing a child, who was used to riding a horse or riding in a buggy, a space ship, and telling her to push certain buttons that would blast her off into deep space. I remember my own encounters with this phenomenon... suddenly "all that is solid melts into air."

Kathryn Harrison, whose book *The Kiss*, about her affair with her own father, caused such a sensation several years ago, was also, not really coincidentally, raised as a Christian Scientist, and her brief passage about this kind of experience is one of the most lucid and accurate accounts I've ever read:

> The practitioner was a woman with gray hair and a woolly, nubby sweater that I touched as she prayed over me, my head in her lap and one of her hands on my forehead, the other over my heart... .I felt myself separated from my flesh, and from all earthly things. I felt myself no more corporeal than the tremble in the air over a fire. I had no words for what happened—I

never will have—and in astonishment I learned, at six, a truth dangerous to someone so young and so lovelorn. I saw that transcendence was possible: that spirit could conquer matter, and that therefore I could overcome whatever obstacles prevented my mother's loving me. I could overcome myself (Harrison, 105-6).

Did Mary Goode love my mother? Or was my mother an impediment, a sign of shame, a continually-present symbol and reality of something that had gone psychotically wrong within her family? Later evidence clearly suggests Mary Goode's ambivalence about my mother; whatever she may have felt when my mother was six, it was clear that T.R. Powell, Philadelphia, Germantown Friends school and, above all, Christian Science constituted the cure. With one grand gesture, my grandmother acquired a husband, more than adequate wealth, social position, a forward-looking religion, and a direction in which to propel her unintended child. More than that, she found her own calling: studying Christian Science intensively, she became, within a few years, qualified according to the Christian Science Mother Church to practice the healing ministry of Christian Science. My grandmother officially became a Christian Science practitioner, duly listed in The *Christian Science Journal*. It was one of the highest honors she could possibly have imagined.

Still, my guess is that, overall, after a rough several months or even a year of adaptation, Mary Scott Goode began to settle in. The miracle in the equation was not Christian Science—that, in the end, was the evil—but rather Germantown Friends School; by tradition and as an extension of their honesty piety, Friends schools tended to be well-structured, strict yet compassionate, rigorous intellectually yet full of small kindnesses, and good places to meet kindred spirits. My own experience of Friends Community School in West Chester, Pennsylvania from fourth through sixth grades confirmed this, and everything that my mother ever said about Germantown Friends made it clear that, if her new home was not actually a home, her six hours a day five days a week at a Quaker school were almost an adequate substitute. At Germantown Friends my mother would have found that she was smart, a quick learner, a voracious reader and a painter of notable incipient talent (since, despite rumors to the contrary, Friends schools did provide excellent education in the arts, including music and theatre); funny, vivacious in her own way, slightly mischievous, and with an excellent imagination, she would have made friends quickly, and they would have lasted: in fact, they lasted throughout her life. One of my late memories of her, within two years of her death, was a reunion she attended at Germantown Friends; I believe it was her class, the class of 1938's, 40th reunion. She returned with photographs of at least 20 people her age, and had stories about them all, although she had not seen most of them for over a decade. Germantown Friends clearly was a mediating reality between Christian Science and home—a practical, quietly religious, no-nonsense place of exploration and play, remarkably subversive when placed side-by-side with Christian Science; fortunately its reputation as a school won out over doctrinal concerns, and in any case my grandmother was quickly becoming too busy to worry about her daughter: besides becoming a practitioner, she had three other children in quick succession—Dick, David, and Sandy. With three young boys in the house, a husband to tend, and a Christian Science practice to uphold, my grandmother clearly had her hands full. To some extent I expect the care and feeding of my mother fell to her new stepfather, T.R., which somewhere along the way raised certain questions that probably never will be answered, but whose impact altered my mother's life.

Only one album of pictures of the extended family remains—my father threw out the rest in what was effectively a family purging in 1984, four years after my mother died—but among those pictures are three of my mother, taken when she was 13, 17, and 21. They tell an extraordinary story. At 13, my mother is sitting on the front stoop of a small house in Avalon, New Jersey, where the family used to vacation in the summers. Dark-skinned—one might wonder about the possibility of African-American blood far in the background of her Confederate family—radiantly smiling, with brilliant eyes and a look that suggested someone trying to think of some amusing new way to torment her younger brothers, my mother is one of the most beautiful 13-year-olds I have ever seen; indeed, her beauty closely resembles that of my own 14-year-old daughter Georgia. What most radiates from the photograph, however, is a naive yet knowing confidence: whatever she has been through, however the family has changed, whatever she has encountered in Germantown Friends or in Christian Science or on the beaches of Avalon, the net effect has been good. This is a strong, happy girl, barefoot again, in a simple, collared short-sleeve shirt and shorts, clearly on her way to or from the beach.

Four years later, it is clear that something has gone drastically wrong. At 17, posing in a long white gown for her high school graduation photograph, my mother cannot disguise her troubled look; her effort to smile only makes the troubled character more profound. Her gaze is indirect, furtive, half toward the camera and half past it; her eyebrows rise slightly, as if in alarm, and her brow is furrowed in a way that suggests, not merely anxiety, but panic: the look in the face of this young woman is the look of one on the verge of flight. Clearly she has been told how to pose, and the folds of her dress flow prettily over the bench on which she sits, but her hands, folded in a position of mock repose, show agitation in they way they're clenched, in the way the fingers are crossed. This young woman does not look, with confidence, directly into the camera; her posture is forced and awkward, not natural; her skin is unnaturally pale, regardless of the time of year; her hair is not happily wild nor perfectly coiffed, but rather slightly askew, as if even that detail could not be brought under control. It is the picture of a caged animal. One cannot look at it—and my sister and I have commented on this to each other repeatedly—without feeling fear for the well-being of this girl.

Again, another four years pass, and the college graduation photograph captures what appears to be another transformation. The young woman in this picture, now 21, sits again in a white gown with apparently perfect ease. The gown flows around her to the floor; her hands lie in her lap open and calm, in seeming serenity; her face, not confronting the camera, is rather downturned as she looks toward her open palms with a quiet, secure smile. Her pose is at once regal and deferential; it is a modeling pose, a stock piece, yet she has fitted herself perfectly to it. She is already engaged to my father, an ensign in the Navy and a flight instructor; it is 1942, the darkest night of World War II; she knows that, barring a cataclysm, she will marry Warren Simmons at the conclusion of the war. The photograph suggests a young woman who sees her life laid out before her and accepts it, without anxiety or passion; a secret knowledge infuses the picture.

The progression has fascinated me for years. Clearly the picture I love most is the informal shot of her at 13—such a kid; such a seemingly happy kid. Whatever might have been going on, something was balance. In general, in fact, in my memory, whenever my mother was in Avalon, New Jersey, her mood seemed to lighten: clearly being by the ocean was restorative, and being in a place she'd loved from the time she was seven, the compensation for losing her Georgia childhood, was a more than adequate compensation. But, because in some ways it is the 17-year-old girl I knew most often as my mother, I come back to that photograph with a sick feeling in my stomach. How you interpret it depends a great deal on certain pieces of information, and on certain gaps that now cannot be filled.

By that time it was clear that T.R., who within the family had acquired the affectionate nickname of "Poppy," had taken charge of her life. Once, when I was a teenager, she told me the story of how she had happened to attend Wheaton College in Norton, Massachusetts. She herself had wanted to go to art school, if not in Philadelphia then in New York, or, astonishingly, Paris, but her father absolutely forbid it: art school did not lead to a respectable profession for a young woman, nor was it a proper training ground for a wife-to-be, which in 1938 America was the underlying reality for most women of my mother's social class. Art schools were immoral, my mother reported my grandfather as saying; they celebrated the body; they had nude models—nude models!—in the classroom; it was possible that my mother might have to examine cadavers to study muscle formations; all of this clearly attracted, not only the wrong sort of women, but particularly the wrong sort of men to such schools. My mother would never make an appropriate marital match with someone from an art school. Moreover, with their emphasis on the body, art schools taught unreality—they taught what Christian Science clearly indicated was unreal. No, despite exceptional artistic talent, which her teachers at Germantown Friends had repeatedly commented upon, my mother would not study art as an entryway to adulthood. Poppy decided for her: she would go to a good college, not a great one—for in his view the human intellect, such as it was practiced at Radcliffe or Smith or Wellesley, was also an affront to Christian Science, a substitution of the human mind for the divine mind. Thus, on the verge of young womanhood, my mother found her most important decisions lifted from her hands by the man who had introduced the family to Christian Science, whom her mother adored and revered for having saved her, who saw himself as having the right and obligation to control completely his children's futures in accordance with his understanding of his religion, and who tolerated absolutely no dissent. Having performed so ably and accomplished so much at Germantown Friends, having been so admired and having found friendship and comfort, my mother suddenly found that everything she had done best in school served as her stepfather's fodder for destruction.

That alone, one might argue, would be enough to explain the profoundly disturbed face in the portrait; indeed, that face reminds me of the look of depression I see in my own face at crucial moments when, in emotional extremity, I realize I must still get up and teach a class, attempt to focus a discussion or respond to a group of student essays, or otherwise pretend that life is normal. But my sister particularly, and I too, wonder if there may be more.

Poppy was, on the surface, a jovial and entertaining man; he liked to play little games with his children and grandchildren, and in one of these he liked to have you sit on his lap while he jiggled his legs faster and faster, to see how long you could stay on. For a small child, or rather for a small boy, the thrill, of course, was trying to stay on as long as possible, eventually falling. I remember that my mother played this game with me, too, a few times, though it was never the same with her. But I know that Poppy played it with her. And I have come to suspect that, with her, he may have played it slightly differently, so that she would stay on rather than fall off, and I suspect he would have commented on her flushed response as she grew older, approving of it and reminding her how much fun the game was. And there may have been other games, more shadowy and, psychologically, far more complex. One record my sister has kept over the years is a group of letters from Poppy to my mother that I found while sorting through the random assortment of her papers left in the aftermath of my father's vindictive housecleaning. These letters date from my mother's early years at Wheaton. What's most striking about these letters is their tone: they are love letters. Though they include bits of advice about what classes to take or how to approach certain problems with studying or how not to worry about the future, they are also letters about love— about God's love for his creation, and how fortunate my mother has been to grow up with the truth of Love in Christian Science, and how fortunate both she and Poppy have been to have shared that love, through so many moments together. The the prose style is deft, complex, and literary, elegantly couched in religious visions and keen hopes; the background voice is eerie: it is deeply manipulative, and its spell is exactly the spell Kathryn Harrison describes when she describes her father's effect on her at the time he initiates his seduction, one specific kiss:

> In years to come, I'll think of the kiss as a kind of transforming sting, like that of a scorpion: a narcotic that spreads from my mouth to my brain. The kiss is the point at which I begin, slowly, inexorably, to fall sleep, to surrender volition, to become paralyzed. It's the drug my father administers in order that he might consume me. That I might desire to be consumed (Harrison, 70).

Did my stepfather sexually abuse my mother? My sister is convinced that it happened: "There's just too much circumstantial evidence," she says. "And then there's how Mom acted." This is a slightly different subject, but it raises the legitimate issue of working back from the symptoms of a specifically-ill person to the possible or probable causes. In the case of Anne Sexton, for example, who early into therapy had memories in which her drunken father had come into her room at night, after she had come into puberty, and had sexually molested her, the patient who is Anne Sexton has symptoms that, while not classic symptoms of hysteria, combine some of those symptoms with psychotic dissociations or personality "splitting," trances or fugue states, abrupt failures or seeming erasures of memory, a borderline personality disorder and problems with personal boundaries in general, so that—for example—one of the difficulties of hospitalizing Anne Sexton was that she would take on some of the symptoms of other patients. All of these psychological characteristics are consistent with a patient who has suffered sexual abuse. Whether one believes in the physical reality of the abuse, when actual physical evidence is absent, depends in part upon one's training and one's pattern of interpretation. In Sexton's case, as Diane Middlebrook reports, "Lois Ames, a psychiatric social worker who has treated incest survivors and who was very close to Sexton for many years, said unhesitatingly, 'I could never believe anything *but* that Anne was a victim of child sexual abuse by both Nana [her great-aunt] and her father'" (Middlebrook, 58).

In response to this view, Sexton's psychiatrist for many years, Dr. Martin Orne, responded, "I dealt with it in therapy as a real event, because there were times that it was real to her... .If you ask me either as a psychiatrist or a scientist, however, I would have to say that I'm virtually certain that it never occurred. It's not plausible the way she described it, and it wasn't the father's style when he was drinking. But it fit her feelings of her father having abused her..." (Middlebrook, 58). Middlebrook's own suggestion is this: "Perhaps the question needs to be rephrased: not was the incident fantasy or memory, but what kind of experience was it?" (Middlebrook, 58). As Middlebrook argues that, behind the reality of Sexton's "memory" lay a true experience of abuse, one might argue that Poppy's "games," his pattern of complete control over his daughter's life, and his letters to her at college that can only be described as a lover's letters, ensnared my mother in the more-than-parental attentions of a parent she could not escape, even in college. It was his manliness that defined manliness, his emotional needs that encompassed hers, his provocative body that certainly, at least in fundamentally compromising ways, provoked hers, and his verbal evocation of her strongest feelings that crossed far over from parental into erotic love. Whatever panic she was feeling at 17, it must have been akin to what Sylvia Plath writes about in her terrifying poem "Pursuit."

How, then, does one explain the transition from the 17-year-old's photograph to the 21-year-old's? On the one hand no comprehensive explanation will suffice; on the other hand, knowing what one knows, one could argue that the 21-year-old's picture, though lovely, is in fact the most frightening. For it is this young woman who has learned fundamentally to dissemble: she has taken on all of the demands of her captors; she has become the almost-perfect Christian Scientist; she has incorporated her stepfather's behavior as an extension of Christian Science teachings about love and devotion; she has learned not to be frightened by what frightened her before, because the body is unreal and one should not fear its violation or the crossing of its boundaries. Only spirit is real, and in this photograph she is almost evanescent, pure spirit. Yet one senses, underneath, the overwhelming power both of the lie and of the child who lived before the lie; one senses what this young woman has learned about lying, about dissembling, about theatre, about appearances, about appearing so powerfully to be and seem good that one almost is: one almost escapes the noose. And then, at the same time, behind this learned dissimulation, a plan has formed; the young woman will escape the family, she will marry a man with prospects, a highly-regarded Naval flight instructor. Constrained and abused, she has made a niche for herself in college, and has made a future for herself that not even her father can oppose. How little she seems to know, then, that even as she has evaded the father, she will step into the life of another man almost equally wounded, and will even so have not solved the problem of her larger bondage—to her mother, and to the world of Mary Baker Eddy. The 17-year-old had sense enough to flee, but nowhere to flee to, no one to tell, and indeed, no one who at that time could probably have helped. The 21-year-old has, in a sense, given up. But beneath the serene surrender one understands the presence of the child's furious heart; as Kathryn Harrison writes,

> Rebuked by my grandmother, sitting in silence beside her, I began to teach myself to define what I really feel toward my mother—a desperate, fearful anger over her having abandoned me, an anger that has left me stricken with asthma and rashes—as love (Harrison, 36).

To survive, a Christian Science child must define a parent's abusive behavior as love; it is the only way to prevent a worse, ultimate rejection. But when, somewhere in one's heart, one knows that one is lying, not only about a particular circumstance but about love itself, and about one's own identity, a furious anger and a furious dissociation begin to build at the same time. One's rage at what one must do to survive is almost overwhelming; one's ability to dissociate oneself from that rage creates two of oneself, one warring against the other. This begins to become a classic definition of depression, but it also explains powerful dissociative states in which one's parent, having been abused as a child, suddenly vanishes—either figuratively or literally; suddenly leaves the room, suddenly goes to her room and shuts the door and refuses to come out for two or even three days, suddenly flies into a rage or a fit of crying, does whatever is the opposite of what one expects—because there is always the other parent, the one one scarcely knows and most fears, because it is the one most like oneself.

* * *

My mother tended to conceive babies, my sister once observed, when she faced a crisis in her marriage. Certainly my brother and sister, only 18 months apart, came during some of the worst moments, early on—after my father had dropped out of college, following World War II, and with no college degree fruitlessly applied for jobs, finally working ignominiously as an accountant for a tyrannical uncle; or, a few months later, after my father had finally landed what looked like a solid job as a product manager for the textile division of FMC corporation. In fact it was an appalling job, one that guaranteed that my father would be on the road three days out of five and would never be able to satisfy anyone—not customers, not plant engineers, not bosses—and over time, as he traveled, my mother began to find evidence of his affairs on the road. In 1955, with incontrovertible evidence, she called a practitioner, desperate for a divorce; she writes about this in the earliest diary of hers that survives. The practitioner reminded her of the sanctity of marriage, the importance of the woman as the homemaker and keeper of the family, and the importance of the family itself, as well as the importance of my father's income and the stresses he faced. And so, instead of a divorce, my mother had me, her third child, the child intended to keep the marriage together.

It worked, although it was the wrong thing to do. Whatever instinctive capacities my mother brought into this world in Georgia in 1920, she had kept intact at least through her 13th year; but by the time I was born, in 1956, she was 38, tired, and far from instinct. Her instincts had told her to flee the marriage with two children...but to flee where? Her mother the practitioner, back in Georgia, would have only been full of advice, admonitions, and failed prayers; her brothers would likely have sided with her mother, and in any case it would have been humiliating, for various reasons, to move in with them; and my mother had few friends close enough to confide her sense of the scope of the difficulty and danger. I was the solution.

It is interesting to have learned this years later, in 1981, the year after my mother's death, as I began to confront her voluminous diaries—which she kept from 1955 until near her end—in part because, at some level, I have always sensed that I never wanted to be here. Never wanted to be *here*—on this planet, in this incarnation, however you would like to call it. There have been times and dreams when all of this has seemed remarkably accidental, when my arrival here was almost not to be, and I have often wondered, as my mother pondered the evolution of her pregnancy in 1955-56, if part of this sense that runs so deeply through me comes from her own ambivalence about her solution to her larger problem. But abortion was difficult to come by and dangerous in 1955, and it would not have been consistent with her particular instinctive nature to have considered it for long. The fact that, as I read between the lines, she did consider it only confirms my own sense that, in a certain way, I was almost not here.

Nevertheless, with a third child, and two other children aged nine and eight, my mother faced a daunting task. Surely each of us reminded her of the anomaly of her own family, her own birth and upbringing, the seeming accident of this branch of the family...and yet everything in Christian Science assured her that, as spiritual embodiments of the one Spirit, all of her children were "cared for watched over." Why, then, did I particularly cause so much unintended trouble? For I was sick, as far as I can remember and as far as my siblings can remember, regularly from about the age of 2 1/2 on, and I was also unusually and dramatically accident-prone. I was the child who, at the age of four, climbing up a wall of stacked cinder blocks to sit next to my brother and sister, managed to slip and fall so that my back scraped against the blocks all the way down, severely abrading much of the skin. It was mid-summer in Pennsylvania, our house had no air conditioning, and my mother stayed up most of the night every night for a week, fanning my back to cool the pain and keep away the flies as I lay in a haze of pain made almost tangible from constant agony. I was the three-year-old who nearly drowned in the surf at Bethany Beach in Delaware while my brother and sister, in charge of watching me, fought on the sand. I was, again, the three-year-old who walked directly in front of the metal swing in which my bored babysitter was swinging, slicing open my forehead so deeply that by the time I ran home alone the world all looked dark red because my eyes had filled with blood.

I was the five and six-year-old who, unimmunized because Christian Science prayer was supposed to protect against mumps, measles, and whooping cough, in fact contracted prolonged cases of all three, becoming dangerously sick each time and taking weeks to recover. I was the eight-year-old who almost died from starvation and dehydration during a severe case of pneumonia. I was the ten-year-old who, showing off for neighbors by riding my bicycle off a wooden jump in the middle of street, wobbled in mid-air and managed to land on my left knee, taking the skin off down to the bone. Though I attended Sunday School regularly from the time I was three until my 20th birthday, though—as an older child—I read Mary Baker Eddy's lesson-sermon daily in the mornings, as my mother did and had done as a child—though, in every way I could think of, I sought to uphold and embrace the Christian Science way of life, the world itself seemed continually to demonstrate that I failed, and my failure was not isolated or incidental, but continual and essential. At times, when I imagined that we were each put on earth for some purpose, I could only think, looking back on what I had lived through, that my purpose was to illustrate over and over again either the essential failure and danger of Christian Science or my own simple failure as a created being. And since it took an act of will or faith larger than I could usually manage to concede that the religion itself might be flawed at its heart, I usually, from late childhood on, understood that I myself was the absolute, incontrovertible, appalling failure. Whatever insanity had run through my mother's side of the family, whatever Poppy had seemed to offer my mother and my grandmother by way of release, however normal his other children and their lives seemed, however gracious and generous and blessed Christian Science seemed to others to be, I was the objection impossible to conceal, the evidence of things not hoped for, things prayed against, things wished away. How much better it would have been if I had not been. And yet there I was: here I am.

* * *

There was a game my mother used to play with me on some of those dark winter mornings before first and second grade, when I didn't want to get up and face the physical and emotional coldness of school. In those days I hated and dreaded school—Gay Street School in West Chester, Pennsylvania, a place of cruel children and indifferent, tired teachers, a place where the lunch room smelled of vomit and I routinely found myself either beaten up or physically threatened. Somewhere in all of that is the question of why I continued to go—why my parents waited until fourth grade to move me to Friends Community School. But they did wait, and so most mornings, in first and second grade particularly, I went to school in tears. To try to ease this, my mother would play a version of Poppy's lap game, but it was a little different: sitting on one of the upstairs steps, she would cradle me in her arms, a slightly-too-large baby, and then she would drop me into her lap as she sang a song she'd made up about a child who's dropped but then caught just before he crashes to the ground. The song was a funny one—she had a lovely imagination—and, as she dropped me and caught me in her lap, I couldn't help laughing. We'd do this several times, most mornings, and thus, even if I went to school in a state of high anxiety, I had, somewhere in the back of my head, the funny moments of my mother intentionally dropping me only to show that she'd catch me after all in the end. And she always did catch me. She never failed.

For all the torments my mother endured later in her life, the dreams her father crushed, the marriage that looked like an escape but turned into a long trap, the infidelities she discovered, the continual financial struggles, her two rebellious older children, her own fear that, in some way, she must be failing as a Christian Scientist if I was sick or hurt so often, for all of that, she herself must have had what both Calvin Trillin and Anthony Storr describe at the beginning of this essay—a healthy sense of herself as a created being, someone with an intrinsic and even unquestionable right to be here. Somewhere in those first six years of her life, the idyll she would sometimes wistfully describe of Georgia and her young mother and her young grandmother, she did feel "cared for watched over," and perhaps not only by her relatives but also by some part of herself, the part that takes oneself gently in hand in times of pain or trouble and offers internal consolation, affirmations of being, tolerance of tears, resolutions of grief with joy to follow. The essential strength of the human temperament is based to a large degree on this internal comforter; whether this is a version, in spiritually-minded people, of the Comforter Jesus promised to send—the "spirit of truth" in John 16:13—there is some reality in the truth-based response of one's internal consolation: a voice one recognizes as one's own speaks to oneself truly and says, "you are here, and it is good; though you are hurting now, it is good that you are here."

It was that voice, I believe, however it may have sounded and however obscured it might have been by the passing years, that on occasion brought out my mother's one truly lovely quality, her absolute creatureliness. In these moments, she comforted directly; she invented games that would console me; she broke the unwritten rule of Christian Science against medicine when, in desperation as I lay dying at the age of eight, she took me to a conventional doctor; she did things, from time to time, not with any regularity and always under the concealing cloak of appropriate Christian Science behavior, that signaled some root love. At heart I came to believe that, regardless of the reason or lack of reason for my presence on the planet, there was something of me she loved. If I craved that because it seemed to come so rarely, it is helpful, now, to understand why it might have come so rarely, and how it had its source in something that, unfortunately, I myself may never have received—that intuitive sense of being absolutely in place here, as a child.

Yet this leaves open the larger question of how one lives, after years of meditation, discovering at one's center the absence of an essential feeling of rightness, of belonging. Perhaps the secret blessing of Christian Science, a characteristic it shared, ironically, with the Calvinism that drove the Puritans to Massachusetts in the first place, 270 years before Mary Baker Eddy discovered and founded Christian Science, is the habit of introspection: one prays without ceasing, examines one's soul for signs of true devotion or signs of falling away, speaks to oneself the Lord's Prayer or the Scientific Statement of Being at different times of day for comfort or revelation, waits patiently upon the Lord, and studies one's past for patterns of reassurance or alarm. Autobiography emerged, as we know historically, through what Lionel Trilling describes as a kind of sea-change in the concept of the self in the West: no longer simply an extension of the Church or a feudal pawn, the self became distinct, an agent of action in its own right, worthy of study: Montaigne studied it, and Rousseau in his periodically appalling *Confessions;* by the 17th century the self stood in political and religious relation to the state, the Church—and to itself—as it had never really done before. It was, in a sense, an element of good fortune that Christian Science, though theoretically forward-looking, really in its structure was a kind of enlightened Calvinism with evil sloughed off into Malicious Animal Magnetism and "error" ineffectively taking its place, with self-meditation and self-scrutiny as continual requirements, and with the concomitant insistence on the erasure from consciousness of all that was material and false. Christian Science itself was an authorization to autobiography: diary-keeping and journal-keeping are unusually common among Christian Scientists, and the whole concept of published testimonies of healing—appearing weekly in the *Christian Science Sentinel* and monthly in the *Christian Science Journal*—enforced the principle of self-contemplation with respect to the divine. And yet, ironically, the divine was hugely circumscribed in this religion, and so much—at least in my world—squeezed out through the theological cracks, so much that was harsh and hard and physical and painful and emotional and sad and nearly fatal and also true. And so, almost from the beginning, I was an autobiographer, but also, from the beginning, it seemed I was telling the wrong story, the reprehensible one. To know at, say, the age of ten that, despite one's most ardent efforts, despite memorizing whole passages of *Science and Health with Key to the Scriptures* and the Bible, to know the books of the Bible by heart backwards and forwards and to be able to summarize their most salient moments, to be able to do all of this so that one's Sunday School teachers are both delighted and proud, and yet to know that one nevertheless has failed, one has not, for whatever reason, been admitted to the faith, one cannot perform the expected healings or even receive the healings that others offer, is to be so fundamentally excluded from the world that one easily acquires, around that time if not before, a sense that it would be better not to live than to live the rest of one's life excluded, an outcast.

And now, at the age of 48, with no prospect of companionship—though with three lovely children, none of whom is a Christian Scientist and each of whom, as far as I can tell, does have that innate sense of being in his or her right place on this planet, despite moments of pain or despair—now I turn back to look closely at that early, essential emptiness, that hole that has never been filled. What to do? The question is not one of pity or self-pity; it is really far more ontological. Though never physically fit, I can see the changes in my body over the past 18 years, the way the fierce obligations of university teaching and research and the strains of failing or failed relationships have had physical corollaries: the muscles less strong, the lungs less powerful, the fading endurance, the heart problems, the unalleviated depression still fiercely holding on after a decade or more, the emerging question about intrinsic neurological problems. In another essay I asked, at one point, "What is left to build"? It is a question that has more than one implication; it is not only a question of grief, borne of lost love late in life. It is a question of what one does with an aging body and an empty center. Clearly other American men with different stories nevertheless arrive at a moment such as this, and respond in statistically unforgettable ways: it is not lost on me, at least intellectually, that I am almost exactly at the median age for suicide, in America, that five times as many men of my age kill themselves as women, and that death by suicide at this age is the third-largest cause of death among middle-aged American men. Nor do the statistics themselves register hope: the incidence of suicide among men increases, rather than decreases, as they age, despite the philosophical optimism of "coming out of the dark night of the soul" in such writers as Thomas Moore; although 65-year-olds, for example, comprise 13% of the U.S. population, they accounted for 18% of all suicides in 2000, the latest year for which statistics are available. Roger "Denny" Hansen, the subject of Calvin Trillin's memoir, killed himself in February 1991 at the age of 55.

* * *

One of Denny Hansen's friends, Nancy Mitchell, was talking to Trillin at one point about how much promise Hansen showed at Yale, how revered he was not only for being a golden boy but also for being a man of the future. "The way I see promise is that you have a knapsack," she said, "and all the time you're growing up they keep stuffing promise into the knapsack... .Pretty soon, it's just too heavy to carry. You have to unpack" (p. 25). I've thought of this for peculiar reasons—not only because, with the strong background Christian Science gave me in reading and analytic thinking, I was a kind of golden boy at Stanford and Berkeley, but also because the idea of "unpacking" as a metaphor is intriguing. How do you unpack what everyone else has stuffed into you if, at bottom, you're empty? When the knapsack is empty and you look with horror at yourself to see only weariness and stories of struggle without reward and financial travail and emptiness, how do you continue? Is it possible to unpack even emptiness?

In *New Seeds of Contemplation,* Thomas Merton writes,

> When the time comes to enter the darkness in which we are naked and helpless and alone; in which we see the insufficiency of our greatest strength and the hollowness of our strongest virtues; in which we have nothing of our own to rely on, and nothing in our nature to support us, and nothing in the world to guide us or give us light— then we find out whether or not we live by faith.

> It is in this darkness, when there is nothing left in us that can please or comfort our own minds, when we seem to be useless and worthy of all contempt, when we seem to have failed, when we seem to be destroyed and devoured, it is then that the deep and secret selfishness that is too close for us to identify is stripped away from our souls. It is in this darkness that we find true liberty. It is in this abandonment that we are made strong. This is the night which empties us and makes us pure (Merton, 258).

So it is possible to unpack even emptiness. But to what end? When the world is no consolation, when it feels as if every comfort and every human consolation has been removed, when one's whole being is in doubt, and when any future plans make no sense because they were all contingent on the incredible tenacity and persistence and fierce struggle of the unhappy man who would prefer the miracle that it all simply be taken from his hands—what then? Merton makes two observations: the first is not a promise, but rather a question; when we face the depths of darkness, we discover whether or not we have faith. What happens if we lack faith Merton does not say, and one might reasonably assume that, of all things missing for a child who never, from the beginning, believed in the worth of his life, faith would be absolutely absent; yet it seems that this is not necessarily so, for faith is not really, either conceptually or actually, allied with one's intrinsic sense of creaturely rightness: to be born and to die are not matters of faith. To live is a matter of continual faith; yet, as Merton implies elsewhere, many people function more or less as communal clones of one another because, having some creaturely sense of themselves, they do not perceive themselves as having faith and avoid situations where that kind of test or crisis might emerge.

The second observation Merton makes concerns liberty: in the psychic place where all that is creaturely seems to be ripped away, "we find true liberty." Freedom: it seems to underlie so much of what we want or need as creatures—freedom from cold, from hunger, from sadness, from the sense of meaninglessness, from despair, from loneliness; or freedom to love, to move forward, to live—freedom lies at the bottom of the unpacked knapsack that one continues to unpack. But if one finds faith and freedom, and the world and one's place in it appear nevertheless to be unchanged, how does the change register? Is there yet a change?

Today, as I write at my old computer, looking out the window at a Grant Wood Iowa, with its blue sky and scripted clouds, I wait to find out if certain new physical symptoms require a CT-scan for further investigation. I am officially, today, sick, and away from work. Yet I am writing here, as coherently as possible, having spent much of the past day in meditation on exactly that moment of darkest emptiness, that moment so deeply yearning to be filled. Returning to *Omens of Millennium*, I watch Harold Bloom posit the gnostic conundrum, a God almost unimaginably far from creation, entirely inaccessible, and yet also deeply within us, constituting the core of our being that can never be destroyed, that preceded creation, that is utterly ours and us. We have no God, but we have God; we are born and die, and yet what is essential can never be destroyed, having never been created, and inhabits, one might imagine, a cosmic scene out of the eighth book of Revelation, where those who have suffered so much tribulation sing at the throne of God, who finally, as he did at the very beginning, wipes away all tears from their eyes. I remember those earliest tears, locked in aloneness in the core of my earliest memories, and I know these tears now, as I sit here, half-blind from how I know this will conclude, and so I offer a series of final benedictions: one to my mother, whose cruel life never quite disguised her moments of creaturely loveliness; one to Christian Science, whose intrinsic and ferocious antagonism toward the creation will in some way, through some vehicle, be burned away, whether one imagines the burning as the fires of Hell or the continual, purifying fire of God, which is always present;

and one to myself, faithful, surprisingly, even unto death, weary beyond measure, a creature uncreated, almost—almost—alive to the miracle.

Part II: Death Revisited

Alone

Why, one wonders, is it so much more difficult—indeed, completely terrifying—to be alone as an adult?

Or perhaps that's not quite the right question. Rather: why, when I think back on my childhood, am I predisposed to remember so many incidents of trauma—foreshortened, as memory tends to do, so that they have the immediate feeling of the present, and yet expanded chronologically, as memory also tends to do, so that they seem to occupy far more time than they actually did? My adulthood, perhaps like yours—perhaps not—is ringed with memories I would rather not have. Yet the alternative, as *The Eternal Sunlight of the Spotless Mind* reminds us in its uneven, clunky, frightening way, is so dark that only a happy ending will do: in that film, Jim Carrey awakens without a memory of Kate Winslet, yet must, on impulse, call in sick to work and take the train from Manhattan to Montauk—no small journey—because, in some way, he is fated to have the experience of a relationship with her, fated to have those memories, not because fate works in a certain way but because he could not be who he is in this world without those specific experiences. Essentially, the film argues, Jim Carrey (or rather his character, or indeed either he or his character) is who he is because he has experiences that could not be other than they are, given who he is. It is, from one point of view, a circular argument, but the circle is interesting.

Of course the redemptive moment at the end of the film is artificial, the unreal and unrealistic part each of us might wish for yet never receive: Kirsten Dunst, the jilted office assistant to the physician who erases people's memories, discovers that the physician has erased her memory of her affair with him; because he tapes each patient's initial interview before he erases his or her memory, however, the office is full of potential for exactly the kind of discovery Dunst makes. Dunst thus gathers up all the tapes and sends them back to the patients. The effect, of course, is electrifying to Carrey and Winslet, for each hears the other's fierce and seemingly intractable complaints—the other is dull, boring, inflexible or, by contrast, too impulsive, with too many mood swings, and too unpredictable. Faced with what were, at a certain moment, the words of absolute true feeling about one another, each character re-discovers the nuances of emotion, the way frustration and anger at a certain time often cover a lack of truth: thus, at the end, when Carrey acknowledges that Winslet will repeatedly drive him crazy with her impulsiveness and unpredictability, and she acknowledges that she'll soon feel bored and trapped in the relationship, there's a pause; Carrey says, "Well, that's OK"; and suddenly we are meant to understand that each has come to terms with the limits of the other. Within the imagination of each is the capacity to tolerate what had previously been intolerable; the psychic compensation lies, not only in knowing something true about oneself in relation to another, but in having the other's company through that catharsis. Each character has his or her memories and the ability to accept, to project acceptance into the future.

"We all leave behind memories as our primary legacy," wrote Charles Lachenmeyer in a small volume early in 1982—*Thought Control and Technological Slavery in America (?)*. I have not read this volume, and would not know about it but for Charles' son Nathaniel Lachenmeyer's extraordinary story, published in 2000, of his father's battle with schizophrenia: *The Outsider: A Journey into My Father's Struggle with Madness*. Charles Lachenmeyer is interesting in his own right because, before he began his long slide into a schizophrenic and homeless nightmare in the 1980's and 1990's, he was an eminent young professor of sociology at Hunter College in New York. His two books in the 1970's, *The Language of Sociology* and *The Essence of Social Research*, were both widely admired if somewhat iconoclastic in their field. Having published so much within the first six years of his assistant professorship, Charles would have rightly considered himself an unquestionable candidate for tenure and a lifetime position as an associate and full professor at Hunter College; his most serious deterioration began when, to his shock, his colleagues turned him down. Now, in a different era, that decision would certainly have triggered a formal review within the institution, as well as a lawsuit on Charles' behalf against Hunter College, a suit that—one speculates— would have gained him both tenure and a sizeable monetary settlement. For Charles' main problem, a complicated but not unresolvable issue in academia, was that he did not fit into the Hunter faculty "family," from his colleagues' point of view; he was too abrasive, too outspoken. Tenure is designed in part precisely to protect those who are somewhat abrasive and outspoken from the predations of their more passive-aggressive peers, and the tenure process itself should have come into play to protect rather than to harm Charles. But it may also be true that his colleagues at Hunter sensed something more odd than usual about him, something potentially alarming behind his abrasiveness and outspokenness; they sensed a mind at some level ill at ease with itself. Nevertheless, a serious academic in today's world would have to wonder at the legitimacy of the Hunter College faculty decision in Charles' case.

I deeply value Nathaniel Lachenmeyer's book for two reasons: first, I have a memory of Charles Lachenmeyer's books from the time of their first appearance; one of my professors of sociology at Stanford University, I. Bernard Cohen, recommended them to me as revisionist views of the discipline. And so I sought them out in the Stanford Library and the Stanford Bookstore, full of admiration for the relatively young man who had written them. It would take more than 26 years for me to find out what had happened to that man. But I also value Nathaniel's book because it reveals that, like me, Charles Lachenmeyer was raised in a Christian Science family with a profoundly influential and devout mother. Her devotion to Christian Science clearly exceeded her devotion to her children, and some of the incidents Charles' relatives and former spouse remember from random family occasions—family dinners, off-hand comments from Charles' mother—echo, almost to the word and tone, things that I remember from my own childhood. Interestingly, as Nathaniel notes, while Charles' brother took to the religion and still professes it—blaming Charles' schizophrenic fate on his unwillingness to see the truth in Mary Baker Eddy's teachings—Charles himself not only could not tolerate the religion, but could barely stand being in the same house with his mother, even though he loved her dearly.

Taught from an early age that his intuitive and empirical perception of the world was an illusion of "mortal mind," taught that only spirit was real, yet personally unwilling to doubt the authenticity of the world before him, Charles took refuge in a specific and increasingly elaborate distancing device: he began to use his own family as unwitting experimental subjects. His early work on the "double-bind theory," for example—work that parallels the work of other sociologists he had not, at that time, yet read—emerged from his own experience of the double-bind: once, for example, when he fell and badly skinned his knee, his mother told him not to worry about it, but rather to remember that the wound and the pain were both illusions, and that God would heal him. If the wound remained, as it did, bloody and raw, it would be a sign to Charles' mother that Charles himself had too little faith; thus Charles would be punished. At the same time, however, the unhealed pain was itself a punishment, and no amount of praying would make it disappear. There was, thus, no way to escape some form of punishment. In devoutly Christian Science families, the double-bind was virtually a daily occurrence.

While contemporary researchers into schizophrenia tend to view the disease as primarily neurochemical, including a genetic predisposition, psychiatrists generally acknowledge that environmental stresses will trigger its onset. Though few now hold as radical a view as R. D. Laing's 1969 *The Divided Self,* which Charles certainly would have read (though, like most schizophrenics, he refused throughout to see himself as ill, and because of paranoia believed that the CIA was conducting mind experiments on him—not, really, so far from the truth, if one substitutes "Christian Science" for "CIA"), there is no question that the continual stress of Charles' childhood and adolescent environment substantially harmed his ability to perceive reality and to comprehend the way other people formed close bonds of love and caring. This harm almost as certainly contributed to Charles' alcoholism, a not-uncommon concomitant condition of schizophrenia and other mental disorders, including depression and anxiety. Reading in Nathaniel Lachenmeyer's book about Charles' early life, such a mirror to my own, remembering my own impressions of Charles' brilliant initial career, and following Nathaniel's painstaking reconstruction of Charles' descent into a series of hospitalizations, homelessness, and finally a heart attack at the age of 51 in a small, rented room in Burlington, Vermont in January 1995, I can only pray, in my own way, for whatever good fortune I have, by contrast, created or received.

* * *

"The problem with depression," one of my skillful University of Iowa students wrote recently in his own essay on the subject, "is that it's not even interesting to talk about. It's a leaden, heavy, claustrophobia-inducing sensation, the feeling of being a helpless, passive observer in your own body. It's almost as if there's something else making you walk, eat, smoke, and it's not totally expert at doing so; a cadre of aliens unfamiliar with human society pulling levers and pressing buttons." The irony here, of course, at least to me, is that this small sample of my student's writing—like the rest of his work—makes extraordinarily interesting reading. At its most basic, literal level, these sentences are about feeling alien to oneself. That concept was virtually a pop-culture idea in the 1960's and 1970's, when my high school even taught courses with titles such as "Alienation in Modern Literature"; alienation was fashionable. But my student is talking about an ontological condition, a state of being continually not at home, of feeling invaded; the double-consciousness of depression is feeling the grim, unrelenting weight of darkness all the time and yet also being aware that one is feeling it, that some division within the self makes it possible to feel what one would choose not to feel, or to move through the world knowing that some other essential characteristic of one's being has not given consent to this, does not want this mode of life.

This is part of why, for me, depression itself remains a subject of intense interest. People who suffer chronically from depression are sometimes referred to by psychiatrists as "the walking wounded": they move through the world, in general presenting quite competent or even brilliant facades, like Denny Hansen, but behind the facade is a daily, or rather a moment-by-moment, battle to push away dark thoughts, a sense of meaninglessness, a sense of alienation from oneself and from parts of one's past that are actually good, healthy, or hopeful. To do this year after year, with one medical hope after another dashed, yet another failed medicine in one's record book of failed treatments, is—and I say this with no intention of pride (pride being a characteristic not common among depressives)—to act with considerable courage. One can lament Denny Hansen's suicide, yet one can also read with fascination how profound was his determination to persevere, to engage in the ideas and work that seemed to him, despite his alienness to himself, of fundamental importance to the world. Living with depression is very much like living with a loaded gun to one's head: this is neither an hysterical comment or an exaggeration, but simply a confirmation of how close death feels, how close one continually feels to the annihilation of whatever it is one defines as one's self. And yet one may not in any way be actively suicidal; one may, by contrast, prefer almost any possible way of embracing the life that one has. Yet death is the ever-present subtext to depression. Death and silence.

Taking up the almost-universal misconception that people with depression are just perpetually out of sorts and having a decade-long, self-indulgent bad day, neurologist Joseph LeDoux, author of several influential texts on mind and identity, including the 2002 *Synaptic Self*, asks his psychiatrist friend Greg Sullivan in Manhattan about the possibility that depressives are really just quite clever malingers. Sullivan responds, in part, this way:

> In my experience I do not know of anyone for whom this is true. In general, these drugs (anti-depressants) are not fun to take (it's bothersome to remember a daily pill, they often cause sexual dysfunction, they can lead to slow weight gain, and friends and family sometimes imply that taking drugs for depression is a sign of mental weakness)... .SSRIs are not "happy pills," and people without significant mood or anxiety disturbance do not generally get anything beneficial from them, certainly nothing that would make them sustain the use (Ledoux, 276).

What is of course even more interesting, from my point of view, is the long-term reality of having "significant mood or anxiety disturbance" and yet finding no medical relief: that is the depression that might finally seem so unworthy of discussion, so redolent with hopelessness, that one would rather do almost anything—one would rather retreat utterly from the world—than confront the reality of the disease. But the ironic courage of many people with depression makes this kind of retreat only a last resort—or next-to-last resort, before suicide. With the brain rather like a French resistance fighter during World War II, going to Plan B or Plan C or Plan D when the primary plan collapsed, always improvising, always looking for some route back to a secret safehouse, the whole issue of survival becomes itself quite fascinating—not only to the depressive, but to others who—perhaps not understanding the depth of depressive misery—nevertheless see sufficiently the obstacles in a depressive's life that they too begin to wonder how such people make their way through a day. This brings us back around again, somewhat ironically, to the slightly dark irony of being grateful for the good fortune that one has, even if that fortune seems to come at a very high price.

* * *

The idea of one's own good fortune might be seen, on the surface, to be a moral or ethical issue, but in fact it is much more importantly the keyhole to a much larger subject, memory, both long-term and short-term, and memory is a vexed subject if one suffers from chronic depression, known in the field as "dysthymia." In my case, while there were clearly acute episodes of depression as early as age eight, with others at 13 and 16, along with a near-psychotic episode at the age of 20 and another, shortly after my mother's death, at the age of 24 in 1981, I became aware that something was truly and enduringly wrong in July 1995; that sense of something being truly and enduringly wrong has not abated over the past ten years, despite psychotherapy and the seemingly eternal trial-and-error method of tricyclics, SSRI's, mixtures of the two—Prozac, Paxil, Effexor, Serzone, Welbutrin, Pamelor—the list goes on and on—along with various anti-anxiety drugs, including Xanax, Valium, Ambien, Klonopin, and others; thus the long-term diagnosis. In theory, I ought to be disabled by now, and statistically, my symptoms—chronic anxiety, a consistent sense of dread, difficulty in taking pleasure in normal human activities, difficulty in forming and maintaining close relationships, intrusive or obsessive thoughts, sleep disorders, and problems with the kind of abstract thought and analysis necessary for my job, as well as a tendency toward agoraphobia that makes being in a classroom extremely challenging—are statistically likely to get worse, not better, given my age and the tenacity of my illness. I have read, with envy, William Styron's *Darkness Visible* and Elizabeth Wurtzel's *Prozac Nation,* among several other such books, not because I have not sympathized with each narrator's suffering, but because, in each case, the narrator recovers: time heals Styron, while Prozac shows up just in time for Wurtzel. One must count one's blessings, although it is sometimes tempting, though insidious in effect, to count others'. Nevertheless, I return to the subject of memory because it is at once so elusive and so curiously tied to the character of depression.

As LeDoux explains in his trenchant chapter on mental wounds, "Synaptic Sickness," depression is one outcome of long-term stress—the kind I experienced as a child, the kind now officially diagnosed as "post-traumatic stress disorder," or PTSD—becauses it damages the home of memory in the brain, the hippocampus, "leading to a shrinking of dendrites and ultimately to cell death" (LeDoux, 278). "Not surprisingly, functions that depend on the hippocampus, like explicit or declarative memory, become severely compromised," he continues. The curiosity of this, both for me and in my case, is that, while I confront many of the most painful symptoms of depression daily, my memory—at least as far as I can tell, and as far as personality tests can demonstrate—remains quite good. But that phrase itself—"quite good"—is at least potentially a little misleading. What exactly does it mean? I can clearly remember almost drowning at Bethany Beach, Delaware, at the age of 2 1/2—one of my earliest memories, and unusually far back for most adults—as my brother and sister, who supposedly were watching me, fought each other on the beach; I can remember swallowing water, not being able to breathe, and then a huge arm coming down under and around me—my father's arm, as he ran from the road to the shore, past my errant brother and sister, to rescue me before punishing them. I can remember being presented with two plaques—a second-place and a first-place award—in 1968 for two different categories of the Avalon, New Jersey boat parade;

I can remember a much-loved family photograph of my ex-wife, me, our four-year-old Nathaniel and Georgia, barely two months old, in Yosemite, and what was crossing my mind in the moments before it was taken; I can remember what it was like to land a Piper Warrior on a moonless night on a dark runway in Marshfield, Massachusetts with no onboard lights of any kind. I can remember my first California driver's license—N2191378—although I have not owned it for almost two decades; I can remember my first Mastercard account number; I can remember the price-per-pound of the half-pound steak I cooked for dinner last night. So it would seem that, regarding memory, as with most other things, I am atypical.

But Ledoux elsewhere makes a slightly different point about the hippocampus—or at least offers a slightly different interpretation of it. Patients with serious long-term depression actually have a smaller hippocampus, as well as problems with the amygdala and related areas of the brain; under the pressure of years of excess cortisol, the inner world of these patients is literally smaller than that of other human beings. They live in a circumscribed world. That concept has interesting implications for memory, especially for memory sorting and recall. At any given moment, for example, I can remember—or am forced by the nature of intrusive thoughts to remember—any given agonizing moment of the year-and-a-half following my mother's death, when I believed that somehow I was being punished for not having saved her through prayer: the punishment was that I did things without knowing it—anything from walking around the block to committing murder. Often, during that year-and-a-half, I lived a true double life—the one, ordinary life, to which we don't usually give much thought, and another life, a continual mental double-checking of my surroundings, the clothes I was wearing, the actual sequence of events involved in opening and closing a car door or tying shoelaces, so as to be able to remind myself later that I was consciously in a certain place doing certain things, and not elsewhere doing things I could not remember. The terror of this kind of behavior is surely obvious. But why should I, now, 24 years later, be able to remember this unhappy time in such excruciating detail, while earlier but repeated moments—tree-climbing in the back yard of our house in West Chester, Pennsylvania, for example—require much more effort?

From about the age of four, I was a wonderful climber, and because my parents paid relatively little attention, I was "allowed" to climb trees far larger and more dangerous than I would have permitted my own children to attempt. Chief among these was a very large, very old dogwood tree in our backyard. Its dozens of branches offered dozens of different routes and challenges; and if, sometimes, I fell almost to the ground, only to be saved by one last branch, I also learned my way to the very top of the tree, where I could be an astronaut, a pilot, a mountaineer. Every day of every spring and fall in Pennsylvania, from the time I was four until I was around ten, I climbed this tree—or others like it in the park across the street; each climb was a brilliant adventure. And I can remember some of those now, though with difficulty. But why the difficulty, when I remember terrible things so clearly?

One obvious answer is that—given cellular deaths in my smaller hippocampus, along with a build-up of cortisol and its effects over the years, I—or the internal "I" that precedes whatever self I consciously recognize as mine—tends to equate memory with risk, danger, or terror: the synapses of my hippocampus are thus organized in such a way to give priority to stressful memories. It's an interesting adjunct to any theory of identity: we all admit that our environment shapes us in specific ways, but we rarely tend to imagine the "shaping" at the level of the cell or brain; yet from many studies we have evidence that people who suffer from PTSD and depression have brains that have learned to organize memory, not in terms of happiness, but in terms of disaster. Yet this does not mean that the happiness did not occur, nor does it make the happiness entirely inaccessible. Happiness does, however, become "something different" in this kind of brain.

A couple of years ago, in a particularly dark time, I began to imagine writing a book called *The Book of Joy*, which would be nothing except wonderful moments from my life, re-created in straightforward yet vivid prose. The irony, which I did not realize for a while, was the concept of "wonderful moments": the book, as it evolved, became only a series of vignettes, clips of a life, not life itself. The continuity we imagine, or the fictional yet true devices we engage for the sake of a story—foreshadowing, flashbacks—all of these were missing; it was almost as if part of the self was missing, that "no self" narrated the book. Because this was intolerable, I had to stop.

Again, part of the problem in a literally circumscribed mental world is what takes hold, what holds sway. I may be able to orchestrate a moment that will almost certainly be happy, for example—I may be able to arrange dinner with a friend 70 miles away, in Iowa City, or I may be able to arrange an afternoon with my youngest son, Thomas, or I may be able to go to a movie with my daughter Georgia, or I may even be able to change the oil and filter on my old Subaru Forester. Or, if a different kind of good fortune befalls me, though it is rare, I may be able to go out on a date with someone who at least in theory is interested in being with me. All of these, I know, make me feel happy. The difference, as far as I can tell, between my happiness and other people's is what happens afterwards. After a happy event, people without depression can rest for a time in that happiness, and also trust that those good feelings will recur in the near future: something else will come along to make them happy. I, on the other hand, lose the feeling of happiness almost as soon as the event itself is over: the feeling dies with the event. And if you ask if I "remember" being happy, I have to work at it; a "happy" feeling doesn't come to me immediately in the same way a feeling of accomplishment (climbing a tree, winning a boat parade, landing an aircraft) or terror (nearly drowning, nearly dying of pneumonia, not being able to breathe) does. Oddy enough, those feelings of accomplishment are almost as immediately accessible as feelings of fear, sadness, loneliness, pain, and anger, and I remain curious about how, in my life, accomplishment—my one defense against the allegation that I was a failure, from childhood on, in Christian Science—is linked with danger and distress rather than with positive feelings. Nevertheless, it is so. If someone asks me what it is like to feel "happy," I cannot immediately summon that feeling; I have to remember a specific event, have to reconstruct the event chronologically and in detail from my memory, in order thus to have some feeling that approximates happiness. It appears, contrary to the research of neurologist Antonio Damasio, that emotion and reason are not linked, in my brain, in a way one would expect: emotions that come effortlessly to most people require me to rebuild the scaffolding of a whole world before I can sense what such a feeling might be.

This, then, brings us back to the terror of loneliness—a circuitous route, admittedly, but one hopes worthwhile. For an adult world in which happiness fades almost as soon as the event fades is a world in which both feeling and memory are circumscribed: something that comes naturally to most people as a gift of self, a kind of platform on which they can stabilize their independent existence, is largely gone for me. I'm sure it used to be there, at least until sometime around my twelfth year, when I begin to remember a general change both in my sense of what the world was like and in my sense, in time, of how long it took bad things—illnesses, bullying, wounds—to go away. Before I was twelve, I was happy. I was also sad, frightened, injured, or scared, and clearly Christian Science made all of these worse: instantly at this moment, for example, as I write these words, the memory that pops into my head is one from when I was about three or four, locked into a tiny room for forty-five minutes with six other little children in the back of a Christian Science Sunday School in West Chester, Pennsylvania, not permitted to leave or even go to the bathroom because we had to learn to "behave." The terror of entrapment: that started there, I know. But why should that memory appear at the instant I assert I was a happy child?

Because, I think, in some way, I was fundamentally a normal child, aside from Christian Science, and that normality registered in a normal child's brain that—though overwhelmed periodically with cortisol from stress—nevertheless functioned well in a child's world. It was a lovely world. There were trees to climb; there were boats to sail or row; there were forests to explore, where one could pretend one was far and away from civilization, an Indiana Jones before Indiana Jones existed; there was surf in the summers in New Jersey for bodysurfing, there were bowling alleys and places near the beach where you could jump on a trampoline for twenty minutes for fifteen cents, there was the first snowfall of every year, the flakes coming down in the blueness of night and softening all the sharp edges of late fall; there were Matchbox cars and trucks and imaginary cities and all the other worlds, real and imagined or both, that make up a richly-imaginative and somewhat adventurous child's actual world. They were all there; with effort, I can remember almost every one. The book of joy. An alternative view of incidents from my childhood. Some kind of linkage—something internal, some sense of hope refusing for years to die—made it possible to link those moments together into a trustworthy self. For I trusted myself as a child. That, too, I can remember. And that meant that I could be happily alone for long periods of time. I could live in the joy of the tall sand dunes around 60th street between Avalon and Stone Harbor, New Jersey; I could live in the joy of the dogwood tree; I could live in the more literal joy of an eight-foot rowboat with a 1 1/2-horsepower motor on the stern, trolling into the far back channels of some tiny island among dozens of islands in the back waterways behind Avalon and Stone Harbor. I needed no one else; only the world. In the world, and in the way it made contact with my own being, I was happy.

There is, of course, an alternative way even of viewing this—something a child psychologist would instantly notice—which is, simply, how much time this child spent alone. For it was true: I did not socialize well. And how obvious could the reasons be? Everywhere I went where there were other people, I was in danger. If they were bigger than I and decided to hurt me, I was too small to fight back with much success; if we were playing and I got hurt, they could not take me to a doctor, or even give me aspirin or Tylenol; if I was at a birthday party, and from too much cake or excitement or, though I did not know it yet, anxiety, I became nauseated and actually vomited, I would bring down ridicule upon myself. Other people, and the scenarios of other human lives, meant danger, because through Christian Science I was trained in a social reality that did not exist, and I could not easily find a way to commute over to that other social reality that *did* exist. But, alone, and lifted up through the beautiful natural world into the fabulous world of my imagination, I was fine. I was fine.

How profoundly I miss that. I miss that as much as I mourn anything—the death of my mother—for something altered over the course of memory, and as I grew older those ways of being became less accessible, not only in memory but also in imagination. Or, rather: it was difficult to move into adulthood precisely because—while, for most people, imaginings shift over into actual doings, so that one becomes what one imagines—for me, the shifts did not come with a concomitant imaginative blessing. I became a pilot, and both enjoyed and admired what I could do, but flying was expensive—I had to earn enough money at some profession to afford it—and I could never quite shake the fear I had, knowing as much as I did about airplanes, instruments, avionics, and flight physics, of something going wrong that I could not, finally, fix. Even so, I took myself to Alaska, backpacking and flying there, renting a Cessna 172 and getting as far as the Sheldon amphitheater at the top of the Ruth Glacier in Denali, but I did not, really, become the explorer or adventurer I had been as a child. How could this be?

Perhaps to you the answer is already present and simple, and you will wonder how it has taken me so long to see it. My childhood, though full of unhealed pain and genuine danger, was not, finally, profoundly afflicted with loss. Each day, if I awoke to fear of what the world would bring, I also awoke to a more coherent, more vivid sense of whom I was and what I could do; even periodic childhood trauma could only scar that somewhat, not destroy it. But periodic childhood trauma lays down a subtle matrix on which later loss can build with enormous force. At 24 I lost my mother, who was not supposed to die, although of course Christian Scientists did die, and regularly—but it was nevertheless not supposed to happen; with her death I finally lost my last vestige of faith in what by that time I desperately hoped was religion with some true kernel of meaning, some vision of spiritual joy and reality I had overlooked—but it was not there; nothing was there but years and years of people lying to me; I lost, for awhile, my sense of myself, my ability to be quietly self-aware without having to watch myself every second; I lost, for awhile, my confidence in my own sanity; I lost my playfulness, my sense of good luck, in the hard fight at UC Berkeley to earn a Ph.D., and the harder fight, at MIT, to keep my job, though unlike Charles Lachenmeyer I was finally promoted there, and tenured at the University of Iowa; the battle I fought was only a little different from Charles', and the toll it took on my ability to hope and to take delight in ordinary things was immense.

I lost my hope in the sincerity of feminism, a body of value dedicated to what seemed to me a way of life and a kind of equality I cherished, as I watched myself become my father, the sole breadwinner of the family, while my feminist spouse, unemployed, insisted that I pay for daycare so that she could—at first, perhaps, unconsciously, and then willfully as I confronted her—find ways to avoid finishing her own dissertation and thus going on the job market, even though that arrangement required me to take on extra teaching and ultimately go almost $30,000 into debt, a debt that would eventually end in bankruptcy for me—though not for her, for she had by that time acquired a tenacious attorney and, after divorcing me, began to come into her own financially (and, ironically, years later, she and her new husband, comfortably well-off, were willing to loan me desperately needed money—a partial evidence of reconciliation to reality); I lost my hope in my own judgment, as I sought to re-start my life with other women with whom, for various reasons, I could not form an enduring bond, in part because they had hope, or at least a fantasy, and I had, by that time, mostly just a plan. By the time "now" arrived, my oldest son had left for college, my daughter was happily involved in her high school activities, and my youngest son lived with his mother 70 miles away and saw me once a week. I was alone, and the story of my life was loss.

We should be clear: that last sentence is only half-true. I am alone, but if I were inclined in a different direction, I would be, overall, thrilled with what I had been able to do—thrilled, as I am, at my oldest son's accomplishments and character, equally thrilled with my daughter's accomplishments and character, and delighted with the imaginative brilliance of my youngest son; I would be thrilled to have managed to keep a job through so many dark times, thrilled to have been able to provide a home for my children when they needed it, and even thrilled, if I were so inclined, to have done so much to help give my ex-spouse the expensive launching pad she needed for her career in art history and museum studies. On any given night, alone in my house, I would, in another life, walk proudly through its rooms, looking at the many photographs of happy times with my children, and knowing how much I had given, how much I had overcome.

But that is not how I am. If a mind is somewhat like a long-term financial transaction, then the times of trauma and loss compound interest, re-investing themselves with ever more value, as the assets of the world of beauty and light from my childhood withered and finally became negative balances. Imbalance is characteristic of PTSD, but more specifically with a life so commanded by loss and struggle and more loss. Nevertheless, the idea that even this is fluid—that even the quantity and quality of memories, so conditioned, seemingly so intractable when faced with anything like hope, could potentially alter in an act of "gnosis," a knowing like the knowledge of my childhood, which in some form or another is still "there," still vestigal in the ironically darkest recesses of my brain—this does not lead to hope, but it does lead to a question. Where is that world of light? How did I come to know it so well as a child? How did I live in it so successfully? How did I make it up so skillfully as I went along? How was I so good at being alone? Who was I, then? And where has that person gone? Why—if I were to draw the most immediate analogy that comes to mind—was my childhood so much the way Dylan Thomas lived and remembered his own childhood? And, even as I too often drink to forget the present, why was he, finally, consumed with the need to drink, to forget? How did loss finally come to outweigh gain in his world?

"Loss is gain," Mary Baker Eddy once wrote in one of her hymns, and we often studied those words in Sunday School to get at the core of them, the idea that human loss was spiritual gain. But I would say, now, that what I intuited as a child was the opposite: so-called "spiritual" loss was human gain; the theorizing and positing of my religion could still, then, be replaced with the true world and all its analogues, its angelic presences and comforts, its fragrances and its shades of light, its young child singing in the sun. Thomas—Dylan Thomas that is—was at once a pantheist and a pure idealist, as he reveals in "And Death Shall Have No Dominion" and "Poem in October," among many other similar writings; to be a certain kind of pantheist and idealist, one must essentially be a gnostic, a believer in the living Word where the Word does not go to church, does not pray to a catechized God, shows no interest in orthodoxy from Peter to Luther to Bonhoeffer, and offers no direct comfort to the living, the dying, or the dead. The living Word is a fountain of real water, a cloud and a shaft of real light through it; it is the "perfect nature" of Islamic Sufism, or the world of James the Just, almost eclipsed for two thousand years because the insanity of Paul became the cornerstone on which the human-Christian church was built. Paul was a brilliant deceiver and self-deceiver, eloquent to a fault, and intellectually skillful; James the Just, and his increasingly few and dispersed followers, were at home in the Word alone, the world Jesus knew, the world Thomas knew at some point in the third century C.E. in eastern Turkey, a point one can isolate in time and space and even visit, if one wants. Thomas will not be there, but it is no matter, for he came and went as he knew how, in a glorious imagining that was at once its own reality. One wonders, indeed, how gnosticism still could have so few people knowing so little about it, when it is all around. Children, like me, knew it from the start; and, regardless of the damage to our brains, our hearts, or our hope, we know the look and sound of it still when we see it, and thus, still, go looking for it, even and sometimes especially alone.

Alone, Coda: The Setting

Unlike novelists, essayists, whose minds tend toward the cerebral and the synthetic, will sometimes overlook simple details—setting, for example, or plot. As a plot, this book operates at a level both simple and complex: the plot in its simple form has to do with the continued survival, and quest for meaning, on the part of a dysthymic narrator. The plot in its complex form is essentially a mind turned inside out, as the narrator sees and re-sees the near and distant past, looking for both what was fiercely experienced and what was overlooked, in the hope of finding the next bit of road ahead. The setting, however, though in one sense it varies widely from essay to essay, ironically has behind it a single domain—literary critics might call it a "meta-setting," while dramatists might simply call it "upper stage left." It is the setting in which this book is being written, so far completely disguised. But it may have a certain intrinsic interest, at least in brief.

Near the beginning of his virtual non-book, *Let Us Now Praise Famous Men*, James Agee wishes aloud that what he could create would be, in fact, a non-book: "It would be photographs; the rest would be fragments of cloth, bits of cotton, lumps of earth, records of speech, pieces of wood and iron, phials of odors, plates of food and excrement" (Agee, 13). It is one of the most admirable admissions to the compromise of language that I've ever read, and I would wish it here, too—indeed, would have overall traded my word-hoard for certain specific memories, those of life on the water, for example, if I could only re-live those repeatedly, without discussion or verbal examination. But language is part of our curse; if one follows both structuralist and post-structuralist cultural theory, and the history of linguistics from Noam Chomsky's 1957 *Syntactic Structures* on, and contemporary neurology, and paleoanthropology relating to gesture and language, it becomes nearly inescapable to conclude that language itself is essentially an evolutionary trauma for humans. While the body, according to Antonio Damasio in *The Feeling of What Happens*, has perhaps always had "core consciousness"—"an imaged, nonverbal account of how the organism's own state is affected by the organism's processing of an object" (Damasio, 169)—we don't know how some extension of or alternative to that arose in consciousness to become the powerful cognitive tool we call our spoken and written language. But paleoanthropology suggests that, possibly for millions of years before *Homo sapiens*, and perhaps for hundreds of thousands of years early in our lineage, gesture sufficed.

What James Agee proposed in his 1941 book was, in effect, a wistful and unknowing nod back to that act of gesture as the most redolent form of communication. But most of the time we are too far from that to remember...even Jesus mixed the two, as when he made clay spittle for the eyes of the blind man, a gesture comprehensible even to his most skeptical on-lookers, and when he cried, in a loud voice—the volume a kind of gesture— "Lazarus, come forth." Gesture and language...both still possible, yet separated evolutionarily by thousands or hundreds of thousands of years. And so we speak and think on the cognitive site, not of species freedom, but of species trauma: amazing, on the whole, that we do as well as we do. For a paleoanthropologist or neurologist, the Verizon cellular phone company's famous advertisement—with its representative taking a few steps, like an early man, and saying, "Can you hear me now?"—is exceptionally funny, and not for the reasons usually associated with cell phones. "Can you hear me now?"—what early humans must have been saying from the start, in their own way, and what we, in our own way, are still saying. The question is at once so comic and so touching because, while it should have an obvious answer, which is "yes," it also has a traumatic answer, which is "no."

But in any case, the question of setting: this book is being written in the years 2004 and 2005 in a small house on the corner of 8th and Spring

Streets in Grinnell, about three blocks from the campus of Grinnell College. The town itself is not very large, including only about 9,000 people; 8th Street is important in town because it links, in its three-mile stretch, two of the town's elementary schools and the single high school (one other elementary school is a bit south and east of 8th Street, and the lone middle school is at the very far southeastern tip of town, a newer building resembling a prison and standing next to a large field of corn). In this small house, I generally live alone. This has not always been the case; someone shared this house briefly with me in early December 2001, and someone else occasionally came over in fall 2002 and spring 2003, and someone else shared it briefly with me over the Christmas holiday in 2002, and someone else, who was expected to stay for good, arrived in December 2003, left for England just before Christmas, returned in late January 2004—a week later than expected—and left for good for West Hollywood in late February 2004. The record of companionship with regard to this house, one might say, is rather poor.

I arrived in this house in November 2000; at that time my two children who lived in Grinnell, Nathaniel and Georgia, were 14 and 10, respectively. Those of you with children know that 14 is about the age in this culture when you, as a parent, suddenly become important in the background but virtually irrelevant in the foreground: 14-year-olds take off, among friends and football games and basketball games and band and cross-country and track and science fairs and all the other traveling events that go along with high school, and Nate was no exception. This was a good thing, as it almost always is, for, finding his way through the social thickets of adolescence, Nate turned out wonderfully, eventually serving as field commander for the Grinnell High School Marching Band, playing baritone sax in the jazz band, setting a new personal record for himself in cross-country, and gaining acceptance to one of the most distinguished and distinctive small colleges in the country, Colorado College. That was last year, when, over the course of it, he turned 18. He now spends most of his time, as he should, either in Colorado Springs, or at one of the relatively nearby ski resorts, where he's a dangerous man on a snowboard.

And now Georgia is 14, and the pattern, though modulated slightly on the basis of gender and certain personal predilections, starts again. And so the house is empty except for me.

Any good therapist will tell you that people suffering from chronic serious depression should not live alone, but on the other hand, who else is there? I could say: I live with the house: it is my partner. That would be a lie, of course, in some way, because I do not sleep with the house, wake up with it next to me, share my coffee with it, have conversations with it (probably just as well). Still, as the setting here, it deserves some notice.

Technically one-and-a-half stories in its small (1,000 square feet) rectangular essence, the house was built around the turn of the century. It originally had a downstairs living room and combined dining room and kitchen, with one medium-sized and two small bedrooms up a steep flight of stairs; at some point in the century, the outhouse vanished, and indoor plumbing was added in the basement. Much later, in the early 1970's, a small additional wing, facing south, was built on the east side of the old house; this addition, about 400 square feet, included an actual bathroom with a tub, toilet, and sink, and a kitchen with room for a refrigerator, stove, sink, and some cabinets. In addition, as part of those 400 square feet, the builders added a concrete slab and built a small summer porch. Years later, in 2001, buying insulation and drywall and other supplies with bits and pieces of cash as I came upon them, I enclosed the porch, so that it now functions as the study where I'm actually sitting and writing. Unfortunately, because it faces south, open to the street and all the winds and weather that whip down it, the porch takes the brunt of Iowa seasons; if I had had only a little more money, I could have bought the best insulation instead of only the minimal, R-19; thus, even with the rest of the house heated in winter, the porch gets very cold. But that's how it is.

Though the porch includes, technically, the single front door to the house, most people prefer to enter around the back, through the kitchen door. If you do that, you pass into the period-piece kitchen, make a right down a short corridor where the porch is on your left and the bathroom is on your right, then pass into the dining room, then make a left through a doorway into the living room. Above you, by those same narrow stairs built at the turn of the century, are the three bedrooms.

If you come in at any given moment, unannounced, you will inevitably notice certain things about the house. The first is that the kitchen floor, made of indestructable brown linoleum in a vaguely Moorish style from the early 1970's, is nevertheless pitted and scarred and lustreless: it seems incapable of being cleaned, which is why perhaps it looks as if it hasn't been in some time. By the stove, an ever-changing assortment of crumbs should probably, over the years, have attracted mice; if there ever have been any mice here, however, my cat Spitz seems to have taken care of them. Spitz's food is on the floor on the other side of the kitchen, and tends to spread a little over the linoleum, depending on how hungry Spitz is and also on how long I've been away, during one of my long days at work 70 miles away in Iowa City, and how bored he's gotten.

The countertops are sometimes, though not usually, littered with dirty dishes; more often, these find their way into the sink, where they're washed about every other day. What you think of hygiene in this case really depends on when you happen to show up. Some days look good, some days don't. The counter also usually has anywhere from one to four empty wine bottles pushed to the back, waiting for recycling: somewhere, about ten years ago, I began the subtle shift from having a glass of wine at a party or among friends perhaps once or twice a week, to having a glass of wine myself after work each day, perhaps four or five days a week; and then, after my divorce, clearly without knowing it, I began to have a glass of wine every night, and then two glasses. Even this did not really attract my attention for some time. But after the most recent, and most hope-giving, and most duplicitous lover left, in February, I began to drink between one and two bottles a night most nights. And then, suddenly, I realized. What followed was a willed diminution, not always successful, a normal CT-scan but somewhat high amylase levels, and a kind of limbo marking, perhaps, something physiologically more ominous. I find myself torn between books such as *Rational Recovery* and *Drinking: A Love Story*, each of which reflects a certain aspect of my personality. Meanwhile, the bottles eventually go out in the garage.

Because the house had an invasion of carpenter beetles in the basement about 15 years ago, and because its roof is a rather haphazard affair, with shingles pounded over cedar shakes about 15 years ago, it looks like a major risk to a normal investor, and thus sold for relatively little when I bought it four years ago. But now, of course, I have to think about things like basements and roofs. Sometimes I go down the basement, when doing laundry, and stare at the several beams still apparently in place yet turning to dust if you even touch them gently. Small steel girders from after the original infestation criss-cross the basement, supporting the beams that still are sound and thus supporting the entire house: without the girders, the house would collapse. The right thing to do would be to hire a builder to reconstruct the basement from start to finish, but that could easily cost $10,000, which might as well be a million dollars in my world. At some point I intend to replace certain of the beams myself, though—since they are two-by-eights—handling them solo in the basement, while removing the dead beams, may be a trick. But I tend to handle most things solo.

The roof is another matter. It, too, obviously needs to be replaced, at a cost of at least $6,000, which again might as well be six hundred thousand dollars in my world. But since the roof technically is not part of the setting here, we will ignore it.

Passing from the kitchen past the tolerable though dusty bathroom, glancing into the study, one sees the piles and piles of books that characterize the house. There are over four thousand books here—I'm not sure how many more than that; I've never catalogued them and lost count somewhere around three thousand. They cover everything from contemporary American fiction and poetry to fiction and poetry from the sixteenth, seventeenth, eighteenth, and nineteenth centuries; some biographies and some literary criticism; some texts on eastern religion and on Islam; several Bibles, including one in Greek and Latin (facing pages) and one interlinear, Greek-English; several different kinds of dictionaries, including English-French and English-Italian, and the complete *Oxford English Dictionary* before it went on-line; American Indian texts and ethnographic works; maps, including aviation maps, and map books of all kinds; works on neurobiology, paleoanthropology, animal intelligence, the brain, linguistics, cognitive studies, philosophy; works on ecology and law books on the environment and on constitutional law. There are probably some other categories as well. In the year 2000, I moved four times within half a year; in the course of all those moves, some books got lost, and all of them ultimately were thrown together in various boxes, to be thrown together on shelves once I finally managed to settle. In four years, partly as a refusal to revisit the specific traumas of 2000, I have never gotten around to arranging the books according to subject or period. I've noticed this tends to unnerve people who come to visit.

The carpet in the living room and dining room is as old as the linoleum in the kitchen, and one would have to say, if one were a carpet longevity expert, that whichever company made it deserves a certain kind of congratulations: the carpet has not frayed through or worn down to its underlying mat. But, since both carpets are brown, with a relatively high nap, both carpets show almost 35 years of wear—people walking back and forth, more or less along the same paths over all those years—and no matter how often one vacuums, the carpets always look like a movie set for something terrible waiting to happen. I've almost, but not quite, given up on vacuuming them. Four years ago I repainted the absurdly pink walls in the dining room, so they are now a more soothing if somewhat grubby off-white, and two years ago, in a moment of hope with a partner who wanted to sell my house so she and I could buy something very beautiful on the other side of town, I painted the dark fake wood paneling in the living room off-white as well. Over the years, the chemicals of the fake wood have seeped somewhat through the paint, making the living room look more dingy, rather than less; I suppose I will have to repaint it again and again, if I stay here much longer, in a long-term losing battle against ingrained chemicals. Someone with money would rip down the wood paneling and restore whatever plaster wall lies underneath. But that, like a new roof or basement, is out of the question.

The furniture throughout is what one friend, years ago, referred to as "graduate student special"—two old couches, one old rocking chair in the Arts and Crafts style, its runners partially chewed by two different dogs; an audio "entertainment center," sagging in its middle, holding a record player, a tape player, a CD player, and an amplifier; an old, scarred, imitation Arts and Crafts coffee table from Thailand; an old Danish Modern dining room table from somewhere in Scandinavia, with a mixture of Colonial American-style dining room chairs, most but not all remnants from my mother's house; a desk in the study that used to be a dining room table; a futon in the study for guests; a dozen or so bookshelves from Walmart, mostly four-shelf but two larger; and a Samsung TV I got for free from Charles Gabus Ford in Des Moines in December 2000 when I bought a used Subaru that, over the course of the next three months, required a new front differential, a new transmission, and a new engine. The car is long gone; I kept the TV. The TV is somewhat unusual in another way, however, given the "average" American household, in that it is not connected to cable—which even in its most basic package is too expensive for my budget; nor is the computer on which I'm writing this book connected to the internet, for an internet connection would also be too expensive, and in any case the computer itself—although a Macintosh Performa 6200CD—happens to have a non-working CD-Rom player, meaning that the only way of getting data in or out of the computer—other than typing—is through the 3 1/2-inch floppy drive. No internet provider puts internet data on 3 1/2-inch diskettes any longer. I could probably have this computer repaired and upgraded to something like current status...but that would not only require money, but a new operating system that would in all likelihood wreak havoc with the old Microsoft Word program I use (some later Macs will read this book on a 3 1/2-inch floppy with its old Word program; some will not). So the computer, like the TV, stays in the past.

Upstairs is different only to the extent that it exists contextually in the present; in other ways, rather like the computer, it is a museum. Two years ago, with a little extra money from summer teaching, and hoping to entice my children to come more often to my house, I had the stairway and all the upstairs bedrooms recarpeted, and I repainted them from their various dingy and appalling original colors; they're now yellow, or pale tan, or off-white. A very skillful firm in a place called Montezuma, Iowa (county seat of Poweshiek County, which includes Grinnell) laid the carpet, and it does look handsome. But, as it turns out, almost no one ever goes up there. Nate's room now looks a little like a diorama, with its perfect single bed perfectly made, its desk and chair, its Walmart bureau, its old, old Sony TV and one old video game magazine on top; on the desk sits a plastic model of a vintage car, 3/4 finished. Someday, perhaps, I will finish it myself. Georgia's room, right next to Nate's, shows a few signs of more recent occupation—all the Beanie Babies stuffed into the closet, some old quadratic equations on a sheet of lined paper on the desk, a mail-order catalogue from a teenage girls' clothing store by the bed. But it's been a few weeks since she stayed overnight even once. To be fair, this is in some ways a compliment: her social life is thriving, and as I struggle to find, on line, the kinds of posters that will make her room in my house a more attractive place for her and her friends to hang out, I must also realize that—just as her weeknights are filled with homework—her weekends are filled with sleepovers, and in a town like Grinnell, the rolling pattern of such teenage gatherings can leave the houses of some divorced parents quiet for some period of time.

My room, the larger one across the four-foot-wide hallway from theirs, is painted a soothing yellow—though, for a while, it was orange and magenta, colors my last partner chose in an effort to make the house look more Mediterranean—and it has two small and two very large Walmart bookshelves, a Danish Modern dresser that I remember buying in San Francisco in the fall of 1981 with my then-new wife, a platform bed, and a nightstand with the usual stack of books and a phone. I rarely sleep up here; it's too quiet, and the noise of silence from the two rooms across the hall is too loud. I prefer, in fact, to sleep downstairs on one of the couches in my oldest and most favorite sleeping bag, a North Face Superlight I took with me 12 years ago to Alaska. It has been washed only four times since then, but each washing cuts its warmth a little, so that it is now truly only an indoor or summer bag. But since the temperature in the house rarely drops below 50 degrees, it suffices most nights.

My time in relation to this house is extraordinarily consistent. It has changed slightly this fall, because I have been consulting part-time, as my University of Iowa contract permits, for the Writing Lab at Grinnell College; the overall pattern, however, is the same from day to day. I awaken, unwillingly, around 7 A.M., and try to sleep about a half-hour more, until I feel a gathering surge of determination that even my favorite sleeping bag can't prevent. Making coffee and a small bowl of cereal, I feed Spitz, take a shower or just wash my hair in the sink, get dressed, and then head off either to the College or, in my car, 70 miles to my office in the English department at the University of Iowa. After a day of teaching and meeting with honors and graduate students and other advisees, I return to Grinnell; usually, between October and April, it is dark when I get back to the house. Putting dinner in the oven—something simple, baked chicken and a baked potato—I open a bottle of wine and look over the lesson plans for the next day's classes. Often the rush of ideas after such a rush of ideas earlier in the day is simply too much to bear, and I set my mind to a kind of fast-forward—trying to imagine all the possible questions that will occur the next day and all of the ways I might or might not be able to answer them—and then I close the books, put them all back in my bag, and finish the bottle of wine.

The house is dark; though I leave outside lights on, on the entirely unlikely chance that, perhaps because of some emergency, one of my children or a friend will stop by, I otherwise have only two interior lights on, a small lamp over the kitchen stove and a small lamp in the dining room. On the dining room table I light one favorite oil lamp and, sometimes, a fragrance lamp from Georgia several Christmases ago; otherwise, I light a length of Nag Champa incense from India. Over the course of hours, as the night rolls by, I walk around the silent house, and all around me are stories—like the ones you've read here thus far: stories of my past, happy ones and terrible ones, and musings about how memory works, and speculations about the various evolutionary theories I've read, and ponderings over Sufi and Buddhist and Christian texts and why, thus far, I have never felt myself quite inside them, nor they in me. What I try not to think about, or remember, is what it would be like to have a partner—how the evening, how every evening, would be different. Those thoughts go quickly downhill, of course, and yet a more disturbing corollary also arises, which is simply: this is my home, my life. Loneliness is its characteristic. I am used to it. In a decade, despite considerable effort, I have not been able to change it. The past nine months, perhaps, have been about acceptance: this is my home, my life. The night empties out into pure darkness. I think about when Sunday will arrive, when I will be able to see my youngest son, Thomas, in Iowa City or, sometimes, here. I finish the last of the wine, perhaps put an old, old William Ackerman record on the stereo, walk around a little more, thinking. What I sedulously avoid is self-pity. My home, my life.

What I have described is, I think, neither sad nor not sad. It is what it is. In many quite specific respects I am fortunate. I have no relatives or children currently fighting in what I consider to be an unjustifiable war in Iraq, a war based on intelligence information that was either falsified or known to be unreliable, and which has killed over a thousand young American and coalition men and women roughly the age of my oldest son, not to mention the thousands of Iraqi civilian casualties. For the parents of those children, however they themselves may think of the war, I think of them sometimes as I walk around the house, and sometimes for them I light a candle. I have no aging parents to care for. I have not lost a beloved fiancée to a terrible accident, as one young woman here in town recently lost her fiancé. What tore my life apart last spring has, like grief itself, begun to recede, although I cannot yet tell if it will ever really fade, or if anyone will ever show up to help place it firmly and permanently in the past.

Although I am chronically short of money, and always in debt, I am not facing foreclosure, nor do creditors routinely call. Most months, though not all, I have enough money to pay for heat and light, water and garbage collection—no small details within the infrastructure of American civilization. Most days, despite everything, I can think through what needs to be done for work the next day; most days, when necessary, I can set aside time to grade student papers or read student theses and make intelligent suggestions for revision. Most days, when necessary, I can plan classes a semester or two or three into the future. Walking wounded or not, I am not crippled. My loneliness is not to be pitied. On the other hand, looking at this life closely, as a setting, one can see, perhaps, how it might be increasingly difficult, over the years, for anyone else to decide, or even to intend, to enter it.

Meanwhile the house waits…It has a life, apart from me, yet twinned, when I am not, a life that it might well offer to all comers: a history, stories lodged in beams, corners of the basement, closets, and all open areas, waiting to be more of what it already is, to offer what Agee wished that words would offer. That, perhaps, though an eccentric kind of observation and hope, is why—though the front door is appropriately locked most of the time—the back door is always open.

And Death Shall Have No Dominion

Dylan Thomas drank himself to death in 1953, three years before I was born, in New York City during a national reading tour. This is how it happened:

Arriving in New York on October 20, Thomas had an uneven journey as he made final adjustments to the script of *Under Milkwood* and performed in its audio recording. Near financial ruin, with bills for his two children's tuition and his mother's care waiting for him back in Wales and two American publishers threatening to sue him for not completing promised manuscripts, he alternated between despair and hope in those late October days, staying as usual at the Chelsea Hotel and drinking, as usual, at the White Horse Tavern. Anyone who was watching the downward spiral of his actual life would not have been fooled by his remarkable public performances in those days, nor his expectation of salvation. On November 4, 1953, he returned to his hotel room and said to a friend, "I had the bartender line up 34 shots of whiskey and made it through 18. I think that's a record." Within minutes, he was in a coma; transported to St. Vincent's hospital early on the morning of November 5, he died four days later, on November 9.

But this is not, in fact, exactly what happened.

What is curious, however, is how much of this story remains in public legend. This is essentially the story I received from my most gifted high school teacher's most gifted student, a senior named Andrew Hingston, the resident expert on Ezra Pound and Dylan Thomas (I, as a sophomore, was by then the acknowledged expert on T. S. Eliot; later that year, Andrew would impart bits of literary information with the intent, I think, of reminding me how much I didn't know—a useful thing to remember still). A couple of weeks ago, for example, when I was first contemplating this essay and discussing some of Dylan Thomas' poems with students in my 20th-century American literature class, I asked if anyone knew how he died. Surprisingly, one student knew the year, the place, and virtually the exact quotation I've included above—"I had the bartender line up 34 shots of whiskey and made it through 18. I think that's a record." And so, 51 years after Thomas' death, the legend lives on.

One wonders how. The quotation, for example, does exist in part in some biographies—John Malcolm Brinnin, in *Dylan Thomas in America*, reports that Thomas spoke to his American "assistant," Elizabeth "Liz" Reitell, before going into a coma, and Bill Read and Rollie McKenna report the same incident in *The Days of Dylan Thomas: A Pictorial Biography*. In each of these—and I mention them because they were two of the most popular sources on Dylan Thomas' life when I was a teenager—Thomas is reported to have said to Liz, "I've had eighteen straight whiskies. I think that's the record." How the additional drama of having lined up 34 shots of whiskey came into this quotation I have never been able to determine; I've found no source that records it, yet—even though apparently completely apocryphal—it remains wedded to the legend, as does the site of this final alcoholic implosion—the White Horse Tavern.

But more recent research inevitably complicates the picture. Of the two most current and assiduous biographers—Paul Ferris, whose 2000 revision of his work on Thomas includes much new information, and Andrew Lycett's 2004 *Dylan Thomas: A New Life*—Ferris includes the quotation to Reitell about the whiskey, with one additional comment: "I love you, but I'm alone," Thomas says before at first going to sleep and then slipping into a coma early in the morning of November 5. Lycett simply discounts the entire scene. There are, perhaps, more than sentimental reasons to trust Ferris in the final analysis; among other things, Ferris himself tacitly acknowledges the power of sentiment by noting that Thomas spoke to Reitell "the words that quickly were embedded in the legend." Beyond that, both Ferris and Lytell attempt to reconstruct the White Horse part of the evening of November 4. Lytell finds no evidence that Thomas went to his favorite New York bar that evening, while Ferris quotes "Ruthven Todd and other friends" who actually went later to the bar and spoke to the proprietor, who "concluded, on the evidence of his stocks, that he [Thomas] could not have drunk more than six whiskies, or eight if two regulars who usually took Old Granddad as a nightcap had changed their brand."

The larger issue, however—especially for Ferris—is that, as Thomas' drinking had grown heavier over the past two years particularly, and his health problems had correspondingly increased—gout, liver disease, asthma, gastritis—his doctors had occasionally prescribed morphine to ease his pain. For anyone who has ever had serious surgery—as I have—and has experienced severe post-operative pain, morphine is an interesting drug in the extreme: not only does it mask one's pain, but (for patients fortunate enough not to respond to it with nausea) it also provides an emotional and physical lift; it can, among other things, erase the horrible paranoia and hallucinations common with severe hangovers. I can, unfortunately, speak from experience on this subject. Clearly Thomas could as well, and—reluctant to consign him to the increasing hell of his drinking—his New York doctor, Milton Feltenstein, injected him on November 4 with half a gram, or grain, of morphine.

As a means of comparison, a normal American dose of post-operative morphine is approximately 100 to 200 milligrams every four hours as necessary, combined with 650 to 1300 milligrams of acetaminophen (assuming no evidence of liver damage); thus Thomas would have received in one dose a sizeable amount of the drug, though somewhat less than the "three times" the recommended dose that Ferris alleges. As Ferris goes on to note, even half a gram of morphine—which would, among other things, have depressed Thomas' respiratory system—would not, of itself, have been quite enough to kill him. Combined with almost any amount of residual blood alcohol, however, and asthma, that amount of the drug would pretty much do the trick.

Re-reading these biographies now, I find myself struck by something perhaps odd—how durable Thomas actually was, how much his body resisted death. Two years ago, after an operation, not knowing much about morphine and knowing nothing about its interaction with alcohol,

I took 400 milligrams for extreme pain while downing a bottle of red wine over the course of the evening; around 4 A.M., I woke up as near to suffocating as I have been since that moment on Bethany Beach when, at the age of two-and-a-half, I was drowning. Not knowing what was wrong, trying to keep myself up and walking, choking and vomiting up spittle, I simply thought that, along with everything else, I had either caught pneumonia or a bad case of the flu. In a way, I was probably close to right, since pneumonia is the most common immediate cause of death after chronic and acute alcohol ingestion combined with morphine ("Hypostatic bronchopneumonia" is one of two causes of death listed on Thomas' death certificate, the other being "Acute and chronic ethylism"; there is, as Ferris notes trenchantly, "no mention of morphine."). In a few hours, I was better, but my background was not Thomas'. In any event, it seems clear that Thomas' final comments about 18 shots of whiskey were apocryphal—not to mention the other 34—and the larger story—even if one means by "larger" only the hellish final two weeks of Thomas' life in New York, from October 20 to November 4—is a story of heavy drinking, morphine, desperation and hideous hangovers and blackouts, well-intentioned and less-well-intentioned parties that got out of control (one, involving a dancer, that has alarming echoes of the much later film *Very Bad Things),* magnificent moments of public self-control for the sake of readings and recordings, an underlying sense of utter hopelessness—and one final letter from Thomas' spouse Caitlin, which he received two days before his collapse, announcing that they were through, berating him for "his weaknesses, his lies, his drunkenness, his infidelity [a charge that could also have been aimed at her], and, worst of all, for having left her without money. Her threats to kill herself or go whoring, she said, were not a joke" (Ferris 324). Clearly, in some way, Thomas foresaw all this, whether or not one argues that he brought it upon himself (and that, as a concept, bears some further examination a bit later): when, on Friday, October 23, at a party where he seemed to be staying away from alcohol for the moment, he told Rollie McKenna, "I've just seen the gates of hell, that's all," the comment is scarcely one to be dismissed or, as Ferris does, to be seen as Thomas already taking his current misery and turning it into "material" (317).

Let us imagine, for a moment, that, for Thomas at this time, the gates of hell were cognitively real. What would they have looked like to a man who, in 1933 (at the age of 19—he was born October 27, 1914), had written his first draft of one of the most extraordinary poems in English, "And Death Shall Have No Dominion?" Why—and this is, perhaps, an intentionally naive question—why should such a man find any intimidation at the gates of hell?

As with any vision compelling enough to be haunting, the gates of hell have both a near and a distant prospect: the near prospect was the immediate "view," the words themselves, while the distant prospect was perhaps more difficult for an ordinary viewer to see—it was space and time pulled inward rather than expanded outward, compressed into the atemporal space of the psyche. To an ordinary reader this may seem vaguely laughable, this art-historical way of coming at a psychic terror, but Thomas was interesting in part because he often did not distinguish (as most of us do, consciously or unconsciously) between a thing and a word, something perceived and something spoken:

> Once, in America, Thomas told Alastair Reid that "when I experience anything I experience it as a thing and a word at the same time, both equally amazing." Failure to see that an image is only an image, not the reality, may have been, for Thomas, not a failure at all, but a positive capacity that was at the root of his perception. The state of mind in which a person cannot tell the difference between saying that "Jane is a rose" and "Jane is like a rose" is familiar to psychiatrists. Mescaline and other substances can induce it. In one experiment, "with a loss of insight into the difference between analogy and the literally meant, the responses assumed psychotic-like forms." These are dangerous waters for a biography; no doubt the poet and the madman may both have heightened or distorted perceptions. It is enough to say that Thomas's view of his own body, and thus the poems that made him famous, may have been influenced by the fact that he wrote in a state of mind where words and objects became, for the moment, essentially the same (Ferris, 98).

Leaving aside, for the moment, the conceptual unexploded ordnance of "poet versus madman," this analysis is worth considerable attention because, among other things, it calls into question some essential concepts about language that have been with us since Ferdinand de Saussure produced his *Course in General Linguistics* in 1959. Saussure posited that language creates us; we do not create it; and implicitly, to the extent that language creates us, language may also create the illusion that we, ourselves, are both creating and extending our identities, even fathoming our souls, while in fact we are simply working within the specific limits of an arbitrary sign system whose function is not, in fact, "self-knowledge," but the furtherance of the sign-system group, the culture. As Mark C. Taylor writes in his summary of Saussure's four essential points:

> First, Saussure insists that all signs are arbitrary conventions... .Second, Saussure's concentration on synchronic rather than diachronic aspects of language implies an unavoidable tension between temporality and systemic thought. Since temporal change resists systemization, systems can only be constructed by excluding time. Time, in other words, disrupts every effort to establish a system. Third, Saussure reverses the modern philosophy of subjectivity by suggesting what later is described as the "decentering," "dissolution," or "deconstruction" of the subject. Instead of constituting the language that creates the world, the speaking subject is constituted by its place within the linguistic system.... Finally, Saussure's recognition of the differential nature of signs inverts the traditional relationship between identity and difference. As we have seen, for most Western philosophy, unity and identity are primary and plurality and difference secondary... .Saussure [insists] that since identity is derived from difference, the latter has a certain priority over the former (Taylor, 13-14).

The degree to which Thomas both does and does not fit Saussure's model is one of the strikingly-unstudied aspects of both his life and his art. Certainly, at a visceral level, Thomas rejected the essential Saussurian concept that "signs are arbitrary conventions": when he wrote, the thing became the word, and the word thing: Thomas wrote as if the first chapter of the Gospel of John were actually true, a fact that many readers, even Christians, tend to ignore, a fact that would probably today put Thomas in the madhouse, but a fact that John, at least, believed at heart: the language of the world was the language of God, and God was the language of the world, and while there might be a multiplicity of languages, at any given moment "the Word was with God, and the Word was God." At the same time, this Thomistic (as opposed to Thomist) link between language and thing may have been slightly less rigid than it appears: Thomas loved sounds, rhymes, metrical experiments, and all kinds of remarkable technical subtlety; he was also often translating in his head from Welsh to English to Welsh, although his writings are all in English. Surrounded by two distinct sound systems, Thomas knew that a word and a thing were one, and yet another word and the same thing were also one: this was not a sign of "arbitariness," exactly, but it gave to things a certain fluidity, gave them a more-than-mortal capacity for transubstantiation through language. The Word may have been God, but if so, God and the world were both ceaselessly in flux through the very act of language. That concept, in its comforting moments, might have led Thomas to "And Death Shall Have No Dominion"; in its darker implications, it led to "Fern Hill" and "Poem in October."

But if Thomas rejected a central component of the Saussurian vision, he embraced one other—the concept that "temporal change resists systemization," that to construct a system one must do so outside of time. For Saussure this may be seen as a philosophical problem; for Thomas it was psychological. Time, in Thomas' world, had, not surprisingly, at least two aspects, an internal chronology and an external one; these two were by no means synonymous. The internal chronology in Thomas' world made possible stories in which narrators told themselves stories about what was, what could be and would be, even if, at the very end, they discovered that the function of external time destroyed their internal system; In "Poem in October," for example, it is impossible to know if "the weather turned round" in the chronology of the world, but it is entirely possible to know—in terms of ordinary human knowledge—that "the long dead child" did not return when the weather turned, if it did turn, and that Thomas the narrator did not become himself, himself as a child, and himself as a child and as an adult, but rather registered all these changes through an internal chronology in which time effectively came to a halt. One might argue, if one wished, that "Poem in October" is ingenious because it represents a kind of systemic thought about the roots and spiritual salvation of wonder, and how it is that one must stop time in order to recover those roots; one must resist the intrusion of time into language, which one does in part by defeating language itself, by making its synchronicities turn back upon themselves and disrupt the chronology they themselves seem to have set in motion.

If one were to take Thomas' method as seriously as many philosophers take Saussure's, one might see an actual spiritual method in the primacy of the Word over time. But Thomas himself struggled to see this, and it was not because, as some might allege, of his rejection of the final Saussurian tenet—the idea of difference, rather than identity, as a function of language. For Thomas, the idea of a "decentered" or "deconstructed" self would have made no sense, although one might argue that such a concept could have come to his rescue: a "deconstructed" self, for example, might have placed itself at odds with the sign system of language, dismembering even the concept of "self" through whatever tools existed, even the admittedly biased and damaged tools of language, to find meditatively a different route to whatever might exist outside of the linguistic construct. Even then, of course, the question of whether Thomas would have succeeded at discovering anything other than what he discovered depends on which theorists you listen to—if, in fact, you are unfortunate enough to listen to any of them; for Derrida, for example, there is simply no "hors-de-texte," no "outside of the text" to get to; any sign system, deconstructed, yields another sign system, although a devout Zen or Tibetan Buddhist would— well, not dispute this, because such an adept would see nothing worth disputing—but would find Derrida a sad curiosity at best. Centuries before the academically-popular anomaly of deconstruction, certain Tibetan lamas were positing the existence of Shambala, which might indeed be a specific valley in a remote part of Tibet, difficult to get to by any human means—and yet, should one accidentally or on purpose find oneself there, one would still not perceive the real city or its real inhabitants, because— though all around—they existed in a dimensionality imperceptible to humans. This analogy is, for Westerners perhaps, a stretch, although such an author as Edwin Bernbaum has some things to say about it that might make its presence here less surprising. In any case, Thomas, when he contemplated the idea of self and identity, saw, not a self accessible to deconstruction, but rather a super-constructed self, a self made of its own perceptions through intuitions and language and a self of language, a word-self that promised the paradox of unity and dissolution underlying all pantheism and certain kinds of Christianity. It is this self that narrates "And Death Shall Have No Dominion."

But now we run into one of the great contradictions within Thomas, the paradox that, although the thing was the word, and the word was not arbitrary, the word at some level had a life of its own, and the thing had a life of its own, and the word was immortal, or as close to it as anything in this world might come, and the thing was not. The thing would become old, would become diseased, would falter or disintegrate, would die. The thing was a horror. And the home of the thing, for Thomas, was the very body that also harbored the passion and concept of the word. It is a classic neo-Platonic paradox, slightly different from conventional Cartesian dualism by virtue of the third character, the Word, neither flesh nor mind but at once an intermediary and a sign of transubstantiation. All of this is scarcely new in either philosophy or theology, yet the way in which Thomas lived it showed a destructive side remarkably like the undercurrent of neo-Platonism in Christian Science. Paul Ferris returns to this subject repeatedly. "The physical world was always capable of giving him the horrors," he observes.

> Worst of all was to be "naked in a bath of white mice." A sandwich made of dried eyes was another of his fancies... .Oswell Blakeston, a writer he met in London, said that "Dylan's face would light up and he'd say, 'How *often* have you thought about cancerous meat?'" Or he would talk elaborate nonsense about how he poured boiling water on decaying meat, and the meat screamed. A severed lip with a moustache, lying on the pavement, first appeared in a *Portrait* story, and reappeared in anecdotes... .The stories that Thomas began to write in Swansea, and produced for several years, continued to draw on this vein of shudders experienced with relish.

> Heads burst open, someone drinks a cup of semen and
> bird's blood, intestines dribble from a rabbit, madmen
> howl, a doctor grafts a cat's head onto a chicken (Ferris, 98-
> 99).

Ferris' point here, in part, is that Thomas took what he found horrible
and to some extent "made it enjoyable" through the medium of language,
of storytelling: it is a little hard to say, from Ferris' account, whether the
biographer himself perceives how deeply these grotesqueries moved
Thomas, how profoundly his seemingly entertaining storytelling was a
defense against a world that, if one took it seriously, could not possibly
be the world of the Word. What had happened? Where, exactly, in the
spatial reality of time, had the nightmare begun, and why was language—
potentially a means of escape—so utterly implicated in it? Why was the
home of language the body? "The final horror," Ferris notes, "may have
been his own body."

> His body was a trap. One notebook talks of "man…like
> a mole within his fleshy prison"; another of "the jailing
> skin." A friend in later life recalled him after a three-day
> drinking bout, scratching at his hands and saying, "To be
> able to tear off my flesh, to get rid of this awful, horrifying
> skin we have, to get at the bone and then to get rid of that!
> What a wonderful thing!" (Ferris, 99)

This perception, perhaps more than any other, brings us back around
to the question of what, for Thomas, the "gates of hell" looked like. By
now, of course, the answer scarcely needs to be stated: the gates of hell
were the ordinary world, the non-Saussurian world that had not created
Thomas nor bound him to a specific linguistic sign system, yet did create
the context in which he moved through it, drunkenly and symbolically,
in order to escape what he himself would never have made. Perhaps
Thomas' most evocative prelude to the gates of hell—what they were, and
how they accompanied him increasingly as he drank increasingly in a
vain attempt to escape them—comes, not in any specific story or poem,
but rather in a letter to Vernon Watkins, one of his closest compatriots
throughout his adult life (at times they used to play by writing alternate
lines of a sonnet), whom he stood up on October 2, 1944, when Watkins

was to be married and Thomas was the best man. Written on February 2, 1945, the letter remained undiscovered until 1972, when Gwen Watkins found it at the bottom of an old RAF kitbag (Vernon had been a sergeant in the RAF during World War II). In it, Thomas only indirectly apologizes for his cruel gaffe, but says a great deal about a physical world that was beginning to close in on him:

> I have found, increasingly as time goes on, or around, or backwards, or stays quite still as the brain races, the heart absorbs and expels, the arteries harden, that the problem of physical life, of social contact, of daily posture and armour, of the choice between dissipations, of the abhorred needs enforced by a reluctance to "miss anything," that old fear of death, are as insoluble to me as those of the spirit... .The ordinary moments of walking up village streets, opening doors or letters, speaking good-days to friends or strangers, looking out of windows, making telephone calls, are so inexplicably (to me) dangerous that I am trembling all over before I get out of bed in the mornings to meet them (Ferris, 198).

As Ferris notes rather trenchantly after quoting the letter, life for Thomas—only eight years before his death—"was a torment; that seems true, and real enough" (Ferris, 198). Yet Ferris leaves the specific character of that torment tantalizingly unanalyzed: the details Thomas offers in confidence to one of his oldest friends, though perhaps inscrutable to an "ordinary," "well" person and apparently inscrutable to Thomas himself, are classic details of a profound anxiety disorder coupled with attention deficit and depression. The point here, however, is not to argue that Thomas had diagnosable psychological problems that might, with treatment, have abated (indeed, the first edition of the pyschiatrists' bible, the *Diagnostic and Statistical Manual*, would not appear until 1952); the point, rather, is to illustrate the degree to which Thomas was increasingly in the position of apologizing for problems that were not, truly, under his control, while describing with remarkable accuracy a kind of "ontological insecurity," in R. D. Laing's phrase, that made daily life a horror. For someone with a mind at once prone to vivid visions of what might be and terrors of what is, a walk to the post office, for example, might be a major act of courage and a source of terror: in the world of the ordinary street, one meets ordinary people, is obliged to enter into ordinary conversations about conventional subjects (what would it have been like, one wonders, if someone had stopped Dylan Thomas on the street in Laugharne to say "hello" and Thomas had replied with what was really on his mind, which was "Do you realize that death shall have no dominion?"), must conduct ordinary transactions with government-issued currency and a certain accepted level of politeness—that is to say, beyond most people's general imagining, the nature of daily life is in fact a highly-scripted life, neither original nor personal but performed from morning till night. The consent that most of us give most of the time to this performance is important because it maintains the illusion of contact: we imagine that we are in touch with other people, as we are in touch with ourselves, because we say and do that which, over the years, we have come to expect as the customary sign system of "in-touchness": to that degree, Saussure was perhaps more darkly correct than anyone at the time imagined.

But to a person whose internal life has, for whatever reason, suffered some damage—who cannot count on either mere or complex performance for intrinsic meaning—daily life is an actual portrait of the gates of hell. If one is depressed, one seeks essential contact above all else; daily life— where contact appears real but is in fact fundamentally semiotic or, to put it another way, highly ritualized—is the opposite of essential contact, and futhers one's depression. If one has an anxiety disorder, one knows already that one will fail at the falsehoods of daily life, and thus confronts them not with ordinary equanimity but with terror. If one suffers from attention deficit, then one cannot conduct one's own performance with any degree of reliability; some stray thought, profound or minor, always intervenes to disrupt the expected behavior. For Thomas, clearly, by 1944 if not before, the phenomenal world—the world of people, performances, and time—was riddled with nightmare. And while it is true that, as Ferris suggests, Thomas could turn nightmares into entertainment—look at the underlying nightmarish character of the irredeemably-popular *A Child's Christmas in Wales*, for example, routinely ignored by those who cherish its public performance—it is surely more true that Thomas felt the pressure of what Saussure described with different intentions: the pressure of time made a diachronic world virtually impossible, yet for Thomas a world outside of time was the only world one really could take seriously. Because Thomas—like many of us—could *imagine* such a world, he understood that in some dimension it actually existed. Yet, human as he was, he was constantly negotiating the transition from atemporal to diachronic life, and being fundamentally atemporal, he fared poorly in the transition.

If one looks closely at certain details of Thomas' 1945 letter to Watkins, for example, it is striking how powerfully time allies itself with the body: time may exist in a kind of relativity, going on, "or around, or backwards, or [staying] quite still," but "the brain races, the heart absorbs and expels..." The body registers a strict chronology from birth to death; it is the most unimaginatively unimaginative creation in the realm of creation. It starts at one moment, and ends at another; regardless of the fascinating secrets of its cell structure, its neurons and synapses and dendrites, its muscles and bone and marrow, it is purely time's toy, and in that regard it is—in the inner universe of Dylan Thomas, as well as the inner universe of anyone who has ever suffered from depression, anxiety, "visions," or schizophrenia—an appalling curse. It is God's trick on creation, a dark, dank joke created in the back corner of a satanically divine locker room, the fleshly timepiece that registers a win only at the moment of one's most abject loss.

In a direct confrontation with its fundamental relation to mortality, a diachronic soul will look for a different pattern, something else implicit in creation that permits the possibility of what Saussure calls "a system" outside of time. One such pattern might arguably be an alliance between word and thing, not so that words become things but rather that things become words: the material creation sheds an aspect of its materiality so that a radically different universe might appear. This is what brought Thomas, in the early 1930's, to his first drafts of "And Death Shall Have No Dominion." The final draft appears here, with certain caveats. Most serious poets who read Thomas do not actually consider "And Death Shall Have No Dominion" one of his better poems; its repetitions are polemical, it relies on exegesis and argument rather than epiphanies of language for its vision, its faith is declarative rather than something unfolded and examined; the character of its paradox is not passionate, as in "The Force That Through The Green Fuse Drives The Flower," but rather expository; it lacks the absolute interpenetration of language and perception in "Fern

Hill." Yet "And Death Shall Have No Dominion" is, in its own way, one of the great poems in English; it is one of the few poems that I myself know by heart, and the story of that knowledge is perhaps worth adding here as further evidence of how certain lives follow patterns unknowingly set down through the genius of the recent past.

> And death shall have no dominion.
> Dead men naked they shall be one
> With the man in the wind and west moon;
> When their bones are picked clean and the clean bones gone,
> They shall have stars at elbow and foot;
> Though they go mad they shall be sane,
> Though they sink through the sea they shall rise again;
> Though lovers be lost, love shall not;
> And death shall have no dominion.
>
> And death shall have no dominion.
> Under the windings of the sea,
> They lying long shall not die windily;
> Twisting on racks when sinews give way,
> Strapped to a wheel, yet they shall not break;
> Faith in their hands shall snap in two,
> And the unicorn evils run them through;
> Split all ends up they shan't crack;
> And death shall have no dominion.
>
> And death shall have no dominion.
> No more may gulls cry at their ears,
> Or waves break loud upon seashores;
> Where blew a flower may a flower no more
> Lift its head to the blows of the rain;
> Though they be mad and dead as nails,
> Heads of the characters hammer through daisies;
> Break in the sun till the sun break down,
> And death shall have no dominion. (*Collected Poems*, 77)

Just as it may be worth noting critics' caveats about this poem, it is equally worth noting its Thomistic beauty: the poem is masterful with alliteration both within lines and across lines: "...one/with the man in the wind and the west moon" shows an incantatory devotion to long and short "o" sounds, augmented with short a, short i, and short e; similarly, repetitions that may seem appealing simply because of their rhetorical ingenuity—the repetition of "clean" for example, with the actual meaning of the term shifting from one use to the next—lead to other details that stand out precisely because they are *not* repeated: "they shall have stars at elbow and foot" is a remarkably specific line about the resurrection of the body. The poem includes a neologism—"windily"—and a conceptual neologism—"unicorn evils"—and dares such a cliché as "dead as nails," yet turns that cliché inside out in the next line, as the "heads of the characters" hammer their way out of the implicit coffins in which they are nailed to re-enter the world of the flower; indeed, even "characters" is a double-entendre, as the characters flowing from Thomas' own pen determined the outcome, the resurrection, of this poem. Whatever criticisms one may be inclined to level at "And Death Shall Have No Dominion," it is a strikingly vivid and polished production.

There is a certain irony, I suppose, to my profound admiration for this poem, since one of my own most celebrated college professors was the Anglo-American Donald Davie, a distinguished British poet who had defected, more or less, to America; he taught at Stanford in the 1970's and then finished his career at Vanderbilt University in Tennessee. Though admired as a poet, Davie had actually made his influentially-conservative reputation with his first critical book, *Purity of Diction in English Verse,* a book that directly and vehemently attacked everything I admired about Thomas and willfully refused to see the cognitively-meaningful, if literally inscrutable, juxtapositions in Thomas' syntax. It is curious that Davie, who so detested Thomas and yet who made so much money and such a reputation attacking that poet, went on to study and write in detail about a poet even more famous and even less successful in his "ply on ply" of juxtapositions, Ezra Pound: It never seemed to occur to Davie that the praise he lavished on Pound rested on the same criteria he used to attack Thomas. The word "envy" comes to mind; Davie was a very brilliant intellect, but a cruel, unhappy, mean-spirited man, one of the most appalling professors I was ever to encounter; but it was not Davie's assault on Thomas that either sealed my opinion of Davie or guaranteed my fascination with Thomas. Thomas entered my life much earlier, in the early winter of 1972, when I was a sophomore at Los Altos High School and our magnificent but eccentric English teacher, Warren Wilde, had given us "And Death Shall Have No Dominion" as a poem for close reading and analysis.

As it happened, Wilde's assignment came to me just as my mother was leaving on a trip back east to visit her relatives, and I was home more or less alone: my brother and sister were long gone, and my father, who worked absurd hours primarily to distract himself from his profound unhappiness, was rarely at home. At that point, having lived in Los Altos, California for barely two years and having made few friends, I was about as isolated as I am today—another curious irony—and my main companions at that time were the books and poems Warren Wilde assigned to our class, and the Bible and Mary Baker Eddy's *Science and Health with Key to the Scriptures*, the central texts of Christian Science. As I sat in my loneliness on the couch of the living room, reading and re-reading Thomas' poem, I had a stunning revelation: Thomas had prefigured everything I knew about Christian Science. The poem defined my faith, and my faith defined the poem. Everything was there, everything: the ordinary material world did not define us—"though lovers be lost, love shall not"—nor did the terrible pains of being human mean that human experience was defined by pain—"strapped to a wheel, yet they shall not break." Indeed, one might not even need faith—"faith in their hands shall crack in two"—and one's life might, to other humans and to the world at large, look like a piece of evil—"And the unicorn evils run them through"—yet none of this was any more real than the moment on the cross when Jesus said, "My father, why hast thou forsaken me?" That very human cry of Jesus was also, to a Christian Science reading, merely an error in a time of agony, a mistake: God had not forsaken Jesus. The real Jesus was perfect, eternal, and continual, daily proof that death could have no dominion. Never had I seen a poem that so vividly confirmed my faith.

Even now, 33 years later, re-reading this paragraph, I find myself stunned at the beautiful interstices of Thomas' poem and Christian Science doctrine. If one had, perhaps, learned Christian Science in a less punitive way—if its ugly, even hideous, yet secret dualisms had not tortured me throughout my childhood—one might say that the truth of Thomas' poem was an act of faith too powerful to doubt. At the time, it might have helped me to realize that Thomas was actually converting the "world" into the Word, so that the words said what the words meant, and said what Thomas might pray to be true, though it was already true in word; this did not, however, make it true in terms of the phenomenal world, and had I known that I might have had more compassion for myself, for others, and for Thomas' life. Even so, my Christian Science interpretation of the poem consumed me, as I wrote pages of notes and drafts, and when I received the final paper back from Warren Wilde, it came with an A+—the first A+ I had ever received. Here, finally, in the midst of my loneliness, was confirmation that my faith could be companionable as well as true. For I had loved writing that paper, and had found my own words to be as comforting as any other person, or at least anyone I had known up to that point. Over the course of that tumultuous year, as I met the girl who would, the year following, become my first girlfriend, and as I began to wrestle more vividly with the intense physical power and delight of the body, I would feel the power of those words slip...just as they slipped for Thomas, perhaps. But is the world really the home of the gates of hell? Do the words always slip? Jesus asked only once why he had been forsaken; are we to ask it every day, wondering if anything will make it untrue, wondering what it is that might return us to happiness, to a sense of connection, to a power of the word and the heart? Is the very system Saussure saw as a means of understanding us—looking at the way language created us, rather than the other way around—is that very system bound to lock us into a world in which beautiful words fly away like birds, leaving us old, loveless, companionless, drunk, and alone?

* * *

This brings us rather directly and uncomfortably, not to the continuing subject of Thomas and his poetry, but rather to the subject of the body and the self. For if there is one thing, and perhaps only one thing, that Thomas and I share, and you share, it is the body, and if there is one thing about which we may usefully disagree, it is the self.

I, of course, was taught from a very early age that the body was the equivalent of the gates of hell, and the pain and suffering I endured as a child—often from people who claimed to love me or to want to help me—reinforced my sense that the body, or rather my erring conception of its mortal reality, should be left behind as quickly as possible. In Christian Science, it was often impossible even to speak of "the body," for the material body itself was unreal, an erroneous belief; Mary Baker Eddy cautioned us against even naming a disease, against calling the flu "the flu," for example, or pleurisy "pleurisy," because names conferred authority, and since disease had no authority, it should have no name. Only spirit was real, and only spiritual truths had names in Christian Science. In practice, however, this had the effect of colonizing one's own body: when one was ill, whatever domain the illness occupied was erased, wiped out, made the Other or the unreal one; in its place were the systemic words of Christian Science. Unfortunately, if one was routinely unhealed, as I was, and thus suffered both from long-term pain and from the fear of pain, one's life was taken up with a continual dual consciousness—the awareness of oneself in ordinary terms, in ordinary life, and the fear that, should one become ill, one would become nothing, no one, a bundle of non-existent pain, while people who claimed to care left the room and prayed that one's true spiritual nature manifest itself in one's body.

I use the word "colonized" here with some specific intention, for—of all the critical tools to emerge from the upheavals in thought and politics over the past century—post-colonial studies offers some of the most trenchant and practical insights into ways in which dominant social or political systems take over the cultures and the lives of those less able to wield the specific kinds of power that define those dominant systems. Clearly, within the terrain of post-colonial analysis, an abundance of unexploded ordnance waits to be triggered: a middle-aged white male in the United States in 2005, for example, who suffers from dysthymia, post-traumatic stress disorder, and chronic anxiety, who was tormented as a child and repeatedly told that much of what he loved was unreal, whose adult life has been marked outwardly by a number of successes yet also by dramatic failures and reversals, and whose inward life is a dark register of all that was attempted, despite early torments, and all that came to nothing—that person is, nevertheless, simply not the same as a man of equivalent age from the Congo, or Nigeria, or Nicaragua, or Afghanistan: the experience of having been colonized politically, of having one's cultural self confronted with erasure, of having members of one's family threatened or killed, of experiencing the racism bound up in that colonialism, of fighting for a self one has to invent word-by-word, of enduring a certain post-colonial chaos with its colonial legacy—one has to admit a difference.

And yet, on the immortal register of pain, one knows that one's experience as an Other is always and irrevocably Other: one knows what it is like never to be at home, one knows how much one longs for home, how much one wishes to be home in one's body and in or with the body of a beloved, one can articulate to a degree how much was lost in the experience of otherness, yet there is always something one cannot say that other people, uncolonized or colonizers, can say: one cannot even say what that "something" is, because it is as inconceivable to an Other as it is for a depressed person, for example, to conceive of what it means to be, over a period of time, happy. At a certain point it simply vanishes from consciousness. Nevertheless, one tries to return from the domain of colonization to the domain of the present, and in doing so one returns, perhaps ironically, to that domain of dual consciousness, slightly modified: one sees oneself looking into the past for clues, for answers, and one sees oneself to some extent as others do—one looks at oneself through others' eyes. And one sees, of course, two different people.

I say "dual consciousness" here rather than "double consciousness" particularly because "double consciousness" is W.E.B. Dubois' phrase for the experience of being African American in *The Souls of Black Folk*, and, again, I wish my own language to avoid any assumed connection between growing up as a Christian Scientist and growing up African American in the United States. Such a comparison, I realize, might seem particularly offensive to African Americans, as the history of Christian Science in its early years was a history of wealthy white Americans, grasping a religion that seemed to them to offer the promise of unlimited health and prosperity. That was a view of the religion that Mary Baker Eddy herself promoted; it was a view that caught Willa Cather's attention when she was writing, in 1908 and 1909, from Georgine Milmine's notes, one of the first biographies of Mary Baker Eddy, a biography that so offended the

Christian Science Church that the Church bought all the copies it could find when the book came out and destroyed them all; the book was not reprinted until 1993, when the University of Nebraska Press re-issued it, again over the protests of the Church. By that time, however, the fortunes of the Church had taken a dark turn; membership, which had peaked at around 200,000 in 1926, had been sliding as my parents' generation died off, and the readership of the *Christian Science Monitor,* around 177,000 in 1988, had dipped to about 77,000—despite or perhaps because of Mary Baker Eddy's requirement that every member of the church subscribe— and would dip further as membership declined sharply once again, to perhaps 60,000 in the early 1990's.

Interestingly, however, as the church leadership looked for new blood, it looked, not to North America, or to Canada, or to Europe—but to Africa; in the late 1980's, the church began a major "outreach" program in a number of African nations, increased its coverage of African news in the *Christian Science Monitor,* and worked to enlarge both the number of church members in Africa and the number of African Christian Science practitioners both in Africa and in the United States. This move caught a number of older American Christian Scientists by surprise, although the original rationale made a certain appalling sense: Africa in 1990, overall, lagged well behind the United States or other formerly colonizing nations in the quality of its medical care; it was thus easier to convince people with little access to doctors that the Spirit, properly conceived, could heal. Yet the irony is inescapable: faced with the possibility of its own extinction, the Christian Science church embarked in the 1990's on a foray faintly yet distinctly analogous to, for example, Belgium's domination of the Congo in the 1880's, or France's colonization of Algeria, or the Dutch occupation in South Africa: it sought to colonize, once again, those who were in certain ways most vulnerable. And so, if I think of W.E.B. Dubois in terms of my own upbringing, though I do so with a slight distance and caution—though I do so always with the memory of James Baldwin's sense of an absolute cultural and historical divide between him and the children of the Swiss village in which he wrote, in 1953, "Stranger in the Village"—I do so as well with an awareness that the comparison is not as remote or as historically inaccurate as one might imagine. To be a Christian Scientist is not necessarily to have the "double consciousness" of which Dubois writes, but it is to have at least a dual consciousness—an awareness of oneself as oneself, and an awareness of oneself as one "should" be, or rather, as one "is," the perfect spiritual child of God who thus must never get sick or hurt, must never be hungry or lonely or sad or frightened, must never admit to the reality of death or the reality of this world, because all the other Christian Scientists who are watching for signs of falling away will see one's own slipping, and will turn away, or send letters of reproof, or simply shun…one will become a no one, an Other.

And the body is the site of this battle. The body is the place where this battle of reality and unreality takes place; it is the conceptual field where one is either recognized or dismissed, saved or damned, showered with grace or showered with all the unreal evils of unreality. Good Christian Scientists have "bodies" that are harmonious, lovely, and healthy, because they worship appropriately; bad Christian Scientists, like me—as I always was, apparently, for as long as I can remember, long before I understood the concepts of the religion—had sick, unfit, unlovely bodies. That was the kind of body I had, regardless of how much I prayed or how often I read the Bible and *Science and Health with Key to the Scriptures* or how often I went to church or how often I called Christian Science practitioners. My eyes were the ones that went bad when I was five; my back was the one with scoliosis; my teeth were the ones with continual cavities; my chest was the one missing a central bone at the sternum, making me an embarrassment at the beach; my forehead was too large, my chin too narrow, my legs turned inward so my knees banged together when I ran, my stomach too sensitive and prone to nausea, my muscles too weak regardless of exercise or diet or prayer, my lungs too small and subject to constant inflammation and infection, my immune system defective in some indescribable way. I was the nigger of the family, of the church, of the Mother Church. That was my identity.

So I have said it, at the risk of offending African Americans who have suffered far more than I have suffered for the color of their skin; and I must say, as well, that I cannot fully approve of my own language here, as it effectively co-ops one kind of discourse—that of racial disparity in colonial situations—for the sake of a white child who grew up in a lower-middle-class American family. Such co-oping is only marginally legitimate, as it damages both the essential meaning and history of such a term as "nigger." On the other hand, the historical evolution of that term and its varied implications and communities in the 1980's and 1990's has been the source of considerable discussion; I use the term here for what I hope is a clearly articulated purpose. My position within the family, within my church, and within the larger church, was the position of a colonized Other, and to say otherwise would be to lie. So that is my truth.

It may be easier, then, to see how a poet like Thomas, and a poem like "And Death Shall Have No Dominion," should have exercised such a compelling effect. No one would claim that Thomas was a colonized subject (although his Welshness was in certain ways an issue), but Thomas too came to understand what it meant to play a role, the role of oneself, and this became much more of a pressure as he entered his late twenties. At the same time, he was not a revolutionary; rather than resisting either the role he played or the world that harbored the gates of hell, he went around all this, found the intermediary of the Word itself, and lived, to the degree that he lived, in the world of the Word, a world of describable beauty and light. Had I had a different character, I might well have read, not Thomas, but Richard Wright, Ralph Ellison, Malcolm X, Langston Hughes, Don L. Lee, Denise Levertov, Adrienne Rich, Audre Lorde— poets of color and feminists who saw themselves as being colonized, or as having been colonized, and who used the language of the ordinary world as a weapon against the invisible incarceration that gave the ordinary world apparent and actual power over their minds and bodies. But I did not want to fight; I wanted to transcend. What I loved on this earth I wanted to keep loving, but there was precious little of that, and the world of the Word was so much more beautiful, so much more reliable, so much more redolent with joy and color and light and sound, so sensual, so sexual. Only sex ever rivaled the Word, and, indeed, when sex arrived—as it did somewhat late for me, when I was sixteen and seventeen—it turned my world upside down: for to cherish sex was to cherish the world as it was, and my girlfriend as she was, and this was the absolute break with Christian Science that frightened me: so attuned by years of torment to the nature of the religion, I could not see that I had already let go of it years before, the very first time I lay for three days in torment from an ear infection no practitioner could heal; not seeing that there might be other realities, or other stories of this reality, I hung onto the letter of Christian

Science, behaved as well as I could, and began to believe, like Thomas, in an intermediary Word, a private domain where all was well and all would be well. But with sex I had utterly betrayed Christian Science, and as my allegiance to the religion remained perverse and absolute, as a victim's allegiance to her torturer remains perverse and absolute, I had nowhere to go. I was a freed slave—free; and a slave.

* * *

One might argue, in "And Death Shall Have No Dominion," that in devoting himself primarily to the primacy of the Word—the vision of what remains after all else, even language itself, is annihilated—Thomas actually follows Saussure's dictum that language creates us; we do not create language. But no truly sane person—and certainly no serious poet—would claim that "language created Thomas." Thomas, it seemed—and one could argue about this one's whole life, conceivably, because it is the essential issue—had, at times, a vision of all that could be and its peculiar connections to the imperfection of what actually was. Linguistically speaking, this claim itself is debatable: I could, for example, say, "As I probed my flower garden for signs of spring, a daffodil bud grew within the space of a few minutes into full flower, and in its flowering I heard God's green fuse saying, 'This is the one world, and you are blessed to rejoice in it.'" Should I find myself saying such a thing, I might, among other things, given my characteristic dual consciousness, immediately doubt my own sanity, although a quick immersion into Blake might reassure me (whether or not that action would reassure others is really not, at the moment, the point). Within my linguistic sign system, a method exists to invoke an undefinable higher power in such a way that any given rite of passage is also a right of language: language makes the theory of the passage possible. But this, of course, in a way Saussure neglects, entirely overlooks the instinctive, instantaneous encounter with what one can only call "the real,' a dimension in which the linguistic sign system breaks down. Witnessing the same daffodil bud, I could say "ugh," and I would mean what I would mean, apart from language—as Henri Bergson knew a century ago from his studies of aphasia, as Antonio Damasio understands in his last decade of books, including *Descartes' Error* and *The Feeling of What Happens*—and my meaning would be what Thomas would understand as the Word. Language, then, is more than an evolutionary marker for human beings; and it is distinctly not a colonizing force, although its complicity with the history of colonization may make it seem so: rather, it is a true eccentricity, a force whose center is undetectable and whose circumference is immeasurable, a force that does not create arbitrary differences but rather conjoins latent realities, and does so on one of the most indisputable and disputed sites of all, the body itself. This is what Thomas understood best, perhaps, in one of his later poems, "In My Craft or Sullen Art":

> In my craft of sullen art
> Exercised in the still night
> When only the moon
> And the lovers lie abed
> With all their griefs in their arms,
> I labor by the singing light
> Not for ambition or bread
> Or the strut and trade of charms
> But for the common wages
> Of their most secret heart.
>
> Not for the proud man apart
> From the raging moon I write
> On these spindrift pages
> Nor for the towering dead
> With their nightingales and psalms
> But for the lovers, their arms
> Round the griefs of the ages,
> Who pay no praise or wages
> Nor heed my craft or art. (*Collected Poems*, 142)

Though the poet is unheeded—in part, implicitly, because he does not write for the assumed "great," the "proud man apart" or the "towering dead," but rather for those most ordinary, "the lovers, their arms/ Round the griefs of the ages"—he labors at his craft because he, too, is bringing into longevity that which may be temporally brief. His work, unlike human life, is not spatial, and to the degree that it is temporal, it operates on a different notion of temporality from ordinary human life: it is potentially infinitely repeatable, its vision reaffirmed with each reading, and for all the lovers lost, the temporal reality of the poem refuses their loss. Shakespeare, one might argue, makes a case for this point in Sonnets 18, 19, and 107, but the point here is slightly different: Shakespeare is arguing for the "immortality" of his lover in print; Thomas does not care whether the lovers know that they live on into the eternity of text or not, but merely and quietly observes that such longevity is an inevitable concept of the Word. Yet something about this paradox remains profoundly unsatisfying: one might imagine the Word as something, ultimately, entirely distinct from humans, something with its own chain of being and causality, into which we enter by accident and with a certain earnest abandon. Thomas surely would refute this utterly, arguing that the Word functions as the fundamental mysticism—a word he used truly, with ultimate intent—of human being, a force of redemption allied with the body yet exceeding it. But how? But how?

An academic essay might posit a certain kind of answer to this question, but the question is not academic, and it makes me swerve back to Thomas' later life and last days, his intoxication with the world and the corollaries of his intoxication with drink, until drink became his vision and, beyond his blackouts and poisoned miseries, he nevertheless saw something real. This rendering of Thomas is potentially so Romantic, so close to Chatterton and the 19th-century French vision of the "poëte maudite," that I want immediately to draw back from it to a quite different source, one who lived at the same time as Thomas and who might have comforted him if they had had the chance to exchange work. This is Pierre Teilhard de Chardin, whom I have mentioned before, but here his presence becomes more urgent because the mystery itself is suddenly, at least to my sense, much larger, and because Teilhard sought to reconcile versions of the Word according to categories that either would not have immediately interested Thomas or would not have been available to him. At the same time, as a kind of warning, it seems important to acknowledge that Teilhard had his own blind side, a side blinded, ironically, by faith, so that what he saw as grace might have seemed to Thomas a kind of catechistic child's play. Yet there might have been some meeting ground—

might still be some—if only for this essay, to keep it from teetering into the darkness.

Teilhard, admittedly, still has a peculiar following, in part perhaps because his background was eclectic enough to encourage it: a chemist and paleontologist by training, a devout Roman Catholic, Teilhard was actually prevented for over 53 years from speaking or publishing his most profound views on the relationship between faith and the world. Annie Dillard, whose remarkably lucid biographical sketch of Teilhard in *For the Time Being* is perhaps the best single thing written on this man, notes that "the unhappy prominence of his dull, arcane, and improbably crackpot *The Phenomenon of Man* thirty years ago" has "obscured his intelligent, plausible, and beautiful *The Divine Milieu* and the short, magnificent literary essays 'The Mass of the World" and "The Heart of Matter" (Dillard, 102). Nevertheless, it was Chardin—exiled by the Church to engage in various paleontological studies in remote China from the age of 42 to the age of 65—who envisioned what one might argue is primarily a re-visioning of terminology with relation to the Real. In Teilhard's world, God is immanent as well as transcendent, not through the ritual death and resurrection of His Son Jesus Christ but because the world itself is also immanent and transcendent, itself both the embodiment and the guarantee of God. One of the best summaries of Teilhard's essential argument comes, perhaps ironically, from post-colonial scholar Leopold Sedar Senghor in his essay "Negritude," from Patrick Williams and Laura Chrisman's *Colonial Discourse and Post-Colonial Theory*. Senghor writes,

> It was on the basis...of scientific experiment and inner experience...that Pierre Teilhard de Chardin was able to transcend the traditional dichotomies with a new dialectic... .He advances the theory that the stuff of the universe is not composed of two realities, but of a single reality in the shape of two phenomena; that there is not matter and energy, not even matter and spirit, but spirit-matter, just as there is space-time. Matter and spirit become a 'network of relations,' as the French philosopher Bachelard called it: energy, defined as a network of forces. In matter-spirit there is, therefore, only one energy, which has two aspects. The first, *tangential*

energy, which is external, is material and quantitative. It links together the corpuscles, or particles, that make up matter. The other, *radical energy,* which is internal, is psychic and qualitative. It is centripetal force. It organizes into a complex the center-to-center relations of the internal particules of a corpuscle. Since energy is a force, it follows that radical energy is the creative force, the 'primary stuff of things,' and tangential energy is only a residual product 'caused by the interactions of the elementary "centers" of the consciousness, imperceptible where life has not yet occurred, but clearly apprehensible by our experience at a sufficiently advanced stage in the development of matter' (Teilhard de Chardin). It follows that where life has not yet occurred the physico-chemical laws remain valid within the limitations we have defined above, while in the living world, as we rise from plant to animal and from animal to Man, the psyche increases in consciousness until it makes and expresses itself in freedom. 'Makes itself': that is, *realizes* itself, by means of—yet by transcending—material well-being through an increase of spiritual life (Senghor, 29).

"Radical energy"—the phrase itself has a vaguely New Age echo, yet it implicitly asks us to turn away, not simply from Cartesian dualisms, but from Platonic dualisms, from idealism itself, the doctrine of forms, the split between spirit and matter. Yet it also affirms that the world is: unlike Christian Science, it is not destructively monist. Drawing on what were, in the early 20th-century, new discoveries and theories in physics, Teilhard saw flux where Plato and Descartes saw "either-or" and Mary Baker Eddy saw "something-nothing": that which appeared solid depended on a confluence of forces which, to physical appearance, would move in and out of certain forms on the way to others. It was, perhaps, the curse of human beings to become so wedded to "tangential energy" that they could not experience as real the "radical energy" behind the appearance, an energy that might manifest itself to them in intuitions, dreams, and other realities of consciousness whose "reality" tends to be regarded as dubious or wistful at best. Such a view of the world would certainly have embraced the concept that "death shall have no dominion," but it would have set the speaker on a meditative journey to expect some continuity with the lost lovers, some continuity with the tortured, the tormented, and the dying, some refusal of the absolute dividing line between "living" and "dead." Teilhard, one imagines, might have brought Thomas back from the cliff on which he spent most of his adult life, the edge of which was the turf of Wales or England or America, and the drop of which was the end of the world, of his world, the end.

Yet even so, one has to pause to reconsider: there is always a danger, as any poet knows, in juxtaposing a poet and a philosopher, for no matter how much they may appear kindred spirits, they have a fundamental opposition, simplified here for the sake of argument: one experiences the world analytically, the other intuitively. Admittedly, some of the greatest poets in English—from Thomas Wyatt and Edmund Spenser to John Milton, William Wordsworth, John Keats, Matthew Arnold, T. S. Eliot (who wrote his Harvard dissertation on the philosopher F. H. Bradley), Louise Bogan, Anne Sexton, Adrienne Rich, and Robert Pinsky, just a few examples—have demonstrated remarkable analytic powers. Yet to turn away from the actual image of death, or to understand "radical energy" as the key to an end to mourning, remains to a mourner profoundly unsatisfying. Thomas knew this early on: "The Force That Through the Green Fuse Drives the Flower" is, arguably, a poem about "radical energy." In all that is created and destroyed in that poem, in all of the loveliness of its tragic vision and the way "time ticks a heaven round the stars," what triumphs most is the alternative world of the Word, the defiant "energy" that refuses categorization, recognizes the immense power of loss, exults in the enormous energy of creation, and implicitly laments the way in which human creation is somehow tangential to this essential body of action. To see the other side of "radical energy," to see its abundance beyond the repeated, repeated, repeated losses of the world, the lost loves, the waning vigor, the aging, the traumas and catastrophes and lies and deceits, to see beyond this into something where "death shall have no dominion," is virtually to remove oneself from the very world in which one finds the tools—the words—to make the Word, the tools by which "heads of the characters hammer through daisies."

And this, this point of greatest literal and figurative stress, is the failure of the Teilhard model: Teilhard can write at one point in *Le Milieu*

Divin, "J'ai senti planer sur moi la détresse essentielle de l'atome perdu dans l'Univers"—"I felt gliding over me the essential distress of the atom lost in the Universe"—and could thus, arguably, show compassion for an aspect of creation in limbo, a moment in space and time when matter and energy were neither "radical energy" nor "tangential energy;" to solve this, arguably, he writes, "Et si quelque chose m'a sauvé, c'est d'entendre la voix évangélique, garantie par des succés divins, qui me disait, du plus profound que la nuit: *'Ego sum, noli timere'* ("C'est moi, ne cragnez point")—"And if something saved me, it was to hear the evangelical voice, guaranteed by divine successes, that spoke to me, more profound than the night: 'It is I; be not afraid.'" Such a moment as this seems to earn Annie Dillard's opprobrium, as she picks her way through the vision of Teilhard:

> If science devotes scant attention to human culture... then science, which is, God knows, correct, nevertheless cannot address what interests us most: what are we doing here?
> Teilhard's own notion...moves top-down, and therefore lacks all respectability. No one can account for spirit by matter (hence science's reasonable stance), but one can indeed account for matter by spirit. Having started from spirit, from God, these and other unpopular thinkers have no real difficulty pinning down, or spinning out, or at least addressing, our role and raison d'être. (95)

Yet one must ask: is this a Dillardesque kind of joke? Teilhard's accounting for matter by spirit is, in a certain way, original, yet its fundamental tenets rely still on the Catholic hierarchy of a God, a fallen world, and a Son whose body and whose Holy Spirit redeemed that world. It is, arguably, a lovely vision: but what about the son who effectively commutes between the unsaved body and the Holy Spirit? Would the transition, or continual transformation, not grow wearisome? If, as John tells us, "In the beginning was the Word, and the Word was God, and the Word was with God," then the Word is two things—God himself, and God's own companion, the reverse of Death and Death's dog, Time. For the Word to be God's companion, however, is essentially to name it the Holy Spirit; to see that Spirit indivisible from the world, the life within the Word, is arguably the reality of Thomas' poetic method. But what an extraordinary strain—not only the rapture of the vision, but the continual return to the non-theophanic reality. To awaken each morning only to discover that, as if waking from reality to a dreary dream, one would have to re-invent or re-vision into being those tools of the Holy Spirit— such a fate might make one long for the oblivion that unveiled the domain where "Dead men naked they shall be one/ With the man in the wind and the west moon." To get to that non-existent point in space and time, one would drink until, not only the "tangential energy," but even the so-called "radical energy" of the body became still, an intellectual illusion returned to its nothingness, and all that was left was the vision of love unlost, illumined bodies unbroken on the rack, unicorn evils evaporating like long icicles into the heat of their own unreality, and the sun itself breaking down in the vivid light of what remained after death was proven to have no dominion. And so one would drink, as Thomas drank, despite the terrible consequences as the drinking itself became, ironically, demonic.

A psychologist might argue that this entire essay is simply an attempt to evade the dramatic danger of addiction, although it seems to me that danger has been illustrated quite clearly here. Perhaps another way of phrasing the problem is simply the question of how to construct an adequate world—a world neither too dangerous nor too dull, a world— if dangerous—then full of secret refuges, "the world as meditation," as Wallace Stevens once wrote, meaning "meditation" in a sense quite different, say, from a Buddhist. What is startling, when one faces it directly, is the possibility that, after certain kinds of visions, the world—and one's own body as the site of its competing claims—is simply no longer adequate. Dillard notes the only partially-amusing story of an "Ashkenazi Orthodox immigrant to Guatemala" who told his "adult, secular American grandson, 'If you want to learn Kabbalah, lock yourself in a room with the Zohar and a pound of cocaine'" (95). According to Dillard, this advice "astounded the grandson" and "infuriated his father, the old immigrant's son" (95). Still, the advice translates remarkably directly to Thomas, who did the equivalent: the world-as-Word was his Kabbalah, God's light and goodness poured into ten vessels that lamentably shattered, spreading their shards of God-inflected reality all over the created world. Whether one reacts to that Kabbalistic creation myth with despair or hope depends on how one feels about collecting shards. Thomas, in his own way, was of course terribly good at it; if one imagines every brilliant rhyme as a shard, for example, then Thomas's "Author's Prologue," the 102-line poem that opens his *Collected Poems*, is a Kabbalistic wonder: the 51st and 52nd lines form a couplet; after that, the rhymes spread, so that the 50th and 53rd lines rhyme, the 49th and 54th lines rhyme, and so on, until one discovers that the first and the 102nd lines rhyme. Who could or would do this without seeing in such ingenious structure a rapturous vision? And where in the world could one go to inhabit an equivalent reality? Arguably nowhere.

One might also argue, of course, that Thomas the consummate performer first fell under the seduction, then the terrible diurnal financial burden, the hellish weight, of his own public role as the great, sonorous, vivid, loud, life-embracing poet; the idea that a role consumes its player is commonplace in the world of psychology. Yet surely this cannot explain the power of ascent in "Author's Prologue" or "Poem in October" or "Fern Hill." Perhaps a better question, the one that I of course am dying to ask, with little enough pun intended: why didn't Thomas' visions of the world-in-Word heal him? Why did they ultimately debase him personally? Again, a psychologist might caution against the importance of distinguishing between Thomas the visionary poet and Thomas the ill, addictive personality; from my own tradition, however, it was precisely this kind of faith in the Word that should have released Thomas from the darkness of his daily mortal life. But this accidentally brings in exactly the dualism that Thomas would have rejected: the "daily mortal life" *was* the Word; his release would come like that of all men and women; he had seen more than most, but did not expect to evade his own crucifixion. Yet someone with my background, and a certain residual faith, still wishes to believe in the power of the Word to transform the ordinary world into an adequate world, a world of balance. Did Juliana of Norwich know such a world? Did Saint Teresa of Avila? Did Saint John of the Cross? How long can a dark night of the soul last, and how may it alternate between the ecstatic vision? Thomas knew what was real, but T. S. Eliot may have been literally correct when he observed in *The Four Quartets* that "humankind cannot bear very much reality," and Thomas drank the darkness away from him.

* * *

The wonder of drinking, what makes it so compelling not simply to an addictive personality but to one of great sensitivity who has repeatedly suffered early harm, is the power of forgetting, numbing: drinking leaves one present in the world, leaves one's body as the site of consciousness, yet effectively forces the world to withdraw, and alters consciousness itself so that its visions become essential, paramount, pure foreground. Different kinds of drunks respond differently, of course, and in his latter days Thomas was known for loud displays of self-aggrandizement and temper. My own inclination is to go the other way, to become more and more quiet as the world, after a bottle or two of wine, recedes. "And death shall have no dominion": Thomas wrote the world's and the body's epitaph. Yet, because both world and body remain, the means to release oneself from them matters hugely. At the bottom, of course, is not merely hatred for the world, or hatred for one's past—indeed, one could hardly love the world more than Thomas loved it—but rather a sense of being fundamentally unloveable, of never having been loved. Thomas knew this; it is clearly essential to my own upbringing. But having learned lovelessness early, one grasps only with the greatest difficulty how to find a true medium of exchange between another soul, another whole life playing itself out on the site of the body. It takes only a few failures in adulthood, sexual as well as romantic, to feel as if love is something that belongs in another world: "Though lovers be lost, love shall not." But once one begins to travel down that road, one is in danger of Thomas' own end, or Jack Kerouac's, or Sylvia Plath's, or Ernest Hemingway's. The company of those lost to love or rapture is among the best. Yet one would not, perhaps, want to meet them too soon—or all at once—or, in the most unthinkable of accidents, not at all.

Alone, Coda Two: The Setting Revisited

A Meditation

It is late winter. When I arrive back in Grinnell from a day's and evening's work at the University of Iowa, 70 miles to the east, the town is ghostly under a light snowfall; a few porch lights shine on my street, 8th Avenue; my house is totally dark except for the two small lamps that are always on—one a small fluorescent tube in the kitchen, reminiscent of the light that was always on in my mother's death room in October 1980 at the Arden Wood Benevolent Association, a Christian Science care facility in San Francisco, and the other a small, replica Tiffany lamp in the dining room. Usually, upon these returns, I light up the house in a particular fashion: first the outside back door light, where I enter, then the front porch light, then the second front door light (the house has the curiosity of two front doors—one from 1900, the other from 1970—but the two lights together have a cheerful feel). After that, I light the oil lamp on the dining room table and a couple of other candles around the dining room. By this time the house is comfortably dim, yet what needs to be seen can be seen; it is meditative, quiet. It is a refuge.

Tonight, however—because it has been a particularly long day at the university, with too many people asking too many questions that sound brilliant but, in reality, are merely conventional—I feel my soul slipping away. I try not to think that this is a common occurrence at the University of Iowa, at least for me, try a little longer to maintain the illusion that my own illness and the peculiar limitations of a Big Ten university don't coalesce into something even darker. But it's a tough illusion to maintain. Last semester, in addition to teaching at the University of Iowa, I served as an assistant at the Writing Lab at Grinnell College, three blocks away from my house, exercising my contractual right at the University of Iowa to "consult" professionally as long as it did not interfere with my duties at Iowa. Grinnell was a revelation, another world far less than a furlong from my house. But there was no permanent job there. And so I returned fully, in the winter, to the reality that has been my reality for over 12 years.

That is a long time, as Galway Kinnell once wrote, to live alone. And, of course, the worst danger is self-pity, and the exaggerations that come from that: for, in truth, I have not always been alone, have had my children with me at regular intervals, have had some friends who have stayed near in thought if not in distance. These are good things, important to remember on a night such as this.

But the night feels peculiar: the drifting snow, luminous through the windows, makes the illumined darkness of the outer world a part of the inner world of my house. It is easy, tonight, to leave all the lights off. I drop my school bags full of books and papers in the kitchen, pour a glass of wine, and stand with my back to the kitchen sink, looking into the darkness of the house, the illumination of the fluorescent bulb, the darkness and dark light around it. So much of the past is always present, if one wants to see it; the past is like the snow outside, illumined darkness. Whatever it contains requires only a medium through which to be perceived; then suddenly it is there, here.

Through the gentle darkness of the dining room, with its single lamp, into the snowy darkness of the living room, I move quietly, drawn upwards to the steep stairway where the three bedrooms lie. These are old farmhouse stairs, and within the family their steepness is legendary; they would not pass the building code today. In addition, three steps from the upstairs hallway, they take an abrupt right turn, with one stair simply and suddenly wide enough at its edge to accommodate a 90-degree shift: if one is not prepared for this, especially going down, one is likely to miss one's footing and fall. I myself did this once, while my daughter was here;

she was greatly amused, as, indeed, was I, once I determined at the bottom that nothing was broken. There are reasons one might want, occasionally, to live within a *Monty Python* world.

Tonight, however, the mood is somber. The stairs remain dark; only a little light floats in through the small window just above the stair with the 90-degree turn. I arrive at the top stair, where the short, narrow hallway begins. To the left is my son Nate's room, and then, a little farther down, Georgia's; these are both small, about eight by 10 feet. To my immediate right is my room, a little larger. A little light from the snowy street lamp at the corner of 8th and Spring comes through the windows in Nate's and Georgia's rooms; a small swath falls on an unmapped diagonal of my carpet. Otherwise, I am feeling my way.

Someone is in Nate's room.

I place my glass of wine on his Walmart dresser and sit down on the bed. The person here is sitting in Nate's desk chair, at Nate's desk. He has a tumbler of something with a slight color, probably scotch, and he seems to be in uniform—at least his dark pants show a tight crease in the thin light, and underneath his leather jacket his dark shirt shows similar trimness. It looks as if there may be a name stitched above the breast pocket of his jacket, but it is of course unreadable. On each shoulder are two small, parallel metal bars, catching the light.

"Hi, Dad," I say—for whom else could it be? But then again—this is not how I remember him, this man just entering middle age—for his hair is only just beginning to thin. He can't be more than 25, 27, 30.

He says nothing. He just takes another small sip of the scotch. The tumbler leaves a slight ring on Nate's ancient desk—I can just see it in the snowy light. He is waiting for something. Or not. Though I am tempted to leave the room and come back again, to kid myself about the nature of this illusion, the projection of desire, and all similar academic and psychological categories, I do not. The illusion, such as it is, is far too comforting.

"Most of the time I knew you, you were unhappy," I say.

The direct approach. He nods.

"Do you have any idea how frightening you were? Do you remember that day you and I were at home alone, and you were almost finished building that Heathkit stereo receiver, and your soldering iron slipped and you thought you'd shorted the whole thing out? You were up on the third floor. Remember? And you smashed about half of the furniture between the third floor and the first floor. And you were swearing while you were breaking everything. I hid in the living room behind the big chair in the far corner until Mom got back. Do you remember that?"

He nods.

"Do you remember the time you thought John was a burglar when he snuck in through the basement from a date at 4 A.M., and you took one of his shotguns and loaded it and nearly blew him away? And then you blamed him? Do you remember that?"

He nods.

"Do you remember when you used to beat John and Cin with a leather belt and make me watch, so I'd know what would happen to me if I misbehaved?"

He nods.

We pause. What is the point of this?

"You were one of the best flight instructors in the Navy," I said. "Remember how every now and then you'd get a letter or someone would stop by from the old days? They always said no one flew like you. Remember how the PBY-5A Catalina, that attack seaplane, turned out to have a surprise stall about 50 feet above the water, and all those early crews crashed and drowned? And they transferred you down to Pensacola to figure out a landing sequence so the crews wouldn't die? They gave you a death plane and you gave it life. That was just one thing..."

"I remember." The first thing he says. So there is more than one memory here, perhaps.

"So why didn't you join one of the airlines after the war?" I ask. "You could have made a lot of money...I mean, sure, there were a lot of combat pilots coming back for those jobs, but you yourself trained them—I mean, who would have been more in the running?"

"I wanted to be a professor of engineering," he said. "That was my dream. You know that."

"I know the story," I said. "I know how you went back to Drexel after the war to get your B.A. and M.A. or Ph.D., but you ran into some calculus professor you hated, and he hated you, and he made fun of you in class because of some unconventional way you handled some assignment, and you'd been an officer in the Navy and no one had ever talked back to you like that before, and so you walked out and swore you'd never go back. And you never did. But you had an unemployed wife, and a child on the way, and your G.I. benefits vanished once you dropped out of school. So you were desperate. And you went to work as an accountant for your awful uncle who ran a dairy somewhere around Ardmore or some still-semi-rural place like that. And then things just went downhill from there."

He sits, drinks.

"Have you ever had a student who died because of what you taught him—or her? I guess you teach girls now, too."

I ignore the last part. I think back. No, of course not at Stanford or even Berkeley—it was just composition and American literature—no, but wait—there was the Berkeley student in 1987 who dashed through my fourth-floor office and out onto the ledge of the roof—I had no phone, it took a while for the police to come, he might have jumped—but he wasn't one of my students, wasn't someone I taught. At MIT I had three suicidal students that I knew of; two I helped one way or another, the third I had to hear about after they committed him. But even if they had died, it wouldn't have been from what I was teaching. It would have been because they couldn't see any way through or out of MIT, or through or out of their families, or through or back into lost loves.

"No, I never had any students who died because of what I taught them."

There's just a silence for a moment, unaffected, unpregnant with meaning, just a silence.

"I did," he said. "By the time I was teaching, I knew more ways of getting a plane into and out of trouble than almost anyone. I knew every aerobatic trick in the book. If we'd had Top Gun then, I would have been at Top Gun. You know that story about that one hot shot who thought he knew better than me—"

"Yeah, the one where you let him take you up and then you pulled an outside loop and a double Immelmann on him, and he threw up and never gave you any more trouble."

"Yeah. Well, for every asshole I had twenty great students. We didn't have guided missiles, then—no air-to-air stuff except guns; it was all dogfighting. You had to get in tight and get out any way you could and come back around and get in tight again. It was serious business. I taught well. And they still died.

"They died and they died and they died," he said.

"Not all of them," I say, a slight panic rising, as if this conversation is not after all going to be under my control.

"No," he said. "But I heard from Command all the time. And through the grapevine. Every week it was someone in Germany. Or somewhere in the Pacific. It wasn't just that my best wasn't good enough. It was that guys I knew and came to admire and like, guys to whom I taught everything, they just died. That's it. They got caught on the outside or pulled a spin the wrong way or looped up instead of down, who knows—it only takes a couple of 50-caliber shots from wing guns or a spinner gun and you're dead. After that, flying was no fun."

"But you did fly after the war, a little…" I falter because I know what's coming next.

"Oh, yeah, that Taylorcraft," he sighs. "There was no reason to ground-loop it. How many thousands of flight hours had I had when I borrowed it? It wasn't even a strong cross-wind—just a gust at the wrong time. But all of a sudden I was upside down and I'd destroyed the plane. And of course it wasn't insured."

"So…" I say.

"I might have paid it off, a little at a time, with the money from the G.I. bill, if I'd stayed at Drexel," he said. "But it was just one more burden, and there were thousands of G.I.'s all trying to get ahead, and the fact that I'd been an officer didn't matter any more, and no cared that my students died. I looked at those professors at Drexel and said to myself, 'Your students didn't die. Your training didn't send them out to die. No wonder you can go home each night and put every day behind you. You can live in your nice, big brick houses in Philadelphia and have cocktail parties and publish influential papers every now and then.' I just didn't fit."

"The story of our lives," I say.

"Yes," he says.

"Have you noticed that we talk alike?" I say.

"Yes."

"I always thought I got that from Mom," I say.

"Both sides of the family were pretty well-spoken," he says. "I just didn't have a lot to say."

"Your swear words were pretty effective."

"Well, I'd been in the military."

I shift a little on the bed, trying to adjust. "So all this—that dark feeling that was always in the house when I was growing up, the way John and Cin hated you, the way you always seemed angry or got violent, all that—was from teaching students to die?" A near-fatal slip of the tongue.

"Only great teachers teach students to die," he says. "I taught them to live. To survive. To get out of the worst possible scrapes. And I didn't succeed. People died because of me. Because of *me*."

"Can you remember, at all, being happy after the War? Did any of us bring you happiness? Were you happy in Avalon?"

He brightens a little. "I always loved Avalon. You remember that, when I was a teenager, I used to fly an old Curtiss from North Philadelphia over to Avalon and back. It was always beautiful in the old days—beautiful beaches, those huge sand dunes, and very few people. Not like it got to be later. And it was where I met your Mom."

"What about us?"

"John and Cin were terrors practically from birth," he said. "I don't know—by that time I was working for American Viscose at FMC in Marcus Hook, you know, which had me on the road all the time—"

"In the air, you mean—you were one of United's first 100,000-mile fliers. Remember that plaque they gave you? I loved that plaque. That little airplane in the center, circling the globe—"

"It just got old," he said. "Some of the pilots knew me, and sometimes I'd sit on the flight deck, but mostly I was just commuting between angry customers and angry engineers. And I'd get home and John and Cin would have done some horrible thing, or they would have stayed up all night crying, and your Mom could hardly handle them—"

"She was depressed," I say.

"We were both depressed," he says. "But no one knew that then, of course. And by that time Mom had the family totally under Christian Science control, so even if doctors could have helped, she would never have let them near us."

"You could have changed that."

"Her family was very influential," he says, unconvincingly. "Remember her mother—Naner—the Christian Science practitioner?"

"Never mind," I say. "But didn't we bring you any joy?"

I can see him turning away.

"No," he says.

Well.

"But on the weekends, in the summers, you loved coming down to Avalon," I persist. "You loved waterskiing. And you taught us to drive the boat, to be lookouts—remember that time you had some rich friend let me drive his yacht when I was eight? What was it—the *Tamara*? It was 50 feet long, wasn't it? You had us in the water early."

"Yeah," he says. "I saved you from drowning when you were a little less than three. At Bethany Beach."

"I remember," I say. "John and Cin were supposed to be watching me, but got into a big fight."

"Yeah," he says. "I gave them some beating afterward."

"Why'd you save me?" I ask.

"What?"

"Why'd you bother?"

"What do you mean, 'Why'd you bother'? You were my son."

"You'd have saved me if I'd just been some random kid in the water. It didn't matter that I was your son."

He is silent.

I persist.

"If you hadn't had a family, you know, if you hadn't gotten married, had kids, what would you have done?"

He sighs. "I couldn't imagine not marrying your mother," he said. "It was, it was fated. I was waiting for it all through the war. It gave me hope. Although there were other women I looked at..."

"It seems to run in the family."

"Anyway, we didn't really know anything about birth control then, and everyone was having babies left and right, so, I mean, why not? I didn't really think about what I wanted. It wasn't really a question. What I most wanted was to be free of the memories from the war. And that couldn't happen. So I did what everyone else did."

"And you were miserable for pretty much the whole of your adult life," I point out, from the time you were 30 to the time you died at 77, from pneumonia and drinking, with no health insurance, living in some 24-foot trailer in Florida with an alcoholic third wife whose daughter was murdered in part because you wouldn't let her move back to Toronto with her in-laws, whom she loved."

"Don't you dare go there," he says.

"I'm just saying that 47 years is a long time to be unhappy."

"Yes," he says. "But look where I am now."

"Where are you now?"

"Here," he says, "In your present memory, drinking a very good scotch, and talking. It's a nice night. It's quiet. The snow is beautiful. Tomorrow it will clear, and if you were still a pilot, it would be a good day to fly."

"So you're a ghost," I say.

"Let's just say I'm around," he says.

A slight murmur of alarm begins to fill my chest. "What does that mean, that you're around?"

"You know John 16, don't you? I'm sure you do. You know practically that whole book by heart. I think it's the only one that really still speaks to you."

"How do you know that?"

"I live inside you. I also have, how should I put it, another life outside you, but that is not really always, or even often, subject to anything you do. This is kind of an anomaly, you know—this conversation. I don't know if it will happen again."

"I see," I say, not seeing. "So you're not a ghost."

"That's a silly category," he says. "Phenomena—think how many different kinds there are or might be. Remember when *Jonathan Livingston Seagull* came out, and how you loved it?"

"I had no idea you even paid attention to it."

"Hell, of course I read it."

"But you never mentioned it."

"You never asked."

"It's kind of a hokey book," I say lamely.

"You're lying," he says. "You believe every hokey word in it. It's also got very good aerodynamic observations, as you also, by now, know."

"So what about John 16?"

"'Thou in me, and I in Thee'? Come on...the whole definition of the universe is contained in John 16."

"Are you happy now?" I ask.

"I'm sitting here in this room, with nothing frightening or threatening, and it seems to me like a beautiful night here on earth, and I have my scotch here, which tastes just as good as it tasted when Mom used to find where I'd stashed it and pour it down the sink, and you're doing fine, and I've gotten to tell you everything I have to say. What could be better?"

"But I'm not fine," I say, suddenly overwhelmed. John 16, whatever else it may mean to me, is also a code for being on the edge of leaving, for loving this world but also preparing oneself to leave it. I have known that since I could read, since I first read it at the age of seven. I have known that book and what it meant practically all my life. I have known it through all the worst moments. I do not want to think about it now. "I have no money, I have a job I would never willingly have chosen if I could have foreseen where it would lead, I see my children only rarely—and, as far as I can tell, I love them far more than you loved us—I'm deeply in debt, I'm trying to pull out of the terrible downward spiral of depression that no one seems able to help me with, and I am alone. How is that fine?"

But somehow, as he turns in Nate's desk chair away from me and toward the desk, picking up his scotch for another sip, he recedes into the darkness of the room, and the chair becomes empty, and there is empty darkness where he was. And there I am, here I am, still, on the bed, feeling my heart as if it were actually beating in my neck instead of my chest, sweat rolling down the sides of my body. I sit this way for some time. But nothing changes, except that, slowly, my heart slows.

So it is that kind of night.

* * *

Demons, angels...devout Christians perform what New-Agers and psychotherapists call a "visualization" when they pray, envisioning Jesus right there with them, right there beside them. Tibetan spiritual masters, Sogyal Rinpoche or Robert A. F. Thurman, summon all of the buddhas and all of the boddhisattvas from all the ages to their aid when they meditate, or they fix their gaze on an image of Padma Sambhava, the great compassionate founder of Tibetan Buddhism; others see before them Avalokiteshvara, the great Hindu god of compassion, pure love radiating purely in and through the immanence of one's own being. Islamic Sufis, as Henry Corbin notes, understand that each of us has a "perfect nature" that is the angel uniquely ours, our guardian and protector, the "man of light" who brings us into the light. But C. S. Lewis, writing in *The Discarded Image,* notes of medieval cosmologists that they understood a sublunar category of beings, neither angels nor men, called the "longaevi," the long-lived: but the long-lived what? Lewis notes four categories: "...they are a third rational species distinct from angels and men..."; "...they are angels, but a special class of angels who have been, in our jargon, 'demoted'..."; "...they are the dead, or some special class of the dead..."; "they are fallen angels; in other words, devils" (Lewis, 134-137).

In Marcilio Ficino's *Theologica Platonica de Immortalitate,* Book IV, section i, they are "the spirits of every element," as every element has a divine source : thus, as Lewis notes, in Shakespeare's *The Tempest,* "Ariel... would be a tetrach of the air" (Lewis, 134-135). This "third rational species distinct from angels and men" is interesting, in part because, historically in the west, it has tended toward the notion of fairies before that notion was itself demoted through children's literature and then simply tarnished through New Age marketing; J. R. R. Tolkien's elves, Arwen in particular, are fascinating because they can, in a sense, choose to be present or absent, choose to be mortal or immortal, though they are born—an odd paradox— immortal. My own instinct suggests that there are enough devils, or devilish deeds, in the world without having to separate them out into a category beyond humans, so Lewis' fourth category, though historically accurate, interests me little; and as for "some special class of the dead," that really, if one considers it, comes down to a matter of perception: was the man in my son's room a "demoted" angel, an elvish vision, some special class of the dead? Characteristically, I find myself returning to Ficino, one of the figures in history I would most like to have met (and would still like to meet, depending on how far one carries one's esoteric theology): my father, as "tetrarch of the air"—the concept almost works. A wounded tetrach. A wounding tetrarch. Around, perhaps, because in between the woundedness and the woundng there were words of explanation and apology to be said. A line from one thing to the next, as William Stafford said, quoted so many pages ago: "it interests us." The authentic.

As is often the case in his later works (at least those not having to do with "The Western Canon"), Harold Bloom is interesting on this question:

> Angels were once more ambiguous and ambivalent, and traditionally their roles have not always been comforting or protective in regard to us. But they suit us now for many reasons, particularly because, like us, they suffer from (and represent) a condition of belatedness: they are not ordinary beings (Bloom, 44-45).

And then, of course, there is the question of Metatron:

> At the imagistic center of 3 Enoch is the radical transformation of Enoch into the archangel Metatron, Prince of the Divine Presence (a title from the prophet Isaiah)... I would [suggest] that Metatron is not only the new, primordial, supernal Adam, but also that Metatron becomes the esoteric link in angelology between the divine and the human, fusing these realms in the manner of the Iranian "Man of Light," whether Zorastrian or Sufi (Bloom, 48-49).

Bloom continues by making some seemingly extravagant claims for Metatron:

> I venture that Metatron is the archangel of our moment as we approach the Millennium; all the omens— other angels, prophetic dreams, manifestations of the Resurrection Body—are aspects of his being. As the lesser Yaweh, he is the angel of angels; he is also the celestial interpreter of prophetic dreams; his transfigured form is the astral body of the "near-death experience"; his man-God reintegration restores the supernal Adam and illuminates the messianic aspects of the Millennium (Bloom, 50).

The Millennium has come and gone, but if there is a Yaweh and a lesser Yaweh, if the direction of the Zohar toward Kabbalistic visions and ecstatic Islam toward direct angelic perception takes little note of time or such minor milestones as a millennium, then there is no reason for an angelic presence to be other than how it appears: sometimes electrifying, sometimes terrifying, sometimes merely quiet. The great power and comfort behind any apparition may be all the greater if the apparition itself appears, from a certain point of view, quite normal.

My longaevi.

* * *

The only other light in the house that, by an odd irony, approximates the light over my mother's bed where she died at the Arden Wood Benevolent Association happens to be a small fluorescent reading light built into the headboard of my daughter's bed. The irony struck me so profoundly, when I was first looking for a decent bed and headboard for my daughter, that I almost didn't purchase it; but, in the end, somehow, it seemed inevitable. Like me, Georgia prefers incandescent light to fluorescent light for reading, and thus her headboard light is rarely on. But it is on tonight. I see its faint glow on the carpet in the hallway.

Knowing what I will find, I find, suddenly, that I would prefer not to go in. But I do anyway.

My mother sits on the edge of the bed, uneasily, as if she had a bag packed and hidden underneath the bed and was ready to leave at any moment. There is none of the ease here that came with my father, the ease with which he sat and drank his scotch. I catch myself quickly thinking how, as ironies build on ironies, this is a cornerstone, because my father was so difficult to bear during his lifetime while, when I could, I sought solace with my mother. Perhaps the operative word there is "sought": perhaps that is the problem.

"I have to leave soon," she says.

"I can tell," I say. What do I want to say? The words approach my mind like a freight train moving at speed.

"I'm sorry I didn't get to see you one more time," I say. "I said, 'We'll be back,' when Lesley and I left that evening, and then two days later you died. I'm sorry."

"But you saw me point to the full moon that night," she said. "You saw that I could still do that. And you wrote about it in your first book. How did you describe it? You said it was—an act of 'scorching clarity.'"

"Yes. I did say that."

"What did it make clear?"

"That you wanted me to keep looking at the world. That you didn't want me to give up."

"Have you given up?"

"Almost. But whenever I see a full moon, it is always beautiful, and I always think of you. The moon last night was beautiful. I saw it from the moment it crested the horizon."

"You're changing the subject."

"No I'm not."

"I asked you it you've given up, and you said 'almost.' Why?"

"You know the reasons."

"Do you remember those two times I asked you if you wanted out of the life you were in?"

I think back...the ironies evade metaphors, no longer with a cornerstone, building like thunderheads...I am a professor, but I have almost always hated school. When I was sixteen, and for various reasons completely miserable, my mother once came outside, where I was sitting, and asked me if I wanted to drop out of high school. Four years later, when I was beside myself with the Christian Science-instilled fear that I would never be able to perceive what was real, never know the truth from a lie, never be able to trust my perceptions, never be able to live a human life, she came out to the same chair where I was sitting and asked me if I wanted to withdraw from the Christian Science church. Two times—two similar questions—out of the blue—with no follow-up. And of course, caught off guard and dutiful, I said "no" both times.

"Yes."

"Why did you say no?"

"I was afraid."

"Of what?"

"I was afraid that I wouldn't know what to do if I left high school. That I'd get some horrible job and have a horrible life. And I was afraid that, if I left Christian Science, I wouldn't be able to find my way anywhere.

Christian Science was 'the way, the truth, and the life'—you knew that. You weren't really giving me a choice."

"But I was. I meant it. We would have helped."

"Remember how you were going to help John, when he was drifting? That beautiful cabin in the Santa Cruz mountains? He could have re-started a life there. But Dad wouldn't follow through. You let him down."

"But doesn't it seem strange to you," she says, as if not having heard me, "that you do, now, having done everything that anyone ever asked of you, having gotten every necessary degree, having hung in there until you received tenure—having done all that, you have what you feel in your heart to be a horrible job and a horrible life, except for your children? Think of all the misery you could have avoided."

"Really? Really? Can you see that? Is there some other version of me that you see, somewhere, the one who said 'yes' instead of 'no'?

She begins to shimmer, as if there were some other source of light in the room.

"Mom?"

"I have to go. I loved having you. I didn't mean to teach you to lie."

"I try not to."

"Yes—you're good now about not lying to other people. But you've lied to yourself about almost everything. There's not much left."

She is almost gone.

"I'm sorry I didn't teach you to love the world," she said. "It would have changed everything."

"Did it change everything?" I ask, my voice rising toward panic. "Is there another me who said and did the right things?"

But she is gone. The fluorescent light goes off. I am dark in a dark room.

* * *

We do not get back what we have forfeited, except in imagination. And if one sees, as Coleridge did, the imagination as the repetition, in the finite world, of the infinite act of creation of the great I AM, then one sees how there might be such a presence as Metatron, not a sentimental little waif with wings but a great, powerful, scintillating vision of compassion, bearing us up in this world because it is in this world, and not some other, that we live. My mother, who did not want to be there, knowing all the questions she would not wish to answer, nevertheless was most sorry that she did not teach me to love the world. It was a great loss. But other people have tried, in their varying ways, to do so: my first wife, Lesley, and my son Nathaniel, and my daughter Georgia, and some of my students, and two or three lovers over the past few years brave enough to confront my sadness and my poverty and to stay with me for as long as they could, and not to lie. Would it be possible to say, then, that what I do now is to live in this angelic world?

At the end of his extraordinary poem "At Pleasure Bay," Robert Pinsky, who has been mulling the various lives and stories that make up the reality of Pleasure Bay, suddenly rises into a rapture of what happens at death; nothing in the poem prepares one for it.

> After you die
> You hover near the ceiling above your body
> And watch the mourners awhile. A few days more
> You float above the heads of the ones you knew
> And watch them through a twilight. As it grows darker
> You wander off and find your way to the river
> And wade across. On the other side, night air,
> Willows, the smell of the river, and a mass
> Of sleeping bodies all along the bank,
> A kind of singing from among the rushes
> Calling your further forward in the dark.
> You lie down and embrace one body, the limbs
> Heavy with sleep reach eagerly up around you
> And you make love until your soul brims up
> And burns free out of you and shifts and spills
> Down over into that other body, and you
> Forget the life you had and begin again
> On the same crossing—maybe as a child who passes
> Through the same place. But never the same way twice.
> Here in the daylight, the catbird in the willows,
> The new cafe, with a terrace and a landing,
> Frogs in the cattails where the swing-bridge was—

Here's where you might have slipped across the water
When you were only a presence, at Pleasure Bay. (Pinsky, 98-99)

Could you live in that world? Where would you trip? Where would your heart stick or tremble? Would it be the moment when you floated "above the heads of the ones you knew"? Would it be your wandering off, or would it be the most overt moment, when "you/ Forget the life you had"? For that is a great forgetting. Think of all you leave behind, think of all of them thinking of you...and yet, in a world marked essentially by connections and passageways, the connection here is a love-making so profound, yet envisioned so vividly as something essentially human, that it lifts your soul in a burning out of you...the essences do not change, only the connections and the passageways.

The first noble truth of Buddhism, as most people, oddly, seem to know—even people who don't know the other three—are that life is suffering. An interesting psychiatric social worker in Minneapolis, Philip Martin, writes in *The Zen Path through Depression* that the mythic decision of Siddhartha to sit under a tree in Bodhgaya until he had attained enlightenment contained "a very real element of desperation, of his back being against the wall. He wanted to find out what human life really was" (Martin, 2). Noting that Siddhartha had "gone through the extremes of sensual pleasures, self-denial, and self-mortification," and that "none of those paths had brought him the insight he sought," the man who would be the Buddha, the Awakened One, "decided to stop his seeking and just sit down" (Martin, 2).

To suggest that this is wrong—that the first noble truth of life is that it is *not* suffering—is not only to counter an essential teaching of a great world faith. It is to suggest that, granting the desperation of Siddhartha, his particular vision does not, in fact, necessarily translate to a world vision. Life is not defined by suffering. The extraordinary passages we make, the people we love who leave us, the people we leave behind, the children who grow up and away...yes, one could say that loss is everywhere, and one might even agree with Philip Martin that Siddhartha, at the time of his enlightenment, was not only profoundly determined to the point of release, but also profoundly depressed, when he sat beneath the tree in the foothills of the Himalaya. The simplicity of the Buddha's vision is complicated somewhat by the nature of translation, so that the Sanskrit word that we translate as "suffering"—*duhka*—has implications of what Martin calls "dissatisfaction" and "physical and emotional pain." On the one hand, the point here might be that, were we to survey our worlds in terms of dissatisfaction and all physical and emotional pains, we might well be overwhelmed. Part of Buddhist practice, the meditation, *zazen*, has to do with learning to tolerate even that sense of being overwhelmed without becoming attached to it—releasing ourselves even from it, releasing ourselves to the pure emptiness within and without.

But it is not a cultural anomaly to point out that this is not Pinsky's universe; it was not C. S. Lewis's universe, either during his lifetime or during the time he loved, the European Middle Ages; it is not my universe. In my universe, no one would say what Martin says: "Simple uncomplicated pain is something we cannot avoid" (Martin, 11). For there is no "simple, uncomplicated pain"; the very idea itself is as absurd as it is cruel, and all the more cruel coming from someone engaged in mental health practice. As Elaine Scarry explains at length in *The Body in Pain*, one of the crucial and defining characteristics of pain is that it is never simple or uncomplicated, in part because we cannot communicate it: we cannot, through language or any other means, make others feel the pain that we feel. Pain is an absolute, and while we may attempt to gain help through our expressions of pain in language, language always loses to pain; what a torturer knows, as Scarry points out, is that—the more the pain closes in on the victim, the more it happens in simple ways, or in settings that are domestic—rooms of ordinary buildings, for example—the more inexpressible it becomes. Releasing oneself, in the face of true pain, is not necessarily enlightenment; it may constitute, on the contrary, precisely the kind of trauma that Cathy Caruth describes early in *Unclaimed Experience*, the kind of trauma the mind cannot or will not process *because it was there*, because it witnessed what was terrible and felt what was terrible. To tell someone who has been tortured to sit and meditate may be to continue the torture.

To refuse this instruction—to witness the world as it is, to inhale and live its anguish, to explore its caverns and beacons of light, to take one's body and live through it, with all its increasing restrictions and limits, to breathe in air and breathe out light, to accept the company of spirits, however infrequent, distant, or anomalous they may be—that is to live in the incarnated world, the world of pleasures and presences, of despairs and conjectures, of resolutions. Toward the end of *Unclaimed Experience,* Caruth re-interprets Lacan's re-interpretation of Freud's story of the burning child, placing into the child's mouth words that were never spoken: *"wake up, leave me, survive: survive to tell the story of my burning"* (Caruth, 105). No story will replace the unspeakable nature of pain, just as no story will confirm or deny the enlightenment of the Buddha, or the multiple healings recorded in the backs of hundreds of *Christian Science Sentinels* and *Christian Science Journals,* stories that those who tell them tell with the absolute conviction of the converted. There is a limit to what language can do. But—just as, on the one hand, language cannot convey to anyone else exactly what we are experiencing—so, on the other hand, we may convey, through language, the reality of what has not been felt, does not "exist" or does not appear to exist: we may summon, through our speech, the vision that compels feelings which themselves did not exist before, and we summon ourselves as well to stand within the pale of our speech and witness the reality of feelings brought to life through words we never imagined we would here. Thus the longaevi; thus the bodies, burning in the passion of love until the one passes into the other; thus the miracle of the created; thus Metatron, the lesser Yaweh, and Yaweh, without rivalry, without explanation, and without contradiction.

And thus, in the end, one kind of setting becomes another, and the very material that James Agee imagined for his book—the wood, the bit of cloth—becomes, in a sense, the material of the manger, where candles are always and forever burning, and, unexpectedly, there is music almost too antiphonal to bear.

John Denver

Just as this book begins with a small-plane crash—Jim Croce's, on September 20, 1973—it concludes with another crash: John Denver's, on October 12, 1997, just off the coast of Pacific Grove, near Monterey, California. Where Jim Croce is still clearly remembered for several great pop songs, Denver's legacy appears much more diffuse: one almost never hears any of his songs now, whether on oldies or country stations or as covers by other artists, yet Aspen, Colorado—Denver's adopted home— holds a major music festival in his honor every October 12, and his 1970's chart-topping songs still command respect on "best of" CD's, even at (or perhaps especially at) places like Wal-Mart. The kind of opprobrium and dismissal much of his music received over the course of his career is almost astonishing, given the platinum status of his fourth album, the 1971 *Poems, Prayers and Promises*; critic Allan Jones, writing in *Melody Maker* in 1974, is characteristic when he writes that Denver "seems to have taken over as a metholated, less obviously trauma-ridden James Taylor... full of infantile optimism...There's little in Denver's catalogue of songs that intimates he's in any way sensitive to the complexities of even the most secluded and idyllic reality" (Collis, 108). Given the aura, at once evanescent and tarnished, around Denver's reputation, my devotion of so much attention here suggests either that I myself have suffered a massive lapse of musical taste or that I have my own reasons for a somewhat different way of evaluating both the music and the life than any I've read elsewhere thus far. My hope, of course, is that the latter is true.

John Denver was a pilot; Jim Croce was not, although Croce had no fear of small planes and loved the adventure of life on the move. But simply to say that John Denver was "a pilot" is—as with virtually everything about Denver—to say something both literally true and figuratively false. It would be tempting, for example, to begin to extoll Denver's flying abilities by saying, "Denver was no amateur," and, again, in a certain way, this would be true: at the time of his death, when he was flying a Long-EZ experimental aircraft built by the well-known private aircraft builder Adrian Davis using FAA-approved plans from the Rutan Aircraft Factory in Southern California, Denver had amassed well over 2,750 flight hours (his actual logbooks, which he probably carried with him among an assortment of required papers in the Long-EZ, were never recovered) (NTSB, 2). Considering that it is currently possible to get a job as a first-officer trainee on almost any regional airline with a minimum of 500 hours of flight time, 50 of which are turbo-prop or jet, Denver was more than qualified as a serious pilot.

And yet, curiously, in technical terms he did remain an amateur. Like me, or anyone who starts with a serious interest in flying, he earned his private pilot's license; he then went on to an instrument rating, which is essential if, for example, one is going to fly private jets, because jets are pressurized and designed to fly most efficiently above 18,000 feet, and in the United States all airspace above 18,000 feet is designated as "Class A" airspace, requiring an instrument rating. Though he did not own enough aircraft to create an airline, Denver did own a number of planes, including a Lear Jet (and he did, in fact, create a corporation for these craft, "Windstar Aviation," for which his father was the chief pilot). It was the Lear Jet that would have required Denver to have the instrument rating. But most serious pilots move on quickly to a commercial rating after getting their instrument ticket; some, like me, even seek the combined instrument-commercial rating, which requires 250 flight hours and a complex checkride with an examiner who tests one's ability both to fly on instruments alone and to fly especially demanding maneuvers in the checkride aircraft.

Though Denver, as a highly acclaimed singer with a demanding tour schedule, would have had no professional interest in becoming a "commercial" pilot, the "commercial" designation is important for two reasons. First, it indicates that one has demonstrated unusual competency in the control of an aircraft under difficult conditions. Second, it requires a higher-class medical certificate for its use—a second-class certificate, rather than the third-class required for a private pilot, even one with an instrument rating. Finally—if one follows this hypothetical route a little longer—had Denver really wanted to demonstrate his full proficiency as a pilot, he would have progressed to the highest rating, the air transport pilot (ATP) rating. This would have indicated to anyone familiar with him as a pilot that he was as competent as any given airline pilot. It would also, again, have required him to acquire a different medical certificate—a first-class medical certificate, again with stringencies that go beyond even the second-class certificate. If all of this sounds, at present, a little arcane, the fact is that it all becomes relevant eventually, as it all became suddenly quite relevant on October 12, 1997.

The record shows that, after getting his private license and instrument rating, Denver essentially went sideways into category, class, and type ratings: he was qualified to fly single and multi-engine land aircraft, single-engine seaplanes, gliders, and the Lear Jet. One could philosophize about Denver's strategy; it is not that uncommon among the wealthy, who seek the privileges of the sky with a minimum of official intervention. But such a reading of Denver's ratings doesn't really do justice either to his skills, his sense of risk, his inner disorientation despite his public appearance, or his interests. If one were to speak, again, literally, one might say that Denver simply loved to fly: what he wanted were the planes and the experience, not the fancy ratings. But, again, at a less literal level, this reading does not quite make sense. For to take pleasure in the sky is always, in every flight, to test oneself against the unknown, to confront or even, sometimes, invent simulated situations in which one must use one's skills, not only to one's "best" ability, but to a specific, objective standard: in an emergency, calmness and accuracy may matter above all. This is why, for example, one of the required maneuvers for a commercial rating—a maneuver Denver was never required to fly, although as an unrated aerobatic pilot he flew other maneuvers arguably much more difficult—is a chandelle, a slowly ascending half-circle turn in which the pilot brings the plane out of the turn exactly 180 degrees from the starting point and exactly at stall speed, the speed at which the plane will drop nose-forward out of the sky. This maneuver is important because it teaches essentials of absolutely perfect directional control, pitch and roll control, airspeed control, and attitude awareness under duress, the kinds of conditions one might conceivably face in an emergency.

Pilots who know and appreciate the inherent possibilities—and limits—of their aircraft seek higher ratings because they also seek the skill to understand and internalize those limits in an emergency. Pilots who "love to fly" but also fly with a certain self-centeredness, a mission of vision or rapture, or for the thrill of it, are often pilots other pilots sniff out and avoid the way certain dogs avoid others. Such pilots may love the air, they may fly brilliant maneuvers that dazzle passengers or people on the ground, they may seek ever more complex and demanding aircraft for more and different kinds of experiences or thrills. But if they lack the essential training of the most highly-trained pilots, and if they continue to avoid learning the most demanding skills of pilots who demand much of themselves, eventually the air will kill them.

In a disparately-organized and eccentric "exploration of the spirituality of John Denver," *A Mountain in the Wind*, writer Christine Smith appears to misunderstand Tom Poberezny, President of the Experimental Aircraft Association (EEA)—a combined umbrella group, task force, and political action committee on behalf of the kind of aircraft Denver was flying at the time of his death. Smith quotes Poberezny in the context of how much "John loved flying helicopters [though the National Transportation Safety Board reveals that Denver held no helicopter rating], jets, small private planes, experimental aircraft, and gliders" (Smith, 50). But this is what Poberezny actually says: "I don't think he [Denver] did it with the idea of being serious about it as much as just enjoying the exhilaration and the feeling it brought" (Smith, 50). Looking for good news, Smith finds it here, but from a pilot's point of view, Poberezny's comment is scarcely a glowing assessment of Denver's character in the air. Members of the EEA are among the best pilots in the world; some of them are official test pilots, or former test pilots, for the Navy and Air Force, and they train by the numbers, in simulators and in untried experimental aircraft, using an array of skills honed from years of careful and thoughtful flight. To suggest that a pilot of an experimental aircraft like the Long-EZ was not "serious about it" is to raise exactly the questions of proficiency that dog Denver's list of ratings. Behind Denver's thrill for life and all that it seemed to bring, behind this quest for freedom and the endless possibilities of the human endeavor, behind his joyous music and celebrations of the human spirit, there was a quality of heedlessness that, one might say, courted death.

Or one could put it a different way and, perhaps, come up with a startlingly different conclusion: from the time he found music, as a young adolescent in a rootless Air Force family, Denver knew rapture as he had known before only loneliness and anxiety. And rapture—not technical facility—was precisely what he sought in the air. If one were going to read one of his favorite books posthumously, as it were, over his shoulder— Richard Bach's *Jonathan Livingston Seagull*, which in 1970, the year Macmillan first published it, sold over a million copies—one might well see in Denver the solo seagull, ostracized from the crowd yet full of love and curiosity about life, finding his way through his own experiments to the wisdom of spiritual adept Chiang (in 1970 seagulls could also be spiritual adepts), who counsels him as a buddha counsels a boddhisattva who wishes to return to teach others what he has learned. It is almost impossible to read *Jonathan Livingston Seagull* and not to see how its its progressive vision of what Geshe Sopa calls "cutting through appearances" would be attractive to Denver—especially given his own wide-ranging (some would call it promiscuous) spirituality, his consultations of the *I Ching*, his study of Werner Erhard's *EST*, and other practices.

Yet granting the possibility that, through his own experience, his music, and his meditations on life, as well as his reading of Bach, Denver envisioned this life as a precious moment in the evolution of consciousness, a time when the deepest recesses of the soul and the stars themselves both seemed within reach for the first time—granting all of this, one cannot help wondering if Denver overlooked the quite precise details of flight training scripted into *Jonathan Livingston Seagull*, the intensity with which Jonathan, the much-maligned protagonist, performs his routines over and over, not simply for exhilaration, but for the sake of drawing closer to "perfection." Perfection was a concept that interested Bach in more than one way, but it certainly did interest him literally, for Bach was (and is) a different kind of pilot from Denver—among other things, a rated professional. Denver might not have known that, and he might not have cared, but missing the way that professionalism in execution—a spiritual adept would call it devotion—works in *Jonathan Livingston Seagull* is to miss something that might save one's life. Without it, no matter how much exhilaration one might feel, there would always, arguably, be an inner emptiness, and it would not be the healthy kind of Buddhist "selflessness" or "no-self" but that other kind, that profound Western fear of being alone. It would be a kind that Denver had known from his earliest years. In that context, it becomes impossible to overlook the matter of Denver's two DUI's, and the fact that—though it had not yet initiated legal action—the Federal Aviation Administration had revoked his third-class medical certificate at the time, around 5 P.M. Pacific Standard Time on October 12, 1997, when Denver climbed into the Long-EZ and began his 28-minute final flight.

* * *

My inclination, when I first learned of John Denver in the late winter of 1973, was to dismiss him as a musical lightweight. This response, I have to admit with some shame, came largely because my first girlfriend Janet, after breaking up with me, appeared in one of my high school classes that winter enormously enraptured about a concert she'd been to the night before at Flint Center, a beautiful performance hall at De Anza Junior College in Cupertino, about 20 miles south of where we lived in Los Altos, California. Janet was beautiful, very smart though not intellectual, funny, worldly, and hugely popular; why she chose me as her first boyfriend I will probably never really know, although I must have seemed "poetic" to her. My liabilities, given her background, were comical: because her family was wealthy, she was used to regional and world travel, and I shocked her into what eventually became her reason for dumping me in February 1973 when I refused to go on a skiing vacation with her family to one of the Lake Tahoe resorts. "I really need to write some poems over the break," I said, acutely aware of the absolute, unforgivable lameness of my excuse. No wonder she sounded shocked; she must have thought I myself was pulling away from her.

In reality, my undiagnosed anxiety disorder made it impossible for me to eat in public without becoming nauseated or throwing up, and of course I knew that, if I went to Tahoe, we would be eating in many fancy restaurants. Even if I could have explained this to her, however, she might have heard it as yet another excuse, because one of our earlier dates had actually been to a restaurant—in fact quite a fancy restaurant at one of the Hyatts in Palo Alto. What I could never have described to her, however, was a scene about six months earlier when, in a momentary fury of frustration, my parents had forced me to eat there, and I had indeed survived, and had also, as usual for someone who's also obsessive-compulsive, scoped out the routes to the men's room, thus giving myself a clear shot at escape. Thus, in a way, the Hyatt restaurant was a safe haven, and I must have seemed relatively comfortable there with her, comfortable enough that she might have begun to imagine me along with her on some of her family's travels. But then there was the remarkable fiasco of her birthday dinner, which—even though it had taken place at her house—included me as the second guest of honor; too anxious to eat, I managed to disgrace myself with portions on my plate suitable to a mouse. The fact was that, under most circumstances, I couldn't travel or eat in public because I didn't know how to feel comfortable with other human beings, even those who were Christian Scientists. Janet, a Catholic, seemed comfortable everywhere. So it was hardly a surprise when, after giving it her best shot, she found someone quite a bit more comfortable in his body than I was. Still, it was hard not to resent her profound enthusiasm, as she talked in class about her most recent date where "this really great singer" sang beautiful songs about the mountains and country roads and being in love and feeling the goodness of the sunshine and all kinds of wonderful things. "His name is John Denver," she said, "Oh, and you know what else"? [yes...it is amazing that I remember this word-for-word 32 years later.] "During intermission there were all these frisbees flying around auditorium, you know, it was *that* kind of crowd, totally cool, but you know what else? One of the frisbees landed on the stage and John came out and *played frisbee* with us all for, like, 15 minutes. Half the people were playing frisbee and half were just clapping. I mean, the man was beautiful."

It didn't help that this "beautiful" man looked far more like me than like Janet's new boyfriend, but what the hell. I immediately crossed him off my list. That changed, however, when my second girlfriend—who was to become my wife several years later—brought a John Denver album to a party we were having. By this time, the shock of losing Janet had also shocked me into some kind of parity with other people: I found ways around the restaurant problem, suggesting that my group of friends go on picnics, outings to the beach—anywhere I wasn't actually enclosed, anywhere I could, if necessary, walk away for awhile. And that worked. As the photo editor of the yearbook and a staffer for the literary magazine, I found a crowd that liked things a little off-the-wall and low-budget, so restaurants weren't a priority. And while, at that time, I also still got carsick unless I was driving, my parents were liberal in their rules about their cars, and so I often drove, a detail that didn't go unnoticed. Neurotics who can't bear loneliness sometimes find some way around their own neuroses, and by the beginning of my senior year, in fall 1973, I was doing pretty well. But suddenly, here was John Denver's 1971 album *Poems, Prayers and Promises* playing on the stereo, and it had come, not from Janet, who was long gone, but from Lesley, a concert violinist even in high school who played in the most competitive chamber orchestra in the area, whose knowledge of classical music was virtually unrivaled at the school, whose intellectual acumen vaguely alarmed even the most intelligent seniors, and who happened to have what her violin teacher might have called a "weakness" for folk-pop music. Nevertheless, here, suddenly, was that strong, vibrant voice singing "Almost heaven, West Virginia," and I suddenly realized I'd heard several John Denver songs before and had actually liked them enormously. I just didn't know they were by John Denver.

"Oh," I said. "So *that's* John Denver."

"Don't tell me you haven't heard of him," said Lesley.

I decided not to explain the circumstances.

"What else is on the album?" I asked.

We played *Poems, Prayers and Promises* several times that night, as the evening wound down and Lesley and I wound up sitting together in a chair meant for one, making out quietly to the tune of "Guess He'd Rather Be in Colorado" or the cover of James Taylor's "Fire and Rain" or the cover of the Beatles' "Let It Be." By the end of the evening I was a John Denver convert. And then, of course, there was the one song, not on the album, that somehow I had not yet noticed: Denver's signature song (no, not "Annie's Song"—Denver actually may be one of the few folk-pop musicians with three or four "signature songs," depending on whom you ask), "Rocky Mountain High," which caught my full attention on the radio a few weeks later. In that original recording, as in every remake I ever heard, you can hear Denver's absolute conviction that he was "born in the summer of [his] twenty-seventh year,/ Going home to a place he'd never been before." It's astonishing that all those lyrics flood back to mind all these years later. If a voice can convey love regardless of its subject, Denver's voice conveyed love. Janet had been right, not to mention Lesley. There was something quite beautiful about this man.

* * *

The Long-EZ, in which Denver met his death just off the coast of Monterey, is a difficult airplane to explain to non-pilots, most of whom are used to seeing conventional Cessna 172's and Piper Warriors flying overhead on their way to the nearest small airport. Those Cessnas—like the one Denver first learned in—and Pipers have changed little in design since their original versions in the late 1950's or early 1960's. Fans of these aircraft will immediately take issue with this claim, pointing out the swept-back vertical stabilizer innovation in the early 1960's Cessnas or the full-scale panel redesign, including throttle quadrant, in the 1969 Piper 140B, or the shift in later Pipers from a "Hershey-Bar" rectangular wing to a tapered wing…and it is true, overall, that each of these design changes, even if scarcely visible or invisible except upon inspection, improved these aircraft. But the fact remains that their basic design dates to World War II: they were constructed with aluminum airframes and aluminum, riveted skins, with engines—usually some version of the nearly-bullet-proof Lycoming 0-320 engine, from Williamsport, Pennsylvania—located in the front. The main difference to the uninitated between the Cessnas and the Pipers was that Cessnas had high wings while Piper had low.

The Long-EZ, however, came from the drafting table of Dick Rutan, a longtime aviation innovator and holder of a number of records, including the still-unrivaled record of the first round-the-world flight without refueling. Aluminum was heavy and rivets, even perfectly placed, still caused a slight, cumulative drag: the fact was that conventionally-constructed aircraft were relatively heavy, with a good deal of "parasitic drag," while other kinds of material—new kinds of high-impact plastics or other composites, for example—could be molded less expensively, with less weight, and considerably less drag. Rutan had a number of aims with regard to aviation—too many, really, to list here—but one of them was to force the general aviation industry to pay attention to its arguably antiquated, listless designs. Cheaper, composite materials, among other things, made it more possible for ordinary people with some mechanical skills to build aircraft in their garages, using plans from Rutan's design team and materials and molds available commercially; these aircraft required smaller, much lighter engines than the Cessnas and Pipers, and thus also used considerably less fuel—requiring smaller fuel tanks and also, not coincidentally, smaller budgets. As aviation writer Budd Davisson explains in his long account of the Long-EZ,

> The Long-EZ is going to set standards for any machine which pretends to be a cross-country runner. The big wing strakes of the Long contain enough fuel and baggage that any couple can use the airplane as though it was a Bonanza [one of Raytheon Beechcraft's top-of-the-line private aircraft]. The cruise speeds and excellent inherent stability make it a great XC bomber, and the seats are super comfortable... .The real advantage of the Long-EZ will become apparent when you taxi up to the gas pump after running ten hours nonstop California to Oshkosh [Wisconsin] and the final numbers on the gas pump are $79! (www.pilotfriend.com, 5)

Conceptually, then, with the Long-EZ, Rutan beat the major general aviation players at their game: he produced a kit-type aircraft costing less to build than a comparable Cessna or Piper (not to mention Beechcraft), costing less to fly, costing less to run, with superior comfort and, arguably, superior handling. Rutan's firm didn't wind up putting a dent in the Piper and Cessna business—other composite aircraft companies, such as Glasair and Lancair, managed that—yet Rutan generally always made his point, and he did so with the Long-EZ.

But a serious pilot might buy the Long-EZ for reasons other than roominess and economy. For one thing, it is, very simply, a fascinating airplane to view: though most of us, presumably, have not seen UFO's, one might easily intuit the Long-EZ as something in that category. Its long, narrow fuselage, much like a seagull's body, ends abruptly in two long, thin wings, swept back like a jet's, with rudders extending upward at the ends of each of those wings. The engine, rather than front-mounted, sits in the rear—a pusher—while the horizontal stabilizer and elevator, or stabilator, is actually in the front, a design feature known as the "canard." The canopy, which covers both pilot and passenger, fits as tightly into the fuselage as a jet's canopy; the glass, or plexiglass, is virtually one with the body of the plane. There's no mistaking a Long-EZ for anything else, because it looks as if it might well have come from Mars. If one simply wanted to grab attention, that alone would be reason enough to buy a Long. Denver, however, was well known by 1997 to have had more than enough attention, and this reason might have given him pause—except for the argument, parallel to this, that the Long is very beautiful if one loves airplanes: beautiful to look at, beautiful to see in the sky. It doesn't look "like" anything—not like a bird, except for the swept wings, nor like another aircraft...it looks like a set of mathematical calculations about flight turned into what they often have turned into under Rutan's hands, works of art.

At the same time, the Long has flying characteristics that clearly would have appealed to Denver. It is well-known among pilots for its roll capabilities: in fact, when the National Transportation Safety Board interviewed "the representative from Scaled Composite, Inc.," responsible for many of the components of this aircraft, he reported that "the lateral roll control with the side stick controller is very sensitive in that a 1/8 inch movement will cause a roll" (NTSB, 5). For many private pilots, the idea that their aircraft will begin to flip over with a sideward joystick motion of merely 1/8 of an inch would be a cause for alarm, since one could easily make such a motion accidentally—while reaching to reset a switch on the navigation or communications (nav/com) radios, for example, resetting the transponder, picking up a dropped pencil from the fuselage floor. For Denver, however, the thrill of flight included repeated 360-degree rolls, loops, and other maneuvers for which the sensitive controls and design of the Long were potentially thrilling. Indeed, Denver had, as EAA President Tom Poberezny noted, a penchant for "exhilaration," and some of the maneuvers that thrilled him were those that most aerobatic pilots practice over and over again, learning the nature and limits of each aircraft and the essential characteristics of recovery: precision is key. In his own comments on this subject, Denver is clear about risk and carefulness: As Christine Smith quotes him in comments to Ray Martin, "I feel much better when I'm in control... .Yeah, there's a risk: so you take care of your engine, you're responsible for your airplane, you know what you're doing, you know what your parameters are" (Smith, 50). And yet, following these comments, Smith reports on one of Denver's most dangerous maneuvers (though it's unclear from her text whether she herself realizes this), a "hammerhead stall": "...then after a breathtaking flight in which John took Ray on a ride in his Christen Eagle, falling out of the sky between the Maroon Bells in a hammerhead stall, John said enthusiastically, 'I don't know how to have more fun than that!'" (Smith, 50-51).

Martin's response to this comment is, at present, still unknown, and Smith leaves Denver's words to speak for themselves, but it's perhaps worth noting that, in a hammerhead stall, one brings an aircraft swiftly up to vertical flight, just to the point of a stall; pivots the aircraft in a certain direction depending on the propeller's slipstream (often to the left); then drops the plane to a perfect vertical descent; then either pulls out to straight-and-level flight or pulls up for a second hammerhead. Typical minimum entry speeds for the maneuver are 160-190 mph; G forces are high; possible problems include an accidental tail slide or an accidental tail spin, either of which requires advanced skills for recovery. Such a maneuver, were it done in, say, a Piper Warrior, would destroy the airframe, and the stresses of the maneuver on both pilot and aerobatic aircraft (such as the commercially-manufactured Christen Eagle) usually demand what one might describe as a combination of technical vigilance and reverence from the pilot. Calling a hammerhead stall "fun" certainly fits with John Denver's evolved image as the good old "country boy" of his song "Thank God I'm a Country Boy," but it may not do justice either to his actual feelings about his accomplishment or his own sense of the balance between risk management and death.

Though the Long-EZ was not designed for the full range of maneuvers Denver performed in his Eagle, it had, perhaps, one component more compelling than any other: It flew like an airplane, but had the visibility and effortless control of a glider. Having acquired a glider rating, Denver would have known the birdlike thrill of riding thermals and turning, with unrivaled visibility, in quiet air, but he would likely have been frustrated by the performance limits of gliders, including the slight detail that, no matter how much you might want to continue to stay up, eventually the glider would decide when to come down. Though an earlier version of the Long-EZ, called the "Vari-Eze," had what Davisson refers to as "foxhole" visibility on takeoff and landing, among other flight attitudes, Rutan's group had solved that problem with the Long, and in it one might well feel virtually birdlike—no engine in front, no wings visible to the side, only the vivid sky above and around, and even all the ground below if one chose, as Denver surely would have chosen if he had lived, to spend some time flying upside down in this lively, almost-alive aircraft. The Long did what no other plane Denver owned quite could do: it seemed to live on its own in the sky, neither as aggressive as a Christen Eagle, as procedural as a Lear Jet, or as cumbersome as a Cessna. With the light controls of a glider and the flight characteristics of a seagull, it might have seemed to Denver like the human equivalent of what his hero Jonathan Livingston Seagull experienced in his transcendent moments.

Still, there were problems—one relatively minor, the other more significant—and both ultimately contributed to Denver's death. The small one (perhaps a little ironically at the literal level) had to do with engine size: for economy, Burt Rutan had designed the Long to fly well on a small engine—either a 100-horsepower Continental 0-200 or a 115-horsepower Lycoming 0-235. Each of these engines would have brought in the low fuel consumption Davisson extols. Fairly early on in its history (the first Long-EZ's date from 1977), its owners had begun experimenting with other powerplants: some, according to the NTSB, have attached "engines of up to 200 horsepower" (NTSB, 3). Denver's plane had been modified with a Lycoming 0-320, a 150-horsepower engine that consumed between 8.5 to 10 gallons of fuel per hour, depending on whether the aircraft was in take-off, cruise, or descent mode. Denver's check-out ride with the previous owner in Santa Maria, California on the day before his fatal crash lasted all of 1/2-hour, and it remains unclear if Denver knew exactly what he was buying, including some of the essential characteristics of the powerplant. Indeed, when the NTSB issued its final report on the accident, it noted with some understatement Denver's "lack of total experience in this type of aircraft" (NTSB summary, 2).

To be fair, Denver had flown in the rear seat of this aircraft a month before purchasing it, and had "also flown in the backseat on two other Long-EZ demonstration flights" (NTSB, 2). He was not, thus, a total neophyte with the Long, yet his front set or "pilot in command" time was below minimal. In any case, he might have remembered from his very earliest Cessna days that the engine in his new (it was actually built in 1987) Long-EZ was virtually identical to the Cessna engine, and thus took far more fuel than normal for a Long. But it's possible that Denver either did not know or did not remember this.

The second problem was more idiosyncratic, and since idiosyncratic problems tend to be the truly dangerous ones, it winds up as the smoking pistol in this story. Most Longs have a fuel selector handle between the pilot's legs in the cockpit. Like many aircraft, the Long had fuel tanks in the left and right wings, respectively, and the fuel selector registered these—though in a very odd way: turned to the right, the handle indicated that the *left* tank was in use; turned straight down, it indicated that the *right* tank was in use; turned straight up, it meant fuel shut-off. Even more bizarrely, the FAA required no placard of any kind to indicate which position referred to which tank (or no tank); it was the pilot's responsibility simply to know.

Although most small aircraft have a fuel selector lever, handle, or valve somewhere inside the cockpit (the Piper Warrior, for example, locates it just back of the pilot's left foot), Denver for some reason felt uncomfortable with actual fuel flow through the cockpit area, and—having decided in September to purchase the Long, but having to leave immediately on a North American tour—Denver asked the then-owner of the plane to have the fuel selector switch, and the gauge associated with it, relocated behind the pilot's left shoulder. Though this modification had been done on some other Longs, it did not really solve the problem of fuel lines in or around the cockpit (very little could solve that problem, if it actually was a problem), and it created a serious safety issue. For it was impossible for the pilot, while flying the aircraft, to switch tanks without taking his or her hands off the controls. To accomplish a tank shift mid-flight, the pilot "had to: 1) Remove his hand from the right side control stick if he was hand flying the aircraft; 2) Release the shoulder harness; 3)Turn his upper body 90 degrees to the left to reach the handle; and 4) Turn the handle to another position. Two pilots shared their experiences of having inadvertently run a fuel tank dry with nearly catastrophic consequences because of the selector and sight gauge locations" (NTSB, 5).

It's a truism among pilots that accidents rarely have a single cause; dropping your pencil on the cabin floor while copying an air traffic control clearance is unlikely to cause more than a minor inconvenience to anyone, but inadvertently pushing against the control wheel or joystick or leaning on a rudder pedal while trying to reach the pencil may put you into an unrecoverable spin. In Denver's case, although he may not have been aware of it, his Long-EZ already had two strikes against it by the time he flew it from Santa Maria to Monterey. Though capable of holding 52 gallons of fuel in two 26-gallon tanks at each wing root, the plane left Santa Maria, according to the checkout pilot, with a total of "about 19 gallons of fuel on board" (NTSB, 6). The NTSB estimated that "the amount of fuel required to fly to Monterey from Santa Maria ranged from 6.4 to 9.1 gallons, depending upon the power settings used" (NTSB, 6); given the engine, the higher figure is more likely, and since Denver did not file a flight plan—as he was not required to for VFR (Visual Flight Rules) flight—we have no way of knowing exactly how much time he was in the air. By the time he was on the ground in Monterey on October 11, however, he had, at best, a total of less than one hour of fuel remaining in a plane designed to hold a little over five hours' worth of fuel—strike one. In addition, that remaining fuel was apportioned unequally between the two tanks; the checkout pilot in Santa Maria estimated that about six-and-a-half gallons were in the left tank, and about 12-and-a-half in the right. The checkout pilot also noted that Denver had left Santa Maria with the fuel selector set to the right tank (NTSB, 6), which means that Denver landed in Monterey with perhaps six gallons in the left tank and no more than three in the right—strike two.

By late afternoon the next day, after a round of golf with friends, Denver was reportedly eager to get to the Monterey airport for an early evening flight in his new aircraft. As a pilot whose flight hours rivaled his hours on stage, he would have known to do a specific set of checks on the Long-EZ before even starting the engine. As it turned out, he failed to perform two of these checks, and even though the plane itself gave him a warning on the ground that all was not well, he shrugged it off, signaling a thumbs-up to a concerned airport technician. To most pilots, Denver's behavior on October 12 was simply inexplicable. But beyond the realm of piloting, one can never underestimate the degree to which other things may be occupying a mind as complex as the seemingly simple John Denver.

* * *

In his 1998 *Life: The Movie; How Entertainment Conquered Reality*, Neal Gabler quotes the historian Daniel Boorstin's remarkably prescient 1960 comment that "we risk being the first people in history to have been able to make their illusions so persuasive, so 'realistic' that they can live in them" (Gabler, 4). These "illusions," the product of a mass-media culture, mean that, as Gabler explains, we live primarily in a culture of deception in which that deceit is neither intrinsically moral or immoral, but rather seemingly transcends traditional concepts of morality for the sake of our own release from what Ezra Pound once called the "loneliness and partiality" of everyday life. When life becomes its own movie—when we no longer exit a movie theatre to return to our daily lives, but have finally learned "how to escape from life into life" (Gabler, 6)—then, in one sense, we have fully realized the actual, literal power of escapist fantasy. Although we may owe taxes or face an IRS audit, we may have lost a job and face foreclosure, we may be divorced, alone, with children far away or out of touch, we may be aging and unattractive and—if we dared look—on the verge of another 30 or 40 years of a life consumed with debt, abject loneliness, and physical disintegration—although any of these may be "true," if we live into what Gabler describes our current culture as being, a "culture of celebrity," then we can choose to enter the illusion that the periphery is at the center and the true trials of life are comparatively trivial.

Given the models of celebrity that Gabler lists—not only movie stars and politicians, but also "super-models, lawyers, political pundits, hairdressers, intellectuals, businessmen, journalists, criminals—anyone who happens to appear, however fleetingly, on the radar of the traditional media and is thus sprung from the anonymous mass" (Gabler, 7)—any one of us might conceivably at any moment rise above "the anonymous mass," whether through public commentary on some engaging issue, a personal tragedy pathetic enough to attract satellite TV coverage, or a mass killing at a scene of high fantasy, such as a mall or an amusement park. It scarcely matters what one does or who one "is," if one has any lingering interest in that ontological question, as long as one *does* something vivid enough to earn the label of "celebrity." Lost and alone, we make ourselves into what we need to be to enjoy the profound illusions of companionship and fame. Gabler's America is like the nightmare version of a Buddhist vision of enlightenment, in which we find all that we seek, yet all that we seek is not only illusory but ultimately destroys us. Yet the pull is both subtle and absolutely powerful. Many of my students would rather watch *Survivor* or *Desperate Housewives* or *Queer Eye for the Straight Guy* or *American Idol* than read anything I assign, and their reasons are, in a sense, persuasive: the people they know, in whose world they live, talk about these shows, dream of being on these shows, and treat these shows as a clear form of reality—which, in a complicated sense, they are: the final four of *American Idol* are likely to receive lucrative recording contracts, while the survivors of *Survivor* get bundles of money, and the lucky straight guy in *Queer Eye* more often than not gets the girl, thanks to the intense attention to superficial detail that marks the major skills of the queer consultants and also, inadvertently, serves as a confirmation of what it takes to appear attractive in this cultural moment.

What's perhaps most important to understand, however—and Gabler makes this point in the historical body of his book—is that this transformation of life into fantasy happened gradually in America, as the interweaving of the entertainment and political domains became more complex and subtle; in the realm of the "modern," as modernism began to slide into Gableresque post-modernism, John Denver and others somewhat like him—the ones that come most often to mind in the music world are James Taylor and Jim Croce—came into influential positions within a culture already dedicated to self-abdication. As early as 1970, what mattered was the image. One might argue that this same principle inhered in the 1960's, but that argument is specious: though the Vietnam War was the first "TV war," for example, the impact of its images was a real impact in a world of real families and viewers; the result was increasingly violent, organized, and outraged protest. By contrast, when General Norman Schwarzkopf offered the media his footage from a fighter jet equipped with night-flight cameras, showing rockets hitting Iraqi targets during the first Gulf War, people in the media, the military, and the country at large treated the event as a kind of entertainment, a revelation of fascinating technology and visual wizardry. The political questions that surrounded the images of Vietnam were modernist in the sense that people cared about the full context of the images; the questions that surrounded images from the first and second Gulf Wars, with the exception of the Abu Graib prison photos, were post-modern because they raised no clear or consistent link between what was seen and what the sight implied. "Reality" *was* the image; there was nothing behind that. Thus people shopped and bought gasoline and partied and watched the Superbowl all through the second Gulf War, even as vets on two-week leave passed through major airports looking as grim as only true soldiers can look. The second Gulf War, on the home front, was a virtual war; aside from its celebrities, such as Jessica Lynch, it did not exist.

After Martin Luther King, Jr.'s assassination, however, and after Robert Kennedy's assassination, after the Students for a Democratic Society splintered into the ultra-violent Weather Underground and fearful conservative forces swung sharply toward the amoral Richard Nixon, the country began to pivot, and reality—with which America arguably wrestled admirably in the 1960's overall—began to become too much to bear: T. S. Eliot's observation that "humankind cannot bear very much reality" began to be heard more and more on college campuses. In that environment, the "entertainers" who in fact had done so much to transform the political landscape of America and Great Britain (and, indeed, much of the West)—including Bob Dylan, the Beatles, Joan Baez, Joni Mitchell, the Rolling Stones, the Who, the Jefferson Airplane, the Mamas and the Papas, even the Beach Boys—began to find that fantasies associated with their image were not only more marketable but also more desired than anything else they might produce. This had, of course, interesting results: the pressure to be "The Beatles" arguably led to the demise of the Beatles, with intriguing consequences: Paul McCartney turned to lightweight, largely unmemorable pop recording as generic and seemingly automatic as chocolate chip cookies from a vending machine;

John Lennon went, in a sense, underground, acknowledging celebrity but refusing to relinquish his musical innovation; George Harrison alone managed to continue in a sixties tradition, using the political and social power of his celebrity to create change in the world, as his "Concert for Bangladesh" illustrated; Ring Starr became the "star," the celebrity item. Among the other artists, Dylan also went underground for several years, Baez continued her highly real political and musical crusades at a much lower level and finally bought a small ranch in northern California as a retreat, the Rolling Stones became parodies of themselves, the Who swerved directly into the fantasy world with the "rock opera" *Tommy*, and the Jefferson Airplane, the Mamas and the Papas, and the Beach Boys all imploded in different ways. Only Mitchell stayed completely true to the authentic line of musical meaning and experimentation that lead to such mid-1970's successes as *Court and Spark, For the Roses,* and the very great album *Blue*—yet by the end of the decade, and well into the 1980's, only her most devoted fans were listening to such commercial failures as *Wild Things Run Fast.* Her pursuit of her most ardent routes nearly cost her her career until the 1991 hit *Night Ride Home.* Dylan, of course, re-emerged as well, but never truly overcame Joan Baez's profound chastisement of what she identified as his sell-out in her late 1972 album *Come from the Shadows.* Clearly, if one were a popular musician in the late 1960's or early 1970's, one ran both the hope and the risk of being what Cat Stevens derisively calls a "pop star" on his 1970 *Mona Bone Jakon.*

By whatever chance of fate, John Denver emerged on the pop scene at exactly the moment the pop scene needed a celebrity who looked like John Denver. As Denver's original recording manager Milt Okun observed to *Newsweek* in 1976, "John exploded as all the crud of Watergate and Nixon was unfolding, when the papers, radio, and TV were full of the darkest, unhumanistic things...He evokes the American countryside the way Elgar wrote about the plains of England or Mussorgksy put Russian peasant song into opera. I put him up there with Aaron Copeland and 'Appalachian Spring.' To me, it isn't bland. It's great simple art" (Collis, p. 101). While there's much that could be said about Okun's interpretation, three things emerge immediately: first, the clean-cut, seemingly simple, and hopeful melodies and lyrics of Denver created a clear alternative reality to the political and social decay of America; second, Denver's image had to be sufficiently compelling to offset the intelligent allegation that some or even much of his music was, to put it kindly, "bland"; and third, Denver's image had to accommodate a quality of greatness, earned or not, that placed him, not in the company of 1960's singers, but rather in the company of great composers from the past who'd gone back to "peasant" roots for the sources of "great simple art." Read carefully, Okun's words define Denver's image: a simple, down-to-earth yet musically vivid composer whose love for people and land transcended all conventional boundaries of time and politics. This was John Denver meeting John Denver; for the first John Denver to stray from the second would mean, in 1970's America, the death of both.

But who was that first John Denver? Because his old, close friends and family guard his legacy with probably rightful jealousy, there's little enough available that doesn't already have the ring of pop mythology to it, but Denver's years before stardom have two main characteristics: rootlessness and hard work. For Denver had been playing the folk and, to some extent, the country scene for a solid seven years before *Poems, Prayers and Promises* made him famous, and those years were marked with the hard work of the club scene and the road: stints with the Chad Mitchell Trio, near-misses with the Byrds and the Monkees, and various solo performances in small and medium venues, several Milt Okun-produced singles and three albums—the 1969 *Rhymes and Reasons*, and the 1970 *Take Me to Tomorrow* and *Whose Garden Was This?*—that had disappointing sales. The hardworking musician, with his "hotel rooms with 35 cents in his pocket" and his near-misses, was neither a star nor a celebrity; he was a certain kind of man working on a definable, if inaccessible, dream. And that dream to some extent came from and assuaged the loneliness and rootlessness of his childhood. But because those early experiences were as compelling as they were dark, the dream itself had to have, innately, a compensatory lightness. How that lightness would change from the mid-1970's on is a story that has to do directly with how the first John Denver turned to confront the second. But before that moment was something true and American and, though psychologically complex, narratively simple and direct.

Born Henry John Deutschendorf, Jr., on December 31, 1943, in Roswell, New Mexico, Denver had the classic childhood of an Army brat. His

Air Force pilot and flight instructor father, H.J. Senior, was reassigned regularly: in 1949 the family moved to Japan, when Denver was five, and a year later they moved to Tucson. In 1957 the family moved again, this time to Montgomery, Alabama, and only a year later turned west again to Fort Worth, Texas, where H.J. (known familiarly as "Dutch") became a squadron commander for a B-58 Bomber group. By this time Denver, having just turned 16 and old enough for a driver's license, was also carrying sixteen years' worth of absolutely classic dislocation and what R. D. Laing calls "ontological insecurity": he belonged nowhere, scarcely to himself, and his home life was dominated by a high-ranking, authoritarian, taciturn pilot and commander who flew by the numbers and tolerated no dissent. As early as his time in Montgomery, however, Denver had been known in school as the kid who played the guitar; in his music class his teacher had invited him to come in and perform several tunes, including the then-hit "Diana" by Paul Anka, and by the time he had graduated from high school in Fort Worth he was playing "parties, proms, stuff like that" (Collis, 41). The question is whether any of this attention assuaged the other realities of his adolescence—the parties he threw to which no one came, the absence of girlfriends, and the intrusiveness of his parents, particularly his father. Denver remembers a decisive moment in his 16th year when, having actually arranged a date, he had to cancel because his father needed the car to go drinking with his Air Force buddies. Incensed, John waited till early the next morning, when the household was still asleep, then crept out to the car, filled it with gas, and headed for Los Angeles. The story is interesting in part because, once Dutch discovered John was missing, he actually took off in a plane and scoured the west Texas countryside, back and forth, looking for his missing son on any highway. The maneuver, late though it was, showed an interesting subterranean attachment, but Denver, in fact, had stopped in Tucson and then headed on to L.A. The James-Deanesque adventure ended on a sour note—the car gave out in L.A. and Denver had to call home for help—but he'd made his mark in two ways: he'd broken the chain of command in the household and he'd cleared some space and direction for himself. A year later, enrolling in the Texas Technical Institute in Austin to study architecture while honing his musical skills, he lasted just long enough to scrape together $250 and, in early 1964, headed back to L.A., this time as a young musician looking for a break. It didn't take long: in less than a year Denver, though still "John Deutschendorf," was the opening act for the *Back Porch Majority* at the major folk scene in L.A., the Troubadour club. "That first weekend," Denver said, "I started getting encores and I was extended to 26 weeks there and started getting jobs around the country" (Collis, 48). By late 1964, at the suggestion of Randy Sparks, who told him "Deutschendorf wouldn't fit on the record label," John Deutschendorf was John Denver, and that was that (Collis, 52).

Still, one has the sense from these early years—though crowned with a slow, continual rise in musical success that many young artists would envy—that Denver was a young man using his love of music to cover exactly the kind of inner emptiness that Laing describes in *The Divided Self*. Though one doesn't want to push this too far, especially because *The Divided Self* was primarily a groundbreaking study of schizophrenia, first published in 1959, the distinction is relevant in part because Laing was also interested in larger distinctions between "sanity and madness" in the contemporary world, and how behaviors that might appear "sane" to ordinary people had an element of insanity in them, while "insane" behaviors might have relatively clear, if inaccessible, explanations. "In the context of our present pervasive madness that we call normality, sanity, freedom," Laing writes, "all our frames of reference are ambiguous and equivocal" (Laing, 11). He continues:

> A man who prefers to be dead rather than Red is normal. A man who says he has lost his soul is mad. A man who says that men are machines may be a great scientist. A man who says he is a machine is "depersonalized" in psychiatric jargon... .A little girl of seventeen in a mental hospital told me she was terrified because the Atom Bomb was inside her. That is a delusion. The statesmen of the world who boast and threaten that they have Doomsday weapons are far more dangerous, and far more estranged from "reality" than many of the people on whom the label "psychotic" is affixed (Laing, 11-12).

Though the timing of Laing's observations coincides with Denver's childhood rather than his years of emerging musical success, Laing's words are worth quoting because they identify the kind of "ambiguous and equivocal" climate in which Denver spent the years that shaped him most profoundly. In Laing's analysis, facing such ambiguity and evasiveness over a long period of time, a psyche may well develop a false outer self and a very different inner self: "The false-self system to be described here," he writes, "exists as the complement of an 'inner self' which is occupied in maintaining its identity by being transcendent, unembodied, and thus never to be grasped, pinpointed, trapped, possessed. Its aim is to be pure subject..." (Laing, 94-95). We have seen patterns somewhat like this before in this book—in the life, death, and art of Dylan Thomas, in the life and words of Kathryn Harrison as they applied to my life and to my mother's life, in the life of Denny Hansen. No one, I think, would argue that any of these people, including Denver, was schizophrenic, although Denver does seem to have manifested what are called "schizoid tendencies"; What is clear, however, is that Denver invented a front in which that inner self— inaccessible to ordinary consciousness in a schizophrenic—became the actual subject of his music: in song after song, the self is "transcendent, unembodied, and thus never to be grasped, pinpointed, trapped, possessed." People who love Denver's music tend to point to exactly these characteristics as being at its core: it is music about the freedom of the self. But the paradox of taking one's inner flight, one's inner escape from the intolerable ambiguity and equivocation of ordinary life, and manifesting it as the material of one's "false front," one's emerging role as a popular musician, is effectively to turn one's soul inside out: one turns nothing into something, one turns escape into fixity, one turns terror into soul-touching sentiment, one turns a disguise into a reality. Denver, in many ways, become emblematic of the society in which he lived, not because he was part of the Watergate darkness nor because he was its opposite, but rather because—as a mode of survival—he intuited the essential American attribute from the late 1960's on, the need to become one's disguise. But the cost, inevitably, was high; it showed in his life and in his death. Ironically, however, it also showed in his music, if one listened carefully, and particularly in the lyrics to his pivotally-successful *Poems, Prayers and Promises.*

* * *

Harold Bloom, *the eminence gris* and much-maligned Yale literary critic who nevertheless produced one perfect book in his career—the 1996 *Omens of Millennium*—and thus is the perhaps the closest figure I have ever had to a spiritual mentor, reserves a lovely phrase for what he identifies as the New Age articulation of angels and near-death experiences: he describes it as having "a vacuity not to be believed" (Bloom, 19). Any professor who, like me, has graded over 16,000 student essays in the course of his or her career will inevitably come across as many as 8,000 which represent "a vacuity not to be believed"; indeed, the psychological torture of having to read and respond to such writing is one of my arguments for a "twenty-years-and-out" program in the university, similar to the military's mode of promotion and retirement. After 20 years of such punishment, one can scarcely imagine what being happy is like, even if one is not clinically depressed. Yet I think that Harold Bloom would look quite askance at my interest in John Denver, whose dabblings in various spiritual traditions and mind-control techniques would qualify him as a New Ager in Bloom's judgment.

Indeed, many of Denver's less-well-known lyrics, and some of his famous ones—including most of "Thank God I'm a Country Boy"—would surely incur Bloom's anti-imprimatur: "of a vacuity not to be believed." But Denver was, in his own way, a cagey and astute self-promoter, an indefatigable performer where endurance counted most, and a lyricist who knew, at some level, that to be successful he had to imitate his image, but who also knew at another level things that were true, both about himself and about the experience of being human in this culture. Some of the evidence for this is contradictory; some of it appears in lyrics of unusual sensitivity while the music registers a happy simplicity, while at other times unexpected harmonies deepen what seems to be a relatively innocuous or vapid lyrical observation. The point, however, is that—however much Bloom (at one end of the scale) and the ironically die-hard Aspen New Agers (at the other end of the scale) wish to identify Denver as a New Age phenomenon, what stands out most about Denver is the impossibility of inserting him into such a matrix. With a New Age image that did, in some ways, match his feelings about life and nature and the soul at certain times, Denver also had a more private musical and poetic vocabulary that acknowledged the true pain of loneliness and isolation, relied on the Romantic imagination to attempt to bring into being what did not, in some way, already exist, and acknowledged the occasional, inexplicable, absolute thrill of self-transcendence—as well as the extreme difficulty of returning to ordinary life after such moments.

"Poems, Prayers and Promises" opens side one of Denver's 1971 album, and as a meditation—while not itself truly a poem—it indicates instantly a meditative mind engaged with what Protestant theologian Robert McAfee Brown has called "ultimate concerns." "I've been lately thinking about my life's time," Denver sings, after a three-measure opening harmony that descends to what might seem a point of darkness but then resolves in a low though major harmony. This is a song of retrospection, unusual as the opening cut for a still-little-known singer; attribute the wisdom to Denver's manager, the celebrated but elusive Jerry Weintraub, or to Denver himself, but the conclusion to the first verse is arresting: "And I can't help believing in my own mind,/ I know I'm going to hate to see it end." Thus Denver's first preoccupation in this album is a wistful confrontation with death—not a light-hearted, happy, New Age celebration of eternal life, but rather an acknowledgment of limits, and a wish for whatever meaning people may construct within the absolute constraint of death. The second verse of the song lists things Denver has done that have had, implicitly, memorable meaning for him: he's "seen a lot of sunshine, slept out in the rain"; he's known his lady's pleasures, "had [himself] some friends, spent a time or two in [his] own home." If it's an unremarkable list, it's also a list with a vague echo of Woody Guthrie: Denver makes no claim to have seen "hard traveling," but he makes a claim for knowing the world as it is—a place where beauty can also, given the circumstances, be harsh or dangerous, where too much sunlight and sleep in the rain can pull down one's spirits, can spin one into disorientation. The question is, then, what does the singer of this tale and his friends do when they're together in these interludes between loneliness? Here, admittedly, Denver moves into cliché, but he handles it cleverly: he and his friends "talk of poems and prayers and promises,/ And things that we believe in,/ How sweet it is to love someone,/ How right it is to care." So far so good—the clichés flow like imitation silk, and yet one has to attribute something deeper here, something in the actual resonance of the voice, the faith Denver has in the reality—not the image—of his words; it *is* sweet to love someone, it *is* right—morally and cosmically—to care about the one you love. But then Denver's list becomes slightly eccentric: the refrain ends, "How long it's been since yesterday,/ And what about tomorrow?/ What about the dreams, and all the memories we share?" This refrain ends with puzzlement: time moves quickly (an idea made explicit in the last verse), tomorrow is an open question, but the real problem is psychic: what is the relationship between our dreams, which implicitly occupy both the present and a time not yet arrived, and our memories, which also implicitly occupy the present and a time past? In the present we have dreams and memories, but is this the substance of the present? Does the present have any substance? The Buddhist approach to this question, of course, is to observe that Denver has misunderstood: the dreams and memories are illusions or, as Geshe Lhundup Sopa and Jeffrey Hopkins write, "appearances" that need to be "cut through" (Sopa and Hopkins, 15-17). But if one does not know or does not take this tack, the present seems almost mystical in its elusiveness, something like Laing's inner self that cannot be pinned down or isolated, a refracting surface in the phenomenal world that speaks back with affirmation to all the desires implicit in Denver's song, including his constrained sadness about the fact of mortality itself. Denver's philosophizing here, if one wants to call it that, is of the purest popular kind from the early 1970's: struggling with questions for which no orthodoxy offers adequate answers, Denver prefers to lay the problems out directly and to sing directly of the momentary comforts between the almost-continual experience of evanescence. This remarkably complex substructure to what seems like a pure pop song is characteristic both of Denver's own songs on *Poems, Prayers and Promises*, and of his covers—James Taylor's "Fire and Rain," John Lennon and Paul McCartney's "Let it Be," Paul McCartney's little-known "Junk," and Williams' beautiful "Gospel Changes." The only piece on the album that rings truly false is the cover of Lascelle's appallingly clichéd "The Box," a spoken piece on the evils of war. Yet even in this almost-unendurable piece, one hears, if one listens closely, a passion in Denver's voice for the real meaning behind the cliché—a passion that almost turns the cliché into meaning instead of drivel. Surely for many fans, especially those of the time, this interpretation of "The Box" will seem both cruel and wrong, as Vietnam was still in full swing and Denver might be seen to be doing what he could to support the anti-war movement. If one leaves "The Box" aside, however, and concentrates on a handful of the other Denver hits on this album, one comes to conclusions that coincide with the underlying subtleties in "Poems, Prayers and Promises."

"Sunshine on My Shoulders" is on this album, a kind and gentle, if slightly trite, piece that nevertheless does something clever in its second verse: instead of trying to be a certain kind of song, it announces to its recipient—for it turns out to be a multi-layered love song—that, if the singer had a song for his beloved, it would be "a day just like today"; if the singer had that song, he would sing it "to make you feel this way." Which way? What song? Ingeniously, "Sunshine on My Shoulders" essentially makes the claim in the second verse that it does not exist: the "if"'s in that verse make that implication inescapable. Thus the paradox: of course the song exists, but is it the song that this singer sings to his beloved? Or is there another, more private version, a melody and a set of feelings, for one person and not for an enormous audience? By this time, Denver was acquiring a considerable fan club, and having traveled a great deal from venue to venue, knew how precious and elusive privacy had become. Though most people think of "Sunshine on My Shoulder" as a somewhat vacuous love song, Denver was smarter than that, and the underlying sense that true love demanded a privacy beyond the reach of fans was a profound attempt at wish-fulfillment, a fulfillment that tragically would always elude Denver.

In fact, as one looks more closely at *Poems, Prayers and Promises,* one is struck by how much of the album concerns death and the uncontrollable passage of time. "Fire and Rain," though a great hit for James Taylor with his gravelly, "Won't-you-look-down-upon-me-Jesus" voice, fares less well for Denver, yet still contains the line "Sweet dreams and flying machines in pieces on the ground"—words that now cannot be heard without an eerie background echo of disaster. Perhaps most important, however, is the less-well-known Denver song "Around and Around," which opens rather conventionally: "Time as I've known it/ Doesn't take much time to pass by me." The list of components of time—minutes, days, months, years—all hurry by the speaker; then he comes to the sudden, brief refrain of the song: "Still I love to see the sun go down,/ And the world go around." Something intrinsic about the beauty of creation, its continual motion rather than stasis, its imperfection rather than its impossible perfectibility, its phenomenological presence, drives both these lines and the overall direction of the song. Intriguingly, the second stanza is primarily a stanza of grief: the singer acknowledges that he's had many dreams and "hopes for the future," but then sings: "dreams I can't remember now,/ Hopes that I've forgotten,/ Faded memories." Such a simple, dark list from a man just 30 years old is quite striking: the song requires us to take the list seriously because the song itself has begun as a peculiar commentary on a world that, from the singer's point of view, is not under his control: it spins off into its own domains, carrying him along regardless of his intentions or his consent. The refrain, once again, carries a much heavier weight at the end of the second verse; then comes the real oddity, the bridge and the final verse:

> And I love to see the morning as it steals across the sky,
> I love to remember, and I love to wonder why,
> And I hope that I'm around
> So I can be there when I die,
> When I'm gone...
>
> I hope that you will think of me
> In moments when you're happy and you're smiling;
> That the thought will comfort you
> On cold and cloudy days if you are crying;
> That you'll love to see the sun go down
> And the world go around,
> And around and around.

Quite suddenly the song turns into the singer's meditation on the moment of his death, partly as a characteristic of his tendency to wonder: is it possible to be conscious of the moment of one's dying, to know it the way one knows the morning stealing across the sky? This image, along with James Taylor's "flying machines in pieces" and the reference in "Gospel Changes" to Jesus bowing his head and lying down to die, along with the "quiet cough" of the Coloradan whose time in New York City is clearly bringing him closer to death than to life, indicate an almost-prescient concern with what Tibetan Buddhists call "the in-between," the bardo state between this life and the next. At the same time, the quite pure sense of impending loss—as if there might be no bardo state, no afterlife, or worse yet, nothing one could know about one's death at the moment it occurred—does not register as conventional pop material, despite Denver's generally upbeat melodies in major keys (his producer, Milton Okun, once went through Denver's entire *oeuvre* of 150 songs, on a bet from a friend, and discovered that Denver had written not one song in a minor key). Nor is Denver playing on sentimentally conventional adolescent heartstrings. The structure of his lyrics, in which he weaves an underlying darkness almost seamlessly through moments of affirmation and hope, reminds one of an urgent inner self struggling to emerge from behind the ingenious and polished public disguise—and struggling, too, to pass the vision on to someone who will know or remember him, who will "think of me."

Yet what makes Denver even more complex, and interesting, is the way in which this "disguise"—this clean-cut, backpacking, "Rocky Mountain High" guitarist with his songs of love and companionship, such as "Annie's Song" or "My Sweet Lady"—was not, in fact, a phenomenon isolated from a more "authentic" internal Denver; whether he came to believe his own mythology or that mythology conquered him and penetrated deeper than one might have expected, Denver had an exceptional way of interpenetrating *himself,* making the false self meaningful to the wounded and isolated inner self, forcing a conjunction through what came to seem like a sheer act of will based on a great confidence in the power of mind and magic. It seems entirely clear, for example, that the incident Denver describes in "Rocky Mountain High"—a song that appeared on his sixth album, entitled *Rocky Mountain High,* in 1972—actually occurred: having already begun to make his name with the chart-topping "Take Me Home, Country Roads" in 1971, and having begun to bring in serious money as well, Denver and his first wife Annie Martell moved to Aspen, where Denver and Annie had visited several years before on a college ski tour organized through Annie's college; Denver had immediately fallen in love with the place. In 1971, spending much of his summer backpacking, Denver had an extraordinarily memorable vision of a Perseid meteor shower:

So we were up all night watching the most glorious display I've ever seen in these mountains...and at one point...I stood in this little grove of pine trees and recognised that it was darker in there than it was outside... there was the softest possible, the most subtle shadows from the starlight (Collis, 83-84).

How that experience translated into both personal meaning and song is now, in the Denver world, the material of legend; most people who know anything about John Denver know the first verses by heart:

He was born in the summer of his twenty-seventh year,
Coming home to a place he'd never been before;
He left yesterday behind him,
You might say he was born again,
You might say he found the key to every door;

When he first came to the mountains,
His life was far away,
On the road, and hanging by a song,
But the string's already broken,
And he doesn't really care,
He keeps changing fast,
But it don't last for long,

It's a Colorado Rocky Mountain high,
I've seen it rain and fire in the sky...

The absolute thrill of discovery in the first stanza—made more redolent in the song with a particularly vibrant melody and Okun's clever addition of reverb to Denver's own voice—confirms the sense of having come into himself in a magical world, a world of wonder and beauty so vast as to be almost immeasurable (the Perseids, for example, move northeastward across the mid-summer sky, starting in Andromeda, and have, as Collis notes, a 1,000-year record of human chronicling, leaving aside the thousands of years they were surely seen and perhaps worshipped by those who left no written records). This was a true spiritual reorientation:

the ordinary conditions of Denver's life, the road, the thread of song that might make or break his career, the issues of money, of production and promotion, the materiality of his work, all spun into a context finally dominated by ultimate concerns: Denver was a spiritually immanent being in a spiritually immanent world, a transcendentalist with no Emerson behind or before him, a man both centered and infinitely wealthy. Or at least this seems to be the dominant message of the song. Yet there are those two final lines of the second stanza—the lines having to do with the singer's changes, with changes upon changes—and those can be read in more than one way. Among other things, they carry the implication that this newly-born creature may not, in fact, be fully centered, may have entered a beautiful whirlwind rather than a still point in a turning world.

What might a consequence of such a whirlwind be? One consequence, not inconsistent with Laing's observations, is profound wish-fulfillment: something is true because one believes it to be true, or because love makes it true, or because God authorizes it; something is true because one's transcendent self makes it so. It's difficult, here, not to hear the voice of a child, and not just any child, but—once again—Kathyn Harrison, encountering a Christian Science practitioner after a car accident and experiencing something seemingly good yet profoundly dislocating:

> Mysteriously, unexpectedly, this stranger ushered me into an experience of something I cannot help but call rapture. I felt myself separated from my flesh, and from all earthly things. I felt myself no more corporeal than the tremble in the air over a fire. I had no words for what happened—I never will have—and in astonishment I stopped crying. My mother sighed in relief; and I learned, at six, a truth dangerous to someone so young and so lovelorn. I saw that transcendence was possible; that spirit could conquer matter, and that therefore I could overcome whatever obstacles prevented my mother's loving me. I could overcome myself (Harrison, 106).

Rapture, the overcoming of oneself, the experience of being lovelorn and having something like a method or at least an intuition, manufactured though it might be, of how to ease one's pain—these were Harrison's experiences, and my own, but Denver had a version of them, too. Most people, including those somewhat acquainted with Denver's biography, assume either that his relationship with Annie Martell lasted until his death or that it was, at least, "long-lived," however one might want to define that. In fact, Denver met Annie in the spring of 1966 in St. Paul, Minnesota, during a gig with the Chad Mitchell trio. She was a student at Gustavus Adolphus College; however it was that she caught Denver's attention, he remembers that he "sang every song to her" that night, and ten months later, when the trio was back in the area, Denver ran into some Gustavus Adolphus students and got them to come to the concert; it was a ruse so that he could find out where Annie lived and pick her up as well. By then he was certain; at Christmas he spent time with her family in Minneapolis, and on June 27, 1967, they were married. How the marriage worked, though still largely a private subject, has clear public parameters: "Annie's Song," a melodically-beautiful if slightly trite evocation of romantic devotion, did not appear on a Denver album until the March 1974 *Back Home Again*, although a much darker song—"Good-bye Again"— in which the singer asks plaintively, "Why do we always fight/ When I have to go?" appeared on the 1972 *Rocky Mountain High* album. Clearly all was not well in Denver-land, but one of the things John Denver believed in was true love, and it was almost inconceivable to his sense of that transcendent power that something should go awry. Annie Martell, a strikingly clear-sighted woman, had this to say: "If it wasn't for the big church wedding my father gave me, I would have gotten divorced in a year. John and I didn't really know each other" (Collis, 61). Interestingly, Christine Smith, whose *Mountain in the Wind* begins with a prologue, a foreward, an introduction, an "autograph," a message from "Friends From Our Heavenly Home," and an invocation to the *Course in Miracles* before really getting into its subject, nevertheless gets the character of Denver's romantic disillusionment with vivid accuracy:

> We may, as John did, fill our hearts with love and seek
> only to share it with another, but we must never allow
> ourselves to join with anyone with a different spiritual
> consciousness. We can, and must, be willing to engage in
> relationships with others for the teaching and learning
> experience, but it is a major mistake to accept intimately

another whose heart, values, or priorities in life digress significantly from those of our own heart (Smith, 78).

Acknowledging the 50% rate of divorce in contemporary America, one would have to say that few enough of us know how to follow Smith's advice, but Denver's inability to do so did not inhere in some intuitive incapacity or crippled judgment. Rather, one might see the opposite being true: self-transcending, loving for the beauty of love and trusting love to guide him, Denver radiated a kind of warmth and compassion that many people experienced and commented on, and it would really only take one lovely person to respond in an idiosyncratic and memorable way to Denver's self-presentation to make "love" possible. But, for all her virtues, Annie Martell did not have a "heart, values, or priorities" that truly matched John's, nor did John's match hers, nor was that kind of reciprocity present with John's second wife, Cassandra Delany, whom he met in Australia in 1986.

Though many of Denver's early songs somewhat ironically focus in the fast passage of time, time for Denver from the late 1970's through the mid-1990's moved in some ways with increasing slowness: though always a popular live and television performer, his music sales were declining, and RCA, his long-time label, lost interest in his work in 1986; the humanitarian and philanthropic organization he had created to protect the world and its citizens from the depredations of no-holds-barred capitalist nations and multinational corporations, Windstar, was beginning to drain his resources. In 1982, his father died, and at one point, when Denver was away on tour, Annie cut down a grove of trees that Denver had considered integral to the house he had built for them. Even though Annie and Denver had been estranged for some years (Denver lived in the guest house on their property when he was at home), he was enraged by this destruction of nature and, beyond reason, took a chainsaw to the dining room table of Annie's house and to the bed that had been theirs; he then, by his own account, found his hands around her throat. Amazingly, Denver did no jail time for this assault, but the marriage was officially over. At about the same time, Denver ended his long association with his manager Jerry Weintraub; Denver's attentions now were increasingly on environmental, political, and philanthropic concerns, and worldwide his tours began to be seen as the work of a spiritual guardian for the planet who also happened to have been a famous singer.

But the toll of travel, the music left behind, the love lost, and the loneliness that harkened back to Denver's earliest days in Roswell or Montgomery or Austin, began to coalesce into a dark shadow from which he could not escape. When, in 1989, Cassandra—Cassie—announced that she had had enough of Denver and Aspen and was leaving—first back to Australia, then to Los Angeles—along with their daughter, Jesse Belle, the shadow took on an almost embodied form. When the divorce was final, on August 21, 1993, Denver found himself pulled over in Aspen for his first DUI. Having been born in the summer of his 27th year, he learned what many mystics know all too well: the moment of revelation is stunning; life is long and ordinary; self-transcendence can descend all too easily into self-delusion; without an inner core of true self-love, the kind of compassion that becomes a standard meditation in Buddhist practice, one can walk into the shadow of depair and occupy it as if it were one's own body. Yet how wrong, one has to say, that this should be a characteristic experience for so many lovely human beings. And how wrong that it should have happened to this dear, dear man.

* * *

A first DUI is a significant but usually not unmanageable problem for the well-heeled drinker; unless the offense is flagrant, one is likely to lose one's license for a time, receive a suspended sentence, pay about $4,000 in legal and court fees, and do community service. In Denver's case, he did a local benefit concert for Tipsy's Taxi service, which, as the name implies, takes Aspen drunks safely home.

But to the FAA, any DUI is a serious issue. If the learning curve to become a pilot is steep, the medical curve is steep as well: the FAA wants to be as certain as possible—given the limits of a large bureaucracy—that its pilots are under rational control at all times, and a DUI is clear evidence that, in at least one instance, someone qualified as a pilot was impaired emotionally, intellectually, and bodily. Pilots are required to report DUI's to the FAA or risk license revocation, fines, or jail; the FAA also cross-references its computers to crime data sources around the country, looking for matches between pilots' Social Security numbers and the Social

Security numbers of DUI's. Thus, on October 18, 1995 (evidence that the FAA's wheels do grind slowly, though exceeding fine), The FAA insisted that Denver's "continued airman medical certificate certification remains contigent upon your total abstinence for use of alcohol" (NTSB, 2). There seems to have been some disagreement between the FAA and Denver's own FAA Medical Examiner, Dr. H. C. Whitcomb, Jr., who apparently protested the severity of this decision; Dr. Whitcomb went so far as to write to the FAA that Denver "in general averages two to four drinks of either wine or beer/week when he's traveling," and asserted that this did not constitute an abuse of alcohol (NTSB, 2). But such an assertion cut no ice with the FAA. Thus, when Dr. Whitcomb re-issued Denver's third-class medical certificate on June 13, 1996, for another three years, the FAA Civil Aeromedical Certification Division sent Dr. Whitcomb and Denver a letter by certified mail, dated November 6, 1996, noting that Denver had failed to fulfill the earlier FAA requirements to abstain from alcohol and thus requiring him to surrender his medical certificate—essentially ending his career as a pilot. That letter, as it turned out, was returned unopened to the FAA on December 2, 1996, and it is unclear whether Denver knew of its existence. But the FAA sent a second letter on March 25, 1997, again notifying him that he was "medically disqualified" as a pilot; that letter made it to Denver's residence, where someone did in fact sign for it, although, as the National Transportation Safety Board noted, "the signature of the person who signed for it was illegible" (NTSB, 2).

It does seem likely that, by March 1997, Denver knew that a clock was running on the one thing he most loved to do, the one thing that had brought him a kind of rapture from the start and had never disappointed him—unlike Annie, or Cassie, or his music which, despite his various interviews in which he describes his pleasure in his songs, did not grow into the kind of *oeuvre* that would have made *Poems, Prayers and Promises* a stepping stone to something greater. Whether or not Denver had seen the letters from the FAA, he would have known that they would have known about his DUI—by then, there was a second DUI, in 1994, and while Denver had plea-bargained the first, he was set to go to trial on the second DUI in January 1998. However one attempts to imagine Denver's state of mind, there is no question that he understood the court case— whether it led to massive fines, a permanent loss of his driver's license, or jail time—meant the end of his flying career. Though still performing worldwide, recently back from a European tour in the summer of 1997, still speaking out vigorously on behalf of the environment, on the need to restrain rapacious, profit-driven destruction of species, habitat, and the homes of indigenous populations, befriending the world and earning profound thanks form activists worldwide, Denver was tired, and in the back of his mind the shadow of all that he could not be—a version of the famous lines from "The Eagle and the Hawk"—was troubling the waters of his being. Knowing, as he did, that alcoholism ran in the family, that it tended to grow quietly and steadily over time until it was suddenly out of control, and knowing as well that it was characterized by multiple relapses, regardless of in- or out-patient treatments, AA, or other support groups, Denver clearly was struggling to find a medium, a bare mastery over a demon that, for most people in its grip, resists control. Although, in his March 22, 1996 letter to the FAA, Dr. Whitcomb stated that "in general, [Denver] has done remarkably well... .The patient seems very happy and balanced at this stage of his life" (NTSB, 7-8), Denver himself knew more than a year later that changes were in the wind that he himself could not control. And those changes would change one of his central identities, the one perhaps with the most permeable boundaries between inner and disguise—the identity of flight:

> I am an eagle who lives in high mountains,
> In rocky cathedrals I reach for the sky,
> I am the hawk and there's blood on my feathers,
> But time is still turning, they soon will be dry,
>
> And all those who see me, and all who believe in me,
> Share in the freedom I feel when I fly.

After January 1998, the man might sing this song again, many times, but he would not be able to live it. January 1998 was the date for John Denver's execution, though it may well have been that he alone saw how, at that point, the axe would fall.

* * *

By 1997, Cassie Delany and Jesse Belle had settled in Monterey, California, and Denver had a second home there to make it more possible for him to spend time with his daughter. It was an imperfect solution in an imperfect world, but there were compensations. On the afternoon of October 12, 1997, Denver played a five-hole round of golf with two old friends, Red Dodge and Bill Twist; he told them he was in a hurry to "try out his new plane," but would meet up with them for dinner afterwards. Dodge and Twist eventually went off to dinner, still unaware of why their old friend never showed.

Arriving at the Monterey Peninsula Airport a little before 5 P.M., Denver borrowed a fuel sump tester from the ground technician who helped him pull the plane from the hangar. He then reached under the wings, pressing the sump tester against a small valve that releases a tiny bit of fuel into the basin of the tester. The check is for contaminants: water, the most common problem, weighs more than aircraft fuel, and thus floats to the bottom of the sump; it's easily visible. Indeed, most of the pre-flight checks that pilot does have to do with fairly obvious things that usually are just fine, but every now and then are not: one checks the engine oil, for example, to make sure it's the correct quantity and also (if one is especially careful) the correct scent; contaminated engine oil, or oil that's had something added to it, will smell and feel different on the dipstick. One checks around the landing gear (in the case of the Long-EZ it would only have been the front gear) for hydraulic fluid leaks; one checks the leading edge of the wing, and all wing surfaces, for serious nicks, scrapes, or other damage that might affect the airfoil; one checks the stall indicator; one actually stands back and looks at the whole aircraft from the front just to make sure that some prior hard landing hasn't bent the airframe; one checks the propeller for nicks and scrapes that could conceivably cause the propeller to shatter in flight, given its very high RPM's along the outer edges. Different aircraft require various different preflight check procedures, of course, but Denver's plane was consistent with most small aircraft in that it demanded attention to fuel quantity, fuel contamination, engine oil, airfoil cleanness, propeller smoothness, and flight controls that moved freely, without binding or stopping short of their design limit. Normally Denver would have attended to all of these relatively small number of details. Why he did not depends on how you imagine the nature of his growing shadow, like a kind of glaucoma in its early stages, obscuring one's vision at unpredictable and inexplicable moments.

One thing that Denver did attend to, interestingly—something that was not part of the pre-flight checklist—was the new fuel selector handle behind his left shoulder. Discussing its inaccessibility with the ground technician, Denver borrowed a pair of Vise-Grip pliers and tried to attach them to the handle, giving him a bit of extra reach but also violating an FAA rule against design changes without a TSO (technical service order). As it turned, the Vise-Grips didn't work anyway, and Denver mentioned to the tech that, if he had to change fuel tanks in flight, he'd flip on the autopilot to keep the wings level while turning around to deal with the fuel (NTSB, 1). Though the NTSB says nothing about this, and the tech only remembers that the fuel selector handle was "in the vertical position" (NTSB, 1), the use of the Vise-Grips suggests that the handle was in the straight-down position—the position where it would be most evident whether the grips were going to provide sufficient or reliable extension to the handle. In the Long, the down position means that fuel is flowing from the right tank, the tank that probably had no more than three gallons of fuel left.

Nothing is drilled into a pilot's head more frequently than the adage: "check your fuel before every flight." The rationale is simple: if you run out of gas in a car, you coast to a gas station or pull over and wait for AAA. There are, as comical—or, rather, as stupid—as it sounds, no gas stations in the air. Denver's failure to check his fuel before takeoff is the one detail that leaves pilots most perplexed, especially since he himself had flown the plane in from Santa Maria the day before and knew that it hadn't been refueled since then. The most likely explanation is that he actually did not realize that his Long had the larger engine, with twice the fuel burn of planes with standard Continental or Lycoming engines; his ensuing confidence in the amount of fuel left, however, does not explain his failure to perform two of the key pre-flight checks (he also failed to check the engine oil). What makes more sense is the thread that runs from the beginning of Denver's music to the cathedral mountains of his most shielded heart—the rapture, the intimacy of the air, and the illusion of the Long as a kind of aerobatic powered glider, making a human into something like an eagle or a hawk. By October 12, there was so much for Denver to leave behind, so many "dreams I can't remember now, hopes that I've forgotten, faded memories," and the inescapable curse of the future: rise above it. Rise above it. That was the October 12 mission. It was only supposed to last for an hour, and indeed Denver gave the Monterey tower no indication that he planned to leave the area just off the coast reserved for practicing turns, climbs, stalls, and other maneuvers. The October 12 mission was a meditation, a private affirmation of all that Denver loved in his inner self apart from the predations of a world that could be almost unbearably dark. It wasn't a mission that needed fuel. It was a mission that needed heart.

As in *Jonathan Livingston Seagull*, the rapture of flight is a complex interweaving of release and control. At the Monterey airport, a major regional airport with "Class C" airspace (the FAA's third most tightly-supervised airspace designation), Denver first had to do several cockpit checklist items, which it appeared that he did—the ground tech noticed that Denver's preflight "included checking the operation of the control surfaces" (NTSB, 1)—and then had to radio ground control for permission to taxi for takeoff; that communication would also have included Denver's request for a series of touch-and-go landings, and ground would have responded by giving Denver a four-digit transponder code (a radar code) for his aircraft, and instructions to taxi and hold for takeoff at a specific runway, along with the tower frequency for that departure, wind conditions, and possibly some additional information, all conveyed in a kind of pilot's shorthand at a rapid rate. Denver would have been required both to note all of this information on a noteboard that he probably strapped to his right knee, and would have been required to give an accurate readback to ground; there's no evidence of any abnormality in his execution of these procedures. Clearly, at this moment on this day, he was the pilot in command.

At some point during all of this, Denver had started the Lycoming 0-320; it quit before he received clearance to taxi. Noticing the abrupt absence of engine noise, the ground tech came back out from the hangar to see if Denver needed help. It was Denver's last chance. The ground tech noticed that Denver turned to the left and appeared to change the position of the fuel selector; he then restarted the engine and indicated no need for further help. At that point, assuming he actually managed to switch the selector to the left tank, he had a little less than half-an-hour of fuel left.

Taxiing, takeoff, and landing all take time; takeoffs and landings are especially demanding on fuel, as throttle positions change to accommodate various exigencies during landing and then go full-forward for a touch-and-go. Seven minutes elapsed between the time when Denver was cleared to taxi from the hanger, at 5:02 Pacific Standard Time, to 5:09, when he announced he was ready for departure and holding at Runway 28. Air Traffic Control held him at idle for three more minutes, clearing him for takeoff at 5:12, and Denver stayed in the pattern for three touch-and-go landings "before departing the traffic pattern at about 1727" [5:27 P.M.] (NTSB, 1). Nothing in Denver's radio transmissions or flight behavior during that time show anything out of the ordinary; the only glitch seemed to be with the transponder, a not-uncommon problem; ATC seemed to be having trouble reading Denver's radar identification code, and asked him to recycle the transponder; his last recorded words, at 5:28:06, were, "Do you have those numbers now?" At that point, Denver had left the airport traffic pattern, following the westerly runway heading of 28 (280 degrees, slightly north of west) and was heading out over Monterey Bay for some maneuvers. His six gallons of fuel were gone.

The FAA interviewed twenty witnesses to the crash. Attorneys and others familiar with crash scene investigations note an unusual unanimity among the stories of the witnesses. Of the four witnesses who actually saw the entire event, all four perceived the Long to be heading west, at between 350 and 500 feet above sea level, when it entered a steep right bank (to the north); "twelve [other] witnesses saw the airplane in a steep nose-down descent, and six of them saw the airplane hit the water.... Eight of the witnesses said that they heard a 'pop' or 'backfire,' along with a reduction in the engine noise level just before the airplane descended into the water" (NTSB, 1-2).

It was, as crashes go, a crash without a mystery—or almost without one. Clearly, having run out of fuel at a low altitude, too low to have time to set the autopilot, Denver quickly turned to his left, inadvertently pushing down on the right rudder pedal for leverage in exactly the way the two previous Long-EZ pilots had done; their survival was due to altitude, luck, or both, and Denver had at this point neither altitude nor luck. His sharp right jab on the rudder turned the plane sharply to the right but also, at low speed, caused the right wing to stall and force the plane into an uncontrollable descent to the right. From the moment of the first "pop" or "backfire" to the moment the plane hit the water, perhaps seven to 12 seconds passed; in that time, Denver would have clearly realized the seriousness of the situation but might also have been disoriented from the quickness of his turn, the plane's own sudden turn and fall in the opposite direction, and the astonishing sensory perception of a huge body of water coming at him at high speed; the inclination would not be to marvel or even to feel fear, but simply to observe, to see without necessarily grasping what was being seen. In her study of trauma—*Unclaimed Experience: Trauma, Narrative, and History*—Cathy Caruth observes that one characteristic of trauma survivors, particularly those who suffer from post-traumatic stress disorder, is their inability to be present at the actual moment of trauma, though they may relieve in nightmares or debilitating flashbacks. It's unlikely that Denver had more than a fraction of an instant, if that much, to realize he was slamming into the fatal limit of his own miraculous and literally crushing life.

The one mystery of the crash, the kind of detail that lingers in archives where ghosts live, is the position of the fuel selector valve: when recovered, it was in an intermediate position, about half-open to the right fuel tank supply line and about two-to-four percent open to the left tank supply line. This might seem to invalidate the theory that Denver had started on the right tank, run out of fuel on the ground, and tried to switch to the left tank; on the other hand, the fuel selector handle was sufficiently mysterious and difficult to reach that it's unclear whether Denver knew which tank he was on. Furthermore, investigators discovered that, because of its intermediate position, the fuel handle selection would have caused a vapor lock in the engine if one of the tanks was dry, even if some fuel remained in the other tank (NTSB, 7). Whether Denver did have a small amount of fuel left or not, he sealed his fate when he moved the fuel selector handle to a position that was neither one way nor the other. But then, that was essentially the position of his entire life at that moment, at that moment.

* * *

My oldest son, Nate, now attends Colorado College in Colorado Springs, near Pikes Peak, and though finances permit my trips there to be less frequent than I would like, I see him, and his Rocky Mountain world, three or four times a year. Though Nate has little patience for Denver's music, it's in the car with me when I drive: coming through the highlands of western Nebraska to the wild ranch country of eastern Colorado, climbing up and up slowly until the whole front range of the Rockies suddenly comes into view, I listen to the years of Denver's best music, the years that were also, in some ways, the best years of my life, but also the most volatile, the most desperate, the most hopeful—adolescence, early adulthood, and a kind of trick of time, like an invisible bridge, into the present, whose years are as volatile as those earlier ones yet with such differences as I look at myself in the mirror. I am old. But the music is not, and within the music I am the seventeen-year-old, trying to imagine what it might be like to be born in the summer of one's 27th year, what it might be like to "find the key to every door." When lives on this earth reach their end, it is inevitable that people should summarize, although some wisdom traditions dismiss such summaries as superfluous, since the life itself goes on and on; still, to me, a summarizer, it seems extraordinary to have known, once in one's life, what it was like to be reborn, to come home "to a place he'd never been before." In a geographic sense, California was much like that—I had the sense, moving there as a 13-year-old, that I finally had found a home, after the drear drudgery and darkness of the Pennsylvania years. But to be released into a whole new life: well, in some ways that was the promise of Christian Science, releasing all of us who believed into the full spiritual reality of God's creation, releasing us as well from the illusory limits of this world. Though I was a believer, no such revelation came to me, or has yet come. But I hear it in Denver's voice—the utter thrill of it, the pure and confident delight. Different things tend to amaze older and younger people, but it does amaze me, after all these years, that nothing in that voice or the reality it affirms has changed: for some people, including Denver, no matter how far down his life descended in its varying degrees of darkness, some underlying faith came from a moment of true revelation, a divine gift.

It is peculiar, thinking of his last years and the moment of his death— and the sense of loss among a wide group of friends, environmental and political activists, musicians, philanthropists, and ordinary fans like me, probably a wider group than Denver himself imagined, drawing together after his death for tributes and concerts (Collis, 167-174). Surely in this chronicle the route toward loss begins to look fatal some years before the end comes, and any biographical essayist's mind inevitably weighs the signs of what might have been a saving grace against the signs of a downward spiral that nothing seemed able to arrest. Yet, in a different context—writing about Sylvia Plath and Ted Hughes—the biographer Diane Middlebrook makes an arresting statement at just about the moment in her book when one is beginning to feel the shadow of doom starting to spread:

> Their story is forever simplifying itself into a tragedy and rushing toward its horrible ending, a process to which Ted Hughes gave a strong push in the fatalistic narrative of *Birthday Letters*...But we, the heirs of their work, can now observe that—aside from their lives—nothing *ended!* *(Middlebrook, 86)*

In one sense, it's hard to escape a certain echo of implicit cruelty in the phrase "aside from their lives"—after all, for most of us, what else is there? If the life doesn't work, and doesn't work, and doesn't work, what in the world is it? A curse from God? A monstrous neurobiological nightmare? A coalition of poorly-related behavioral failures? What? Surely something to be rid of, unless, as Yeats said, "Soul clap its hands and sing, / And louder sing for every tatter of its mortal dress": yes, with that possibility, remote though it may be, who would be so quick to choose death? Who would be so cavalier as to dismiss the lives themselves? But Middlebrook's point is an important one when dealing with any act of creation, whether artistic or scientific: the creation does not end when the creator's life ends. It continues with whatever influence it instantly acquired in the moment of its ingenious birth, surrounded by the accumulated associations of each different generation. Most readers of "serious" literature or fans of musical genres that exclude "folk-pop" would no doubt feel a certain discomfort with a paragraph in which Plath, Hughes, Yeats—and John Denver—somehow wind up yoked together. But the yoking is an act of the spirit, not primarily an aesthetic judgment. Nothing ended. Denver knew and sang of something that outlives him, as Plath, Hughes, and Yeats in quite different ways somehow came around, in single moments, to a visionary's road. The curious thing about visionary roads is that one never really knows where they will lead, how far they will carry one, or how, through carelessness or excessive devotion, one may step off the very path that affirms everything one hoped to be true about life. Or, indeed—as is the case for Plath, though that is another story, and in a more muted way was the case for Denver—the visionary road had a dark and obsessive doppelganger, a force driving the artist away rather than toward resolution. Everyone, it seems—except those little-known mystics in unexceptional places around the globe, alive always to the path—steps off at some point, and drops back down to the fierce hard ocean of final impact, to the transition that, for most of us, is unthinkably hard.

Yet I would be lying if I dismissed the audible, translucent presence of a past at once beautiful and immortal that accompanies me on my own darkened journey where, among the shards of dreams and "hopes that I've forgotten," is the rapture implicit in every measure of a young man's song.

Epilogue: Keeping Watch

Last and First Words

Given all the deaths and dislocations in my childhood family, it's curious that my mother not only remembered my first words but mentioned them to me repeatedly as a curiosity. Most children say some version of "Mama" or "Dada" as they try syllabic symbolism for the first time, but I apparently was different. "You didn't say anything for a long time," my mother said once in her longest exposition of the subject. "We were beginning to worry about you. And then all of a sudden one day you said, 'Bessie's cat.'"

Bessie Hoopes was a very old woman who lived next door, the wife of the man who had sold us our old Pennsylvanian house (in one of the world's lovely verbal ironies, Mr. Hoopes ran the last wooden-wheel factory and wooden-barrel factory in the nation, selling his wares, of course, to the Amish and the Mennonites). Bessie, who must have been over 80 by the time I was three, used to like to sit out on her front porch in the spring, summer, and fall, and pet her numerous cats as they climbed on or off her lap or bushed against her ankles. My first adventures in life, or at least the first happy ones, were to go visit her, where—once "Bessie's cat" emerged as a phrase—other phrases came rapidly. It may true that I learned to talk, not from whatever current upheaval was taking place at home, but from the quiet moments on Bessie's porch. Unlike my family, she seemed quite fully rooted in who and what she was, although I clearly could not have explained this as a child, but it was something I knew and paid attention to. I also knew that she was not well, and I wondered about that.

One day, when I came back from her house, my mother greeted me at the door with a memorably angry face. "You are *never* to ask someone when she is going to die, Thomas Simmons, do you understand that? That is a terrible thing to ask someone." Bursting into tears, I fled to my room and locked the door, as I did when I was profoundly upset, but what upset me primarily, of course, was that I did not know what had gone wrong. This would be the hallmark of my childhood, but it seemed to me quite normal to want to know if people, who obviously did die no matter what my Sunday School told me, knew they were going to die, and Bessie looked like someone who might know. Curious, I had indeed asked her that afternoon whether she was going to die, and she laughed and laughed and said, yes, sometime soon, but not today. Ironically, Bessie found the question so charming that she called my mother to tell her about it; it was my mother who, misunderstanding the moment as she often did, felt a horrible embarrassment and translated it into rage toward me.

After that I was told that I couldn't "pester" Bessie any more, although I'm quite sure no one told Bessie why I would no longer set foot on her porch, and I sometimes think that—as I waved to her from the front yard, and she invited me over for milk and homemade sugar cookies, and I, having been taught to dissemble early, said, no, I have to go inside now, and did that—Bessie must have been quite wounded, and must have felt keenly whatever aloneness she was sensing as death approached, and I'm sure she missed our talks, as I did, for she was the only person I had really talked to, the only person who seemed to know the give-and-take of talk, who didn't instruct, expound, or read from the Bible, who answered questions when I asked them. And then, quite soon, she was dead.

* * *

This book, despite its widely varied subjects, extends from one core irony: that I, who was tortured as a child by a religion that promised to heal me of all "sin, disease, and death" and yet left me in chronic pain and misery, with only the rarest access to simple medical treatments, should now, as an adult, be tortured by a medical community that cannot bring its combined wisdom and skill to heal the combined physiological and psychological ravages of long-term depression. When my first book on Christian Science, *The Unseen Shore*, came out, I received, not unsurprisingly, considerable hate mail from Christian Scientists who promised that my backsliding would unleash furies of destruction upon me, and I have often thought, as my subsequent work has appeared, that they must rest content now that their imprecations were fulfilled, the furies were unleashed, and the disloyal subject, however much he had been crippled and wounded by his earlier loyalty, was now in the grip of hell. Surely there are many parts of this book, especially the "Foreward" and "Alone,"that will make them feel their prayers against the "enemies" of the Christian Science church have been answered. For the rest—the doctors, occasional therapists, and psychiatrists —the enormous bills come in and come in and come in, and I pay a little as I can, over time, deeply indebted despite insurance (which is legendarily inadequate in this country with regard to mental health) to the very people who do not heal me. If I were a vengeful fury, I know exactly who would be the recipients of that vengeance; ironically, though I suspect the doctors know it, too, and for those with any real compassion it may cause them some sleepless nights. I doubt, however, that a single devout Christian Scientist really cares about the human destruction done in the name of that religion or realizes that even the outcasts pray, and pray, if not for vengeance, then at least for justice, and subsequently for forgiveness for all.

When the surfaces of one's life contain such remarkable bleakness, however, and the psychological shadows seem themselves old and tired from interrogation, one has the option of looking for a different kind of shadow, the shadow of "the subject" and certain Biblical, Islamic, and Buddhist ideas about how the "I" speaking at any time, including the "I" speaking throughout this book, is not necessarily synonymous with the true or deep identity of the speaker. One could begin intellectually, as I might given my background, and note the numerous conflicting arguments about "the subject" in contemporary literature and philosophy: certain feminists, for example, argue that "the subject" is a Cartesian leftover, a fundamental duality masking an intuitive interpolation of imperialism, and that only understanding the complexity of the Other, the denied subject, will bring one around to anything like self-understanding; post-colonial theorists argue a version of this as well. But it interests me that shadows of this idea—the mutability of the subject—inhabit peculiar literatures, works of art on the cusp of international upheaval, such as most of Jorge Luis Borges' fiction, nonfiction, and poems. In "The Other," for example, the older Borges meets the younger Borges on a bench by the river in Cambridge, Massachusetts, and neither is quite sure which is real; in the end, for idiosyncratic reasons, the narrator suggests that the older Borges was merely the dream of the younger man, but what does this say about the narrator, who started as the older Borges? He has effectively vanished, become something other than either the subject or the speaker of his story; his identity lies outside. If much of Borges' work seems constructed with an element of fear and loathing—the fear of labyrinths, mirrors, repetitions, even the idea of the self—the substratum of Borges' work is the principle that the disappearing narrator is safe somewhere, preferably somewhere inaccessible except to the "Archetypes and Splendors" of God, as Borges writes in his poem "Everness," beautifully translated by Richard Wilbur. One learns, then, as an afficionado of Borges, not to value the apparent self too highly; one learns as well to listen back through one's life for peculiar echoes—"Be still, and know that I am God," or "Thou wast with me before the foundations of the world"—as ways of remembering that the cosmic scale is almost immeasurably great, and it is within this scale, of which our earthly conditions are but a speck and an aberration, that we are protected, uplifted, and known.

An intellectual approach. Could one bring it down to a matter of the heart, a meditation on the ecstasy of the Imagination, which—as Henry Corbin explains in *Spiritual Body and Celestial Earth*—is both accessible to us and is the very medium by which we first come to know the presence of a "supersensory zone," an "imaginal world" which is neither fully material or fully spiritual, yet the antichamber to the spirit, populated by human initiates and by their angels, an affirmation of all the promises one reads textually in the Bible or the Qu'ran? Perhaps...or one could move in a slightly different direction, meditating not in ecstasy but in quiet over the path of the Buddha and his Tibetan adept Padma Sambhava, whose sources of teaching release one from the illusions of the everyday and offer an emptiness, a pure release from ordinary identity, which ironically makes one both more generous and more able to accept generosity, more compassionate and able to accept compassion. I work with both of these traditions now, yet have to say that, whenever I move into them, I am left with a pang of loss—not the *dukha*, the dissatisfaction, of the Buddha's first "Noble Teaching," but rather the sense of not having had a chance to be what most people in this world are at birth: a creature. I miss my creatureliness; I miss the buffer, the gentleness and compassion, with which Buddhists treat their young, understanding that revealing too much of the teachings too soon can be damaging; no one in Christian Science seemed to realize that they were pouring napalm on the bodies and souls of their most devout children. I miss the chance to have been a little boy, for as a little boy I was always escaping—into vast cities I built on the floor of my room, into books, into worlds I knew within my own mind, and later, when I was slightly older, into the miles of backwaters behind Seven Mile Beach in New Jersey, where I would take my small boat at eight in the morning and not return until nightfall, and no one seemed to miss me. I miss seeing what I saw, and knowing now what I knew then, but also knowing that, then, I was already teaching myself not to believe what I saw or felt, not to trust my senses or instincts, not to be who I was. As Anne Sexton says in a different context, some people have the same language for certain kinds of things—they always ask "which tools," she writes; they never ask "why build?"—and this, ironically, was entirely true of Christian Science. But the underside of that method left me, at times, wondering "which tools" in a way Sexton would have understood, when I should have been asking "why build?"

And so, here, in this book-without-an-ending—for that is how I think of it, the one book I have published of five so far that cannot really conclude, because it alone cuts close enough to the pure truth to make the end unforseeable—I would like to add one of the first essays I ever published in a major magazine, about a cat, as it turned out. I wrote the essay in the small humanities center for graduate students in Bancroft Library at the University of California, Berkeley, in 1983; I was waiting for my then-wife Lesley to finish up some work elsewhere on campus, I had about 45 minutes to kill, no desire at the time to read any of the millions of available books, and some old thoughts about a cat who had died in an odd way. The essay first appeared a couple of years later in *California Living*, which was then the Sunday magazine for the *San Francisco Chronicle and Examiner*; it caught enough attention that Gary Soto chose it for his 1988 anthology *California Childhood*, although, ironically, the events in the first half of the essay occurred in Pennsylvania. The essay is now 22 years old, unbelievably (if one is a writer, one sometimes dates one's writings as if they were children, for writings, too, grow old, although they do not age); unbelievably, it is as old as my teaching career, which, had it been simply words on a page, would no doubt have been much more successful. As an essay, it is still the best piece of writing I have done on what it might mean to be a human creature, and how, despite trying over the past 22 years, I still find the process elusive.

* * *

Once, when I was a child, our cat Siddhartha disappeared. I knew that he had injured himself a few days earlier when he tried to leap from a tree branch to my parents' third-story bedroom window. I did not see him fall to the ground, but I did see him shortly afterward, running sideways with an odd and slightly horrible awkwardness. He stayed near the house for several days, more or less eating, more or less all right. Then he vanished.

In an unusual moment of candor, my father explained to me that Siddhartha had probably gone away to die. Something inside him told him he couldn't survive, my father said, and he wanted to go where people wouldn't pester him by trying to help. The explanation astonished me. It had never occurred to me that a living being, a cat or even a person, might sense that it was time to die. My mother was devoutly religious, believing in her heart what my father only professed, and she belonged to a religion that asserted the unreality of death. My first taste of religion came through her: she told me that I was spiritual, not material, and that when people left the earth, they didn't really die; it just seemed that way to us, though we could learn to know better. I'm not sure if, at the age of four or five, I really had any conception of "spiritual" or "material." The world was still whole to me, a welter of experience not yet forced into theological categories. Yet I had already begun to sense that fatal anxiety of things not being as they should be. I had been born into a world that was playing a nasty trick on me. In Sunday School I was told that I had to protect myself from this illusion. But this was not always easy.

I remember, for example, when my grandfather—my father's father—died. I was perhaps six. My father cried during and after the funeral, although he tried not to. My mother remained impassive—though perhaps slightly solicitous toward me—and reminded me that death was something that only *seemed* real. In reality, she said, the perfect identity of my grandfather was eternal. What that meant, she explained, was that he was still alive, although we couldn't see or hear him. As I talked with my mother about this, I glanced frequently toward my father, whose tears awed me. I had no idea what to say to him. Yet I felt the greatest sympathy for him, as he clearly summoned all his husbandly devotion to support, with his silence, my mother's authority.

When, a couple of years later, my father explained to me about our cat, I again felt a rush of sympathy for him—and, oddly, of gratitude. There was something unexpectedly comforting about the view of the world that his explanation implied. Somewhere in himself he knew that no tricks were being played: creatures did what they did from an instinct deeper than fear, from a kind of intelligence at once simpler and more profound than the Mind I was introduced to in Sunday School. His words soothed my sense of loss; I was almost happy. A day or two later he came into the yard with Siddhartha's matted body, which he had found by a hedge while walking the dog. He buried him right there. My mother came out later and, in line with some superstitions which she admitted to having and refused to relinquish, did a little ritual of Christian burial which she herself had created.

Siddhartha's instinct to die alone, as explained by my father, came back to mind about twenty years later, when my mother had grown incurably ill. We were, of course, not supposed to admit her incurability. She had spent so much of her life denying the reality of whatever was animal or material that my father, brother, sister and I were all supposed to be ready to witness her own great realization of her spiritual being, which would also restore her "temple," her body. But I was not to be preached to—nor were my brother or sister. We knew we were witnessing the ravages of cancer, and before that solemn pain we held to our sense of the real—real pain, real love, a depth of feeling that moved from my mother's shrunken body to the blessed fact of our own corporeal existence. What astonished us, however, was my mother's slowly increasing, unmistakable desire to die alone. At first she would tell us what ideas and encouragement the practitioners were giving to heal her. Then she began, so gradually, to complain: how these practitioners would not come to visit her but only talked to her over the telephone, how their ideas were trite or simpleminded, their prayers ineffectual. Then she refused to discuss her faith at all. Finally, when it had become difficult for her to speak, and to lift the telephone receiver, she announced without a trace of either pride or sadness that she now refused to talk to the practitioners when they called. After that, she said very little. For a couple of months my new wife Lesley and I sat regularly in her room, occasionally speaking, earning silence in return. On our next-to-last visit to her, when we arrived, she suddenly pointed, in an act of almost scorching clarity, to the full moon outside the window. From then on she acknowledged no one.

I have never gotten over how this woman, so attuned to the world as illusion, and this cat, utterly absorbed in an instinctual world in which illusion cannot be conceived, should die the same death. My mother was a crusader for the spirit; in her healthy years, had someone suggested that she would want to die the way her animals died, she would certainly have scoffed. In both these deaths—but of course most obviously in my mother's, since it was hers that brought me to these thoughts—a terrible affirmation staked out its claim: the dying took place in defiance of all our strategies for smoothing the transition from the known to the unknown. We who were alive, who might have wished to comfort the dying as a solace for our own souls, were banished: the lines of communion between the dying person, the dying animal, and death, were infuriatingly intimate and profound. They left us speechless even at an enforced distance, from which we might have been expected to pass judgment.

Yet, after the initial shock, even our speechlessness became a kind of comfort. There was a point beyond which—for us, as for my mother— the language of wretched theorizing and solemn dogmatism could not go. There was a time when we could say, with the full authority of the heart, this death is not illusion; this communion between the dying and death is not some metaphysical sleight of the hand. There was no room for euphemism or clever jargon; this death guaranteed at least one taste of what was real. Though our whole intelligence resisted it, it was there. It was the fundamental instinct resolving itself into a kind of pure presence—cat and prey, cat leaping, sheer experience which no external portrait can capture.

Animals crawl toward the privacy of their death from this instinct. I believe that my mother, too, was finally in the hands of this fundamental directive, so much more powerful and straightforward than the spirituality she preached to us, and had preached to her. The heresy that my father once confided to me, regarding the seemingly small matter of a cat, became at last my mother's faith—or, I find myself hoping, something simpler: a way, a quality of light, a full moon in the dark sky.

* * *

As a name for a cat, "Siddhartha" hardly connotes anything as much as the spirit, the emotional climate, of the late 1960's in America. My brother, of course, had named him; my brother had also named two of our other kittens CORE (for "Congress of Racial Equality") and SNCC (for "Student Nonviolent Coordinating Committee"), primarily because both of them were black and white. A witty young man, my brother, though with an undercurrent of rage that would make its own book. Still, even as a child, I knew the story of Gautama, who finally released himself to the depths of his disenchantment with samsara and became, at the edge of death and life, the Buddha, the Awakened one; and I knew Herman Hesse's story of Siddhartha, who in the depths of his own darkness heard the universal syllable of love, "OM," and moved progressively toward the vision of the universe that would, in the end, bring his dear friend Govinda such comfort in their apparent old age. These stories, part of the counter-culture of the sixties, were also part of my vocabulary early on, a rather odd yet not unallied narrative around the intrinsic narrative of Christian Science.

Yet, in my world, however one described it from a ten-year-old's point of view—as divided between real "spirit" and unreal but seemingly real "matter," as divided between perception and reality, as full of immediate sensual truth in complete conflict with my religion, and full as well of longing, hurt, and loss—one fact remained: a cat that I loved had fallen, inexplicably, in his routine jump from a high window to a tree, and had died a few days later. The only consolation lay in my father's words about the intrinsic reality of this creation, vying in its power against whatever I

217

had absorbed from Sunday School. At some level, it was permissible to be a creature. But this did not necessarily mean that one would reach what some might consider the happy ending of *Siddhartha*.

A seeming eternity ago, by my standards as a writer, I began this book with an essay on loss, on dreams, and on the idea, now rarely discussed in intellectual circles, of "authenticity." And as I struggle to find a shape for this book that has dwelled so much on stubbornness in the face of intractable illness, it occurs to me that, as much as I love my old essay on the cat Siddhartha, there may be a potentially fatal flaw in the writing. The essay avers that my father told me about the rightness of Siddhartha's death...but in the years since that essay first appeared, I have found myself listening to the voice of my father's explanation, the words he used that I remembered, and now it strikes me that those words are not the words of my father: he would never have said "pestered," for example, nor would he have been quite so amorphous in his explanation that something within Siddhartha told him it was time to die. No: all these years later, in this—the first essay that began to bring me regional and then national notoriety as a writer—the key players are reversed. It was, I believe, my mother who explained to me that Siddhartha needed to die. Those are her words that I heard under the old pine tree by the house—not my father's. It was that extraordinary crack in my mother's faith, that rare revelation of true humanity in the face of Christian Science dogma, that emerged because she saw how sad I was, and because, I think, she herself remembered how she had punished me for asking when our neighbor would die, and saw, years later, that death was something I desperately needed to understand. In its own way, of course, this created more problems than solutions, because it meant that my mother's life had a subterranean current, a truth counter to Christian Science to which I had almost no access: I would never know when the lies would fall away, and for a brief moment, some vivid truth would emerge. I lived my life in part out of hope for those crumbs of truth. I think now, perhaps, that the profound and enduring sadness of chronic depression has to do with this unfinished ending between us, this inability on her part to speak to me plainly, the way she lived in those six years of her life in Georgia before beginning sold into the bondage of Christian Science up north, and my inability or fear of asking, because as a child I knew the response would be predictable and the punishment swift if I deviated from the doctrinal norm. There was an unfinished healing between my mother and me that defied *Siddhartha*, Christian Science doctrine, the idea of samsara and release from samsara, and every other construct for the ordinary reality of human life, in order to say simply: we are here and I love you. That would have been enough.

To acknowledge that loss, however, brings me back around to dreams, and to the dreams I have been having lately, as I sense this book drawing to a close. They have been particularly vivid and disturbing. In one, my father is throwing a huge party, to which I am neither invited nor disinvited; I am simply there. My father is serving alcohol to everyone; everyone, including him, is completely drunk—everyone, that is, except me (an interesting and somewhat ironic detail, although characteristic of my ascetic youth). As the party continues, and I try to speak to my father, to take him aside and ask what's going on, he not only brushes me off; he simply doesn't register my presence at all. And it suddenly occurs to me that this man is so enraged with life, is so enraged with having had children, that he must deny them absolutely, must drink them away. As he does so, I become aware that, in the dream, I am beginning to shimmer, as if I no longer exist. My first wife arrives, miraculously, to take me away, but her pull is not strong enough, and the dream and my own life fade together into a blankness that shifts suddenly to an elevator without a shaft: I am standing on top of a device that is going up and up and up, meteorically, and all the floors where we're not stopping are floors of distinction: universities, books, doctorates, classrooms. The only thing I know, as we rise higher and higher, is that we are going absolutely in the wrong direction, and what I most need is to go down: if we go much higher I will cease to exist. The craving to reverse direction, to go down into the darkness that I know constitutes the origin of this ascending vehicle, is overwhelming. But just as I find myself praying for release, I hear the voices of those at the upper level, assuring me that I am welcome, that my books and teaching and intellectual presence are exactly where they should be. And all I know is that they are completely wrong.

Desolation. These are dreams of desolation, but within each is what William Stafford called the line of the authentic, the thing that interests us. I understand now, as I did not at the outset of this book, that my father hated me, hated my brother and sister, hated marriage and family and the world that transformed his life during and after World War II. Whether he himself was a victim of post-traumatic stress disorder, depression, and alcoholism is, in a sense, irrelevant: the stark undercurrent of my life with him was a life of fear, and the roots of that fear lay in my intuitive certainty that he wished us all dead. However Oedipal this may appear—or, in a sense, the obverse of the Oedipal—it meant that, whenever I was in his male presence, I learned a little more about what self-hatred meant, about what it meant to wish never to have been born. It was not just Christian Science that offered me a closed door to the universe; the father figure one so wants to admire and emulate was emotionally homicidal. And in response to that explosive terrain, I did the only thing that I could do, given my various talents: I sought to rise above it, literally, with words and ideas and books that would carry me out of my life, and out of his, to a safer place. But in the end, it was a place with few if any male figures of authority or empathy, where feminism dominated and men, despite claims to the contrary, were viewed as hegemonic and potentially if not actually dangerous. I launched myself from one enemy terrain directly into another.

Perhaps ironically, I also launched myself into a world where love, which I had experienced rarely if at all as a child, would need to be the rescuing device, the trope, and since my own private and best encounters with love were what we might call classically romantic, I sought those over and over, sought redemption in the eyes of another. There is plenty of feminist scholarship, including the works of Jessica Benjamin and Luce Irigaray, to explain how that quest, without more careful examination, is doomed to failure. Yet there are countervailing perceptions as well, indications that the impulse itself, though perhaps doomed structurally, had at its core a truth. But to find these countervailing perceptions, one must look beyond criticism and theory, beyond the pale of depression and its failed treatments, to stranger terrain. And if I find myself ending this book on that terrain, where few of you, perhaps, would follow, you will understand that the words of encouragement come from men I never met—William Stafford and Lionel Trilling—who ask again and again about "the authentic," who believe in a line from one thing to the next that interests us for important reasons, who understand the need to take a less genial view of the social circumstances of life, and who realize that the exigent self, as difficult as it may be, is the only rational ground from which adventures into the super-rational may occur.

* * *

Olga Kharitidi, a Russian-trained psychiatrist who first came to western attention in the mid-1990's with her book *Entering the Circle: A Russian Psychiatrist's Journey into Siberian Shamanism*, might seem—if only from the title of her book—like the kind of person one might turn to during a crisis of reality, a potential New Ager who just happened to hail from the fallen Soviet Union rather than, say, from the depths of Albuquerque or Willits, California. Followers, lost souls, come out of the woodwork for such people—much as the 130 people who showed up, along with me, at Michael Harner's 1997 workshop on shamanism in San Francisco reminded me of people who were either one step from the grave or one step from the asylum. It is a complicated matter psychologically to admit that one might be, at least on the fringe, a part of such a large contingent of despairing yet hopeful people; one may be comforted, under such circumstances, by Harold Bloom's magnificent gnostic sermon at the end of *Omens of Millennium*, in which he reminds us of the cosmic distance we have traveled and the tiny spark of divinity within, the one reality that has never left us. Under the weight of a seemingly boundless yet quiet despair, one might, as an adult, come to know that reality as a form of mourning: as Alice Miller explains in *The Drama of the Gifted Child: The Search for the True Self*, one mourns the childhood one never had, the moments when one might have understood oneself and one's true feelings but repressed them for the sake of parents one knew intuitively to be profoundly needy. In my case, a mother bound up, through her mother, in a totalitarian religion, perhaps sexually abused by her stepfather, and a father who wished nothing more than to be released from his wife and children, created ample territory for a child's emotional disaster. In such a case, intellect naturally comes to one's aid, even when one is young: one learns to behave for specific reasons, to rationalize away the pain, to chase after parents who are always leaving—my father, for example, routinely threatened to leave me at truck stops when I was little if I took too long in the bathroom—until, as an adult, one has a career, family of one's own, and a certain kind of life, yet the profound emptiness of a place where real emotions should be and are not. To begin to re-inhabit that place—to return to it, feeling its emptiness keenly, its losses, both in childhood and in the adult hopes of romance, its need to be filled, or its population of what Tibetans sometimes call "hungry ghosts"—this is no small labor. If this book ends at a moment when such places are being re-inhabited, it ends because there is no clear outcome, only a slightly different direction that may promise a certain hope in the face of profound loneliness.

In *The Drama of the Gifted Child*, Miller writes of her adult patients who manifest considerable worldly success yet experience "depression, the feeling of emptiness and self-alienation, and a sense that their life has no meaning" (Miller, 6). One behavioral characteristic common to all of these people, interestingly, is "the art of not experiencing feelings, for a child can only experience his feelings when there is somebody there who accepts him fully, understands and supports him" (Miller, 10). This book has been, if nothing else, a series of journeys toward feelings that were unthinkable or unfeelable early on, because the author existed in childhood only in two ways—within the carefully-crafted mold his parents had made for him and within the lonely but internally-consistent flights of imagination that became his refuge. The main line from childhood to adulthood, however—the line of true feeling—was closed to him, to me. Yet, as an adult, there are only certain things one can do about this. As an adult parent, one can, at the very least, examine one's own behavior for ways in which it replicates one's parents, and one can try to put a stop to it: my own three children, ages 18, 14, and six, may inevitably have suffered to some extent from my own struggles with inauthenticity, not to mention those of my two ex-spouses, yet each of these children thus far evinces an independence of thought and feeling that far exceeded mine when I was their age, and it seems possible to hope that, whatever curse was visited upon my generation, it did not fully carry over into the next. Even if one is unable to love oneself, true love for the miracle of one's children as they are can assuage many potential forms of damage, and if one of the great pleasures in my own life is trying to see and to be with my children as they themselves are, I have both given and received a gift that I myself, as a child, was never offered.

At the same time, in those moments of adulthood when life seems to stretch endlessly and pointlessly ahead, with nothing but more work and more or less distinction—when, as Miller writes, one "suddenly get[s] the feeling that [one] failed to live up to some ideal image and measure" (Miller, 6)—one feels oneself in the domain of those hungry ghosts, those primal, unfulfilled longings of one's own ancestors, predatory, incessant, devouring, and to the extent that they are both "real" and mythic one looks for responses to that myth. One such response comes in Olga Kharitidi's second, and potentially more disturbing, book, *The Master of Lucid Dreams:*

…."We love storytelling here. Can you tell me a story now? Tell me the most puzzling story you know." I thought Sulema asked me that just to help me feel comfortable, and I was grateful to her for that.

"Now?"

"Sure, why not?"

I thought about her suggestion for awhile, and then suddenly the story of Hamlet, a story that had been puzzling me since high school, came suddenly to my mind.

"All right, I know such a story. It has been puzzling me for years since I never was able to find any final, complete, and unambiguous meaning to it. This story happened long ago.

"There was a prince who lived in a faraway land. His father had died recently. His mother married his uncle and the uncle became king, and the prince lived in his kingdom. He wasn't a particularly sad prince and he wasn't particularly lonely. He definitely wasn't mad, until one day when everything changed and the prince began to change.

"That day, or more exactly that night, he met the ghost of his dead father, who told him a story of how the reigning king, his own brother, poisoned him to death to get the kingdom and the queen. His father's ghost demanded revenge, and there was no more peace left for the prince after he learned that story.

"He invented a clever trick: he invited wandering actors to perform for the king and queen with a play the prince created himself. The play was the story of his father's murder, played out by actors before the prince's mother and his uncle. He saw the proof of guilt in their faces as they watched the play, and then he became truly mad."

"He was killed, right? The prince is killed at the end of the story, right?" Sulema interrupted me without waiting for me to finish.

"Actually, yes, he was. You know the story?"

"That ghost killed him, the ghost of his father."

"Actually, no..."

"Actually, yes. He started to play by the rules of the ghost. He let the spirit of trauma in, into himself; he allowed the demon to invade his memory with the hurt of his father's death and to become part of himself. He started acting from the spirit's command, so he had to be killed. He didn't become mad, as you say. He was just fighting the spirit of trauma. He lost, I guess. He didn't have any wife, did he?"

"No. But he had a fiancée with whom he was very tender at first, but then she killed herself because of his rudeness and madness."

"Whoa! Were there more dead people in this story?"

"Actually, yes. The bride's father and..."

"Oh! A really hungry ghost he was, that father lookalike. That was a good story. The one who wrote it knew about the battle."

Sulema grew silent and her squinting eyes looked straight at me through the fire as if she was seeing through me...

I started to feel how my bodily sensations changed. It felt as if some invisible power penetrated my tensed muscles and untied the old painful knots stored in them. Along with that, I felt that my memory was liberating and changing itself into the same substance of which dreams are made, and soon a stream of images was flowing through my mind. They flowed in abundance, but there was no chaos in it; they were all connected by an invisible, profound order and my perception followed this...I tried to stay still, very, very still, until I heard the noise, like a gate opening, and Michael's voice said:

"Fear nothing and remember that it is the Father who punishes and it is the Mother who forgives. I will be with you when you need me" (Kharitidi, v-vii).

Within the frame of *Hamlet*, Kharitidi begins her own "good story," a profoundly disorienting and alarming tale of traumas endured and ghosts encountered, a passage through time and space from Siberia to Samarkand in Uzbekistan and to Michael, the "master of lucid dreams" whose gifts of envisioning and healing the deepest connections and darkest webs of the mind become part of Kharitidi's own practice. While Kharitidi's 1995 *Entering the Circle* met with both interest and skepticism in the west, her 2001 *Master of Lucid Dreams* raises the question of whether, by any western standard, she could still be considered a practicing psychiatrist. Yet, even as the terrible visions of trauma in Kharitidi's book become themselves haunting, the practice of confronting those visions and seeing past them—to a domain of ultimate forgiveness and release—lies at the heart of the book. And if one had, indeed, a punitive father and a submissive, angry mother, so that the phrase "the Father...punishes and the Mother... forgives" makes no literal sense, within the domain of conscious myth the distinction becomes important and potentially liberating. But he or she who seeks to follow Kharitidi's path is on a long journey with psychic perils that should not be underestimated. In the meantime, one other story comes to mind, and it is the story with which I will conclude.

* * *

It is, given the nature of this book, the story of a dream, but it is also more than that.

As a child, I had few recurring dreams, and those were all terrifying, but one was both terrifying and inescapable to any act of conscious memory. In that dream, I was in a dark cave with many corridors, far underground and without light, feeling my way toward any path that felt as if it were an upward path, drawn by faint currents of air toward the world I craved and could not see. In the end, I found myself at what must have been, at some remote point, a portal, where blocks of stone had fallen on the path; yet through those blocks was a single fissure, and through that fissure light shone. I could not get to it; I could not move or break the blocks; but I could see light, taste the air. It was there.

I have the suspicion that that dream came originally from an illustration to a children's book that I cannot remember at all, for the image of the fissure of light amid the darkness of the cavern is so strong as to be almost overpowering, even now as I near 49, and my sense of such visual power still lies with the visual arts. Yet it may well have simply been created internally, with that degree of vividness, as an account of what my life was and would be. To be so close…even for a child, there is grief in knowing something intrinsic to oneself that one cannot have. But one also knows that it is there—it exists—and its presence is enough both for a certain hope and a certain stubbornness.

This book began with a fissure of a different kind—a near-fatal crack in a relationship that, characteristically, I had hoped would ground me in what I considered to be the normal human world of love and interconnectedness and vivid thought and art, of careers started or revitalized, of children, of hope itself. And all those words, all those ideas, had been exchanged between the two of us; it was not an illusion on my part. And yet it was all, apparently, a form of play to her, a form of experimentation, another curiosity. The psychological character of this behavior is of little interest now; it would be a mere academic exercise. But the crack in that relationship, when it came, left virtually the equivalent of nuclear fallout in a life that already had weathered more than its share of hardship (though surely many of us would say as much—what is, one wonders, the correct "share" of hardship?). How or why one might survive what might have seemed like the last unbearable trauma was really the question underlying this book. But the answer, and I think it is not a poor one, has to do with that very idea of fissure: for just as there are catastrophic cracks in one's own life, there are also fissures of memory, fissures of narrative and vision, and these sometimes bring, not more pain, but light. The fissure of memory that enabled me to see my own eight-year-old self as Freud's burning child, interpreted in a somewhat different way through Cathy Caruth, became a way of reconstructing a story of childhood that did not fundamentally make sense.

The fissure of meditation on something as seemingly benign as hide-and-seek yielded a vision of why one might need to be found, and about how the assumptions of the game, though seemingly harmless and entertaining, embody a way of looking at the world that connotes harm. The fissure of meditation on drinking and addiction, though seemingly dark with relation to Dylan Thomas and John Denver, reminded me again that—in a society plagued with monolithic thought about addiction—there is, underlying the compulsion to drink, a need both for rapture and for oblivion from past pain, and neither of these motives should be treated with anything but respect. And, finally, the fissure of memory that yielded something likely to be true about a memory likely to be false—the fact that my mother, and not my father, told me about my cat Siddhartha's death—is perhaps the most crucial rupture of all, because it also means that, throughout my childhood, my entrapped mother was trying to send me signals that Christian Science was dangerous, that it worked against a natural world she loved, that it did not have all the answers or even any of the answers, that its secret punitive side could kill. If I could not listen, because I was so dutiful and because the institutional force of the religion weighed on my soul from the very beginning, that did not mean that my mother was not scattering breadcrumbs, like Hansel and Gretel, to show me a way back to the realm of the human. The cracks in the stories, and not the stories themselves, are the domains of authenticity; through the fissures of memory, and not the smooth walls of their continuity, one finds another way.

But there is the question of time. This book began with a brief but envious reference to William Styron, whose harrowing depression nevertheless yielded over a period of a year; ten years with the same oppressions makes one wonder, clearly, about the worth of almost any treatment, and one hears the echo of Anne Sexton's "Live or Die," in which she exhorts herself to "ride out any which way you can": somehow the mind must release itself from the circumstances and diagnoses that incarcerate it in medicines, breakdowns, and madhouses. But how, but how? Sexton's decline into suicide is a matter, still, of considerable debate: the upheavals in her last two years—her divorce, which she had thought she wanted but which Dr. Martin Orne, though no longer her psychiatrist because of his move from Boston to Philadelphia, had counseled her against; her sexual relationship with another psychiatrist; her age, as she passed 40, and began to think of herself as unattractive; her alcoholism; her poetry that many critics, used to what she had produced before, found too amorphous, too driven by drink, and too apocalyptic to be good work—all of these could be said to have contributed to her death by asphyxiation and drug overdose in 1974. Yet Dr. Orne's argument, at the beginning of Diane Middlebrook's *Anne Sexton: A Biography*, that—had it been possible for Sexton to continue under his treatment, she might well have lived—is not necessarily self-aggrandizement: there is some clue that a continuity of thought and faith between Sexton and Orne helped her, as one who might never have been well, yet might have had the time she needed to do what she had to do.

For psychic time is not like the world's time, nor like the world's chronology: that, above all, may be the most difficult curse for one who suffers from profound and chronic depression. In "Ourselves or Nothing," the last poem in Carolyn Forche's *The Country Between Us*, Forche quotes Holocaust survivor and scholar Terrence Des Pres: "Vast numbers of men and women died because they did not have time, the blessing of sheer time, to recover" (Forche, 56). How much time is that? Six months? A year? Ten years? The rest of one's life? One forgets so easily how the world turns on the schedule of business: a normal day lasts from 8 A.M. to 5 P.M., and even variant careers, such as a professor's, operate on specific deadlines, sometimes multiple and overlapping, with profound intellectual commitments. The assumption behind all this is really no different from the assumption a first-grade teacher has on the first day of school: his or her students will show up at eight, ready to do the work of the day. But this bizarrely-accepted artificiality, so wedded on the one hand to the industrial and post-industrial society and, ironically, to the rise of the labor movement in the 19th century and sociological and educational theorists in the late 19th and early 20th centuries, has no basis in the psyche. Nothing internal mandates this. Once, nine years ago, on a medical leave of several months, I fled by car regularly to the northern California coast—eight times in four months—because only there could my whole self feel at home, so lost was I in my career and in Iowa. Whether shivering in a tent and sleeping bag by the beach or walking the sands of early spring or the back trails of the Pacific coastal range, I felt my body dissolving back into itself, knowing itself home. On those trips, I would inevitably forget to take the anti-depressant and anti-anxiety medications prescribed for me, and would return to my psychiatrist in Iowa happy, comforted, seemingly stable, and hopeful. It would take about three days in Iowa for all of this to vanish, and then, quite suddenly, my body would crave the prescribed drugs once again. "I have never before seen a patient with such a profound environmental response," the psychiatrist acknowledged at one point. But there was no way to stay there without abandoning my children to Iowa...and now, at this point, the choice to stay for their sakes has come to make much sense to me, as each of them has become someone utterly wonderful. Yet I missed the place and time of my healing.

But it is not over. Terrence Des Pres also wrote, "They turned to face the worst straight-on, without sentiment or hope, simply to keep watch over life" (Forche, 56-57). Few would tolerate the comparison of ordinary American life to any Holocaustic experience, yet anyone who has suffered a chronic and acute psychic illness for a long period of time will know the resonance of "the worst," always a form of torture, and yet will also know that the act of "keeping watch" may be an important, even essential, compensatory act. Out of place, divorced from the roots of its physical and imaginative strength, the psyche may, over many years, nevertheless find a kind of healing, but it may look very different—or cause its beneficiary to look very different—from the character of ordinary American life: there is a reason, after all, that Carolyn Forche almost goes mad in a Safeway, looking at all the heads of lettuce, the other produce, and the coffee, and knowing what it has cost in lives, a knowledge utterly erased in the vivid light of the sparklingly clean store ("Return," 19). One can look at one's midwestern American world and have to talk oneself out of madness, knowing its cost. Yet even in that story there may be fissures, places where a single idea or spark showers a different reality upon the darkness, where—if Harold Bloom is correct in his reading of gnosticism—if we are thrown into a world that God did not actually create, as beings that God did not create because we are co-eternal with Him or Her, uncreated, purely ourselves, eternal—then any moment is potentially the moment of resurrection before death, and every earthly story is really nothing but a tattered garment with the illusion of wholeness, waiting to be rent in service to the soul who needs to go home. This book was the story of a soul who urgently needed to go home, and who has promised himself that, one day, he will; in the meantime, it is time to keep watch, because in the end—apart from one's own remote yet immanent aloneness with God—there is no one but those one loves, those who actually love one back, and those who need one's help, however imperfect it may be, for the next part of the journey.

Sources

The works and websites listed below refer to sources whose specific mention within the text requires further elucidation. The sources are listed, not alphabetically, but in the order in which they are mentioned in specific essays; where a source appears more than once, the subsequent listings are abbreviated with the somewhat archaic but lucid *op. cit.*

Foreward

William Styron, *Darkness Visible: A Memoir of Madness* (New York: Vintage, 1992).

Elizabeth Wurtzel, *Prozac Nation: Young and Depressed In America* (New York: Riverhead Books, 1995).

Barbara Wilson, *Blue Windows: A Christian Science Childhood* (New York: St. Martin's Press, 1998).

Caroline Fraser, *God's Perfect Child: Living and Dying in the Christian Science Church* (New York: Metropolitan Books, 1999).

Nathaniel Lachenmeyer, *The Outsider: A Journey into My Father's Struggle with Madness* (New York: Broadway Books, 2000).

Jeanette Winterson, *Sexing the Cherry* (New York: Vintage, 1989).

Jean-Jacques Rousseau, *Confessions*, cited in Lionel Trilling, *Sincerity and Authenticity* (Cambridge: Harvard University Press, 1972), pp. 58-59.

Part I: The Burning Child

The Unbroken

William Stafford, *Someday, Maybe* (New York: Harper and Row, 1973).

Lionel Trilling, *Sincerity and Authenticity, op. cit.*

Marilynne Robinson, *Housekeeping* (New York: Bantam Windstone, 1982).

Sarah Harasym, ed., *Levinas and Lacan: The Missed Encounter* (Albany: State University of New York Press, 1998).

Donna Brody, "Levinas and Lacan: Facing the Real," *Levinas and Lacan: The Missed Encounter*, ed. Harasym, *op. cit.*, pp. 56-78.

The Burning Child

Cathy Caruth, *Unclaimed Experience: Trauma, Narrative, and History* (Baltimore: Johns Hopkins, 1996).

Harold Bloom, *Omens of Millennium: The Gnosis of Angels, Dreams, and Resurrection* (New York: Riverhead, 1996).

David Lee Miller, *Dreams of the Burning Child: Sacrificial Sons and the Father's Witness* (Ithaca: Cornell University Press, 2003).

Sigmund Freud, *The Interpretation of Dreams*, trans. and ed. by James Strachey (New York: Basic Books, 1953); note that the page numbers given in the Freud citation from David Lee Miller are, in this edition, pp. 509-511.

Hiding

Henry James, "The Jolly Corner," *In the Cage and Other Tales,* ed. Morton
Dauwen Zabel (New York: Norton, 1969).

E.V. Gordon, ed., *Pearl* (Oxford: Oxford University Press, 1953).

J.R.R. Tolkien and E.V. Gordon, eds., *Sir Gawain and the Green Knight*
(Oxford: Oxford University Press, 1967).

Nathaniel Hawthorne, *The Scarlet Letter,* ed. Sculley Bradley, Richard
Croom Beatty, and E. Hudson Long (New York: Norton, 1962),
pp. 183-184.

The Disappearing Mother

Calvin Trillin, *Remembering Denny* (New York: Warner Books, 1993).

Anthony Storr, *Solitude: A Return to the Self* (New York: The Free Press,
1988).

Mary Baker Eddy, *Science and Health with Key to the Scriptures* (Boston:
Christian Science Publishing Society, 1903, 1917, 1971).

Kathryn Harrison, *The Kiss* (New York: Avon Books, 1997).

Diane Wood Middlebrook, *Anne Sexton: A Biography* (Boston: Houghton
Mifflin, 1991).

Sylvia Plath, "Pursuit," *The Complete Poems of Sylvia Plath,* ed. Ted Hughes
(New York: Harper and Row, 1981), pp. 22-23.

"Depression Research at the National Institute of Mental Health,"
National Institute of Mental Health website: www.nimh.gov/
publicat/depresfact/cfm

Thomas Merton, *New Seeds of Contemplation* (New York: New Directions,
1961).

Part II: Death Revisited

Alone

Nathaniel Lachenmeyer, *The Outsider., op. cit.*

R.D. Laing, *The Divided Self: An Existential Study in Sanity and Madness* (New York: Penguin, 1969).

Joseph LeDoux, *Synaptic Self: How the Brain Becomes Who We Are* (New York: Penguin, 2002).

Alone, Coda: The Setting

James Agee and Walker Evans, *Let Us Now Praise Famous Men*, with intro by John Hersey (Boston: Hougton Mifflin, 1941, 1988), p. 13.

Noam Chomsky, *Syntactic Structures* (The Hague: Mouton, 1957); see also, among many possibilities, Ferdinand de Saussure, *Course in General Linguistics*, ed. Charles Bally and Albert Sechehaye in collaboration with Albert Riedlinger, trans. by Wade Baskin (New York: McGraw-Hill, 1959); David F. Armstrong, William C. Stokoe, and Sherman E. Wilcox, *Gesture and the Nature of Language* (Cambridge: Cambridge University Press, 1995); Terence W. Deacon, *The Symbolic Species: The Co-Evolution of Language and the Brain* (New York: Norton, 1997); Elizabeth Closs Traugott and Mary Louise Pratt, *Linguistics for Students of Literature* (New York: Harcourt Brace Jovanovich, 1980).

Antonio Damasio, *Descartes' Error: Emotion, Reason, and the Human Brain* (New York: Penguin, 1994).

Antonio Damasio, *The Feeling of What Happens: Body and Emotion in the Making of Consciousness* (New York: Harvest Books, 2000).

And Death Shall Have No Dominion

John Malcolm Brinnin, *Dylan Thomas in America* (Boston: Little, Brown and Co., 1955).

Bill Reed and Rollie McKenna, *The Days of Dylan Thomas: A Pictorial Biography* (New York: McGraw-Hill, 1964).

Paul Ferris, *Dylan Thomas: The Biography, New Edition* (Washington, D.C.: Counterpoint Press, 2000).

Andrew Lycett, *Dylan Thomas: A New Life* (Woodstock, New York: Overlook Press, 2004).

Mark C. Taylor, "Introduction," *Deconstruction in Context* (Chicago: University of Chicago Press, 1986).

The historical background on the *Diagnostic and Statistical Manual* comes from www.psychcentral.com.

Dylan Thomas, *Collected Poems, 1914-1952* (New York: New Directions, 1953).

Donald Davie, *Purity of Diction in English Verse* (New York: Schocken Books, 1967).

Some of the colonial and post-colonial meditations in this chapter rest on essays in Patrick Williams and Laura Chrisman's *Colonial Discourse and Post-Colonial Theory* (New York: Columbia, 1994); direct intellectual debts are acknowledged below.

W. E. B. Dubois, *The Souls of Black Folk* (New York: Vintage/Library of America, 1990), p. 8.

James Baldwin, "Stranger in the Village," *Notes of a Native Son* (London: Michael Joseph, 1964), p. 156.

The membership figures cited with relation to the First Church of Christ, Scientist (the Christian Science Church) come primarily from Caroline Fraser's *God's Perfect Child, op.cit.;* my interpolations from the number of branch churches, Christian Science societies, and Christian Science practitioners listed in the *Christian Science Journal* were also used.

Annie Dillard, *For the Time Being* (New York: Vintage, 1999).

Leopold Sedar Senghor,"Negritude," Williams and Chrisman, *op.cit.*

Pierre Teilhard de Chardin, *Le Milieu Divin* (Paris: Editions de Seuil, 1957).

Alone, Coda Two: The Setting Revisited

Galway Kinnell, *When One Has Lived a Long Time Alone* (New York: Alfred A. Knopf, 1991).

Richard Bach, *Jonathan Livingston Seagull*, with photographs by Russell Munson (New York: Macmillan, 1970).

C. S. Lewis, *The Discarded Image: An Introduction to Medieval and Renaissance Literature* (Cambridge: Cambridge University Press, 1964).

Harold Bloom, *Omens of Millennium, op. cit.*

Robert Pinsky, "At Pleasure Bay," *The Figured Wheel: New and Collected Poems, 1966- 1996* (New York: Farrar, Straus and Giroux, 1996).

Philip Martin, *The Zen Path through Depression* (San Francisco: HarperSanFrancisco, 1999).

Elaine Scarry, *The Body in Pain: The Making and Unmaking of the World* (New York: Oxford University Press, 1985).

Cathy Caruth, *Unclaimed Experience, op. cit.*

John Denver

John Collis, *John Denver: Mother Nature's Son* (Edinburgh, Scotland: Mainstream Publishing, 1999).

National Transportation Safety Board accident report on John Denver's

fatal crash, number LAX98FA0008, at www.ntsb.gov; follow the
prompts to aircraft accidents, then to October 1997. The report,
when printed, is eight single-spaced pages long; the summary is
two single-spaced pages.

For information on pilot ratings, see the *Federal Aviation Regulations/*
Aeronautical Information Manual (FAR/AIM) (Washington,
D.C.: United States Government Publication, 2005), Part 1—
"Definitions and Abbreviations," and Part 61—"Certification:
Pilots and Instructors."

Christine Smith, *A Mountain in the Wind: An Exploration of the Spirituality*
of John Denver (The Park, Findhorn, Scotland: Findhorn Press,
2001).

Richard Bach, *Jonathan Livingston Seagull, op. cit.*

Geshe Lhundup Sopa and Jeffrey Hopkins, *Cutting through Appearances:*
The Practice and Theory of Tibetan Buddhism, with forward by His
Holiness the Dalai Lama (Ithaca: Snow Lion, 1989).

John Denver, *Poems, Prayers and Promises,* produced by Milton Okun
(New York: RCA Victor Records, 1971).

Background on the Long-EZ, including a complete list of published
reviews and articles on the aircraft, can be found at the
Experimental Aircraft Association's website at http://members.
eea.org/home/homebuilders/selecting/kits/Long-EZ.

Budd Davisson, review of Long-EZ, www.pilotfriend.com/aircraft.

Neal Gabler, Life: The Movie; How Entertainment Conquered Reality (New
York: Vintage, 1998).

R.D. Laing, *The Divided Self, op.cit.*

Harold Bloom, *Omens of Millennium, op. cit.*

John Denver, "Around and Around," song four, side two, *Poems, Prayers*
and Promises, op.cit.

Kathryn Harrison, *The Kiss, op. cit.*

For information on the FAA's penalties for DUI's and other drug use, see
the *FAR/AIM*, Part 61.15, "Offenses involving alcohol or drugs,"
op. cit.

Cathy Caruth, *Unclaimed Experience, op. cit.*

Diane Middlebrook, *Her Husband: Sylvia Plath and Ted Hughes—A Marriage*
(New York: Penguin, 2003).

Epilogue: Keeping Watch

Thomas Simmons, *The Unseen Shore: Memories of a Christian Science
Childhood* (Boston: Beacon Press, 1991).

Henry Corbin, *Spiritual Body and Celestial Earth: From Mazdean Iran
to Shi'ite Iran,* trans. By Nancy Pearson (Princeton: Princeton
University Press, 1977).

Herman Hesse, *Siddhartha*, trans. Hilda Rosner (New York: New
Directions, 1951).

Olga Kharitidi, *Entering the Circle: A Russian Psychiatrist's Journey into
Siberian Shamanism* (Albuquerque, New Mexico: Gloria Press,
1995).

Olga Kharitidi, *Master of Lucid Dreams* (Charlottesville, Virginia:
Hampton Roads Publishing, 2001).

Harold Bloom, *Omens of Millennium, op. cit.*

Alice Miller, *The Drama of the Gifted Child: The Search for the True Self* (New
York: Basic Books, 1981).

Diane Middlebrook, *Anne Sexton: A Biography, op. cit.*

Carolyn Forché, *The Country Between Us* (New York: Harper and Row,
1981).

About the Author

Thomas Simmons, associate professor of English at the University of Iowa, has published four previous books, including *The Unseen Shore: Memories of a Christian Science Childhood* (Beacon Press, 1991), *A Season in the Air: One Man's Adventures in Flying* (Ballantine, 1993), *Erotic Reckonings: Mastery and Apprenticeship in the Work of Poets and Lovers* (University of Illinois Press, 1994), and *Ghost Man: Reflections on Evolution, Love and Loss* (AuthorHouse, 2001). Having previously taught at Stanford, UC Berkeley, MIT, and Grinnell College, he has won several teaching awards, including the Everett Moore Baker Award for Excellence in Undergraduate Teaching at MIT, and the University of Iowa "Thank a Teacher" Award from the Center for Teaching. He currently divides his time between his family in Grinnell and Iowa City, Iowa and in Colorado Springs, Colorado at Colorado College.